Everyday Reading

Everyday Reading

*Print Culture
and Collective Identity
in the Río de la Plata,
1780–1910*

William Garrett Acree Jr.

Vanderbilt University Press ■ *Nashville*

© 2011 by Vanderbilt University Press
Nashville, Tennessee 37235
All rights reserved
First printing 2011

This book is printed on acid-free paper.
Design by Dariel Mayer

Library of Congress Cataloging-in-Publication Data

Acree, William Garrett
Everyday reading : print culture and collective identity in the
Río de la Plata, 1780–1910 / William Garrett Acree, Jr.
p. cm.
Includes bibliographical references and index.
ISBN 978-0-8265-1789-0 (cloth edition : acid-free paper)
1. Books and reading—Social aspects—Río de la Plata
Region (Argentina and Uruguay)—History. 2. Publishers
and publishing—Social aspects—Río de la Plata Region
(Argentina and Uruguay)—History. 3. Book industries and
trade—Social aspects—Río de la Plata Region (Argentina
and Uruguay)—History. 4. Printing—Social aspects—
Río de la Plata Region (Argentina and Uruguay)—History.
5. Río de la Plata Region (Argentina and Uruguay)—
Intellectual life. 6. National characteristics, Argentine, in
literature. 7. National characteristics, Uruguayan, in literature.
I. Title.
Z1003.5.A7A47 2011
070.509163'68—DC22
2011003008

Contents

List of Figures   vii

Acknowledgments   xiii

Introduction   1

1   Words, Wars, and Public Celebrations: The
Emergence of Rioplatense Print Culture (1780–1830)   15

2   Words, Wars, and Gauchos: Print Culture
and Cattle Civilization (1830–1870)   43

3   Sowers of Alphabets (1870–1910)   85

4   Lessons for a Nation (1880–1910)   121

Epilogue: Spreading the Word and Image (1880–1910)   165

List of Abbreviations   195

Notes   197

Bibliography   215

Index   239

Figures

1.1   The 1813 Argentine coat of arms.   36

1.2   The coat of arms of the Provincia Oriental.   37

1.3   *Jura de la Constitución de 1830* (Swearing in the Constitution, 1830) by Juan Manuel Blanes.   40

2.1   A scene of cattle branding on the title page of *Colección general de las marcas del ganado de la Provincia de Buenos Aires*.   48

2.2   A page of brand marks in *Colección general de las marcas del ganado de la Provincia de Buenos Aires*.   49

2.3   A woodcut of a gaucho with pen and paper in hand, from *El Gaucho*.   52

2.4   A woodcut of *La Gaucha* surrounded by different breeds of cattle and dogs, at the top of a loose-leaf sheet of gauchesque verse.   53

2.5   *Interior de una pulpería* (Inside a pulpería), *Buenos Aires*, by León Palliere.   54

2.6   "Interior de una pulpería."   55

2.7   The top of an 1846 pasaporte with the Blanco slogan and the Uruguayan coat of arms.   60

2.8 *Divisas* featuring the profile of Rosas and the Federalist slogan: "Federation or Death! Long live the Federalists! Death to the savage, filthy, scoundrel Unitarians!"   63

2.9 The liberal gaucho Jacinto Cielo whirling his *boleadoras* on the front page of an Ascasubi newspaper.   72

2.10 *El Gaucho en Campaña*, another of Ascasubi's papers, sporting a character similar to Jacinto Cielo on its front page.   73

2.11 A peasant greeting a friend on horseback on the front page of Isidoro de María's gauchesque paper.   75

3.1 Female students in 1893 reading in the Hall for Recess and Reading, Internato Normal de Señoritas, Montevideo.   103

3.2 Male students at the Arts and Trades School in Montevideo, circa 1895, painting the Argentine coat of arms and preparing chalkboards with alphabets.   106

3.3 Students at a school outside Montevideo in 1912 learning to write in cursive with fountain pens.   107

3.4 The covers of two notebooks widely distributed in Uruguay, circa 1900.   109

3.5 The cover of notebook 1 (of 5) in J. V. Olivera's *Método de Caligrafía*.   110

3.6 A young student sharing a book with his mother, on the cover of Emma Catalá de Princivalle's *Ejercicios progresivos de lectura, ortología y ortografía, primer libro*.   112

3.7 A scene of reading in the home.   113

3.8 An invitation to read, on the cover of Figueira's *¿Quieres leer?*   115

3.9   The poetic cover of a notebook belonging to Raudelinda
      Pereda, from Tacuarembó.   119

4.1   A heroic gaucho riding across the grasslands of Uruguay,
      bearing a flag with the slogan "Liberty or Death."   133

4.2   Juan Manuel Blanes's representation of what José
      Artigas looked like on the eve of independence.   134

4.3   A lesson illustrated with a print of Blanes's *Juramento
      de los Treinta y Tres Orientales*, depicting the pledge
      of the group to liberate the Banda Oriental.   135

4.4   The Argentine coat of arms and flag appearing with
      the date 25 May 1810 on the patriotic cover of
      gón's *El mosaico argentino*.   136

4.5   The front cover of a Cuadernos Nacionales notebook
      in the historical series, portraying the exodus of
      the Orientales.   139

4.6   The back cover of the same notebook, with "The
      history of independence explained to children."   140

4.7   An exercise in one of Carmen Biasotti's notebooks,
      where she repeats "Artigas was the first leader of the
      Uruguayans."   143

4.8   A postcard of male students, circa 1900, marching
      through downtown Montevideo.   146

4.9   A postcard of female students, circa 1900, marching
      through downtown Montevideo.   146

4.10 Students participating in the *fiesta de promoción*
      at the Escuela de 2ndo Grado, Rivera, Uruguay, 1923.   147

4.11 Lesson on Hygiene: The Corset. Escuela de Aplicación
      para Señoritas, Montevideo, 1912.   150

4.12 A daughter reading to her mother, on the cover
of Amelia Palma's *Consejos a mi hija*. 155

4.13 The lady of the house arranging the table, on the cover
of *Lecturas sobre moral, higiene y economía doméstica*,
by Alejandro Lamas and Elvira Lamas. 157

4.14 Young students, circa 1893, learning to weave
at the Internato Normal de Señoritas, Montevideo. 159

4.15 Students in 1893 in a music class at the Escuela
de Aplicación, Montevideo, singing the national anthem. 160

4.16 A sewing class at the Escuela de Aplicación, Montevideo,
circa 1912. 160

4.17 A reading lesson at the Escuela José P. Varela 3er
Grado No. 2 in Montevideo, 1912. 161

5.1 A postcard with poetic lines sent to a woman in Melo,
Uruguay, 1905. 167

5.2 A Happy New Year postcard from 1901 depicting the
Plaza de Mayo in Buenos Aires in 1800 and 1900. 169

5.3 A postcard from 1901 celebrating the expansion
of rail lines in Uruguay. 169

5.4 A colorful postcard from 1907 of a colorful "country
memory," with a woman "handing her man a gourd
of bitter mate" as a rooster looks on. 170

5.5 A postcard, circa 1905, from the *Reminiscencias
Camperas* series, representing "a rest along the trail." 170

5.6 A postcard from 1908 showing the Palacio Legislativo in
Montevideo. 171

5.7   A postcard from 1905 with the Uruguayan coat of arms
      and a spread of Uruguayan stamps.   171

5.8   Stamps from the 1895 *Catedral* series in Uruguay:
      a gaucho, the Teatro Solís, and a locomotive.   173

5.9   Stamps from 1883, 1884, and 1910 showing the evolution
      of José Artigas's image toward a bold, youthful look.   174

5.10 The Banco Nacional's 1887 hundred-peso bill.   177

5.11 The Banco de la República's 1896 ten-peso bill, with a
      sailor and Lady Liberty on the front, and Montevideo's
      port and the ubiquitous railroad on the reverse.   179

5.12 A luminescent Artigas decorating the Banco
      de la República's 1896 500-peso bill.   180

5.13 The not-so-subtle imagery appearing on
      Uruguayan cigarette boxes.   181

5.14 Scenes from *Juan Moreira* as told in the criollo dramas
      series of cards included in cigarette boxes.   183

5.15 One of the many creative ads for *Cigarrillos
      Centenario*, 1910.   185

5.16 A 1910 ad for a portlike wine.   187

Acknowledgments

■ My mother is from the Mississippi Delta and my father was born in northern Florida. As my parents, they had little idea that their first son would end up spending so much time in the distant Río de la Plata, much less write a book about the region. But they and many others have guided me along the way, and my few words here demonstrate only a fraction of my gratitude.

To begin, my sincerest thanks to Eli Bortz, Michael Ames, Ed Huddleston, Sue Havlish, Donna Gruverman, and Dariel Mayer of Vanderbilt University Press; the Press's editorial board; the readers who evaluated the manuscript and whose detailed comments and constructive criticism helped me improve it; and Peg Duthie, for her careful, skillful editing. Special thanks to editorial board member William Luis, who kindly shared his expertise and drew my attention to aspects of the book that needed greater emphasis. Working with the team at Vanderbilt has been an absolute honor as well as a pleasure.

Research for this project was made possible by a grant from the Graduate School at the University of North Carolina at Chapel Hill, a Fulbright-Hays grant from the U.S. Department of Education, generous exploratory and research grants from the Institute of Latin American Studies at UNC (now the Institute for the Study of the Americas), and a Dana Drake research travel award from the UNC Department of Romance Languages. Without this financial and institutional support, this study would not have been possible.

Several mentors helped me during my time at UNC, and since then as a fledgling assistant professor: Stuart Day, John Chasteen, Juan Carlos González Espitia, Alejandro Mejías-López, and Greg Dawes. I cannot thank them enough for their time, wisdom, friendship, and advice, as well as the freedom and support they gave me to take this study in the directions I felt it needed to go. Suffice it to say that were it not for the attention and dedication of these individuals, the seed for this book might never have been planted. I also thank Marc Meyer, who showed me the inspirational role of education and the intellectual value of a good laugh.

Other colleagues and friends have likewise provided various forms of crucial support. To begin, my colleagues in the Department of Romance Languages and Literatures at Washington University in St. Louis offered guidance, stimulating conversation about interests in common, and, simply put, open ears. In addition to listening to me talk through ideas for this and other projects, Christopher Conway offered his keen editorial eye and sense of what's good writing (and what isn't), as well as encouragement. Alex Borucki, who knows the history of the region like the back of his hand, answered countless questions, gave great feedback (as well as a healthy dose of constructive criticism), and has been a steadfast friend across disciplinary lines. I'm grateful to Jean-Philippe Barnabé for his enthusiastic interest in the development of this book, for facilitating contacts throughout the Río de la Plata, and for his friendship. Mike Huner, Alda Blanco, Beatriz Vegh, Ana Frega, Hugo Achugar, Ignacio Infante, and Gilbert Merkx generously read and critiqued parts of this book in its early stages. Ricardo Marletti, Adriana Rodríguez Pérsico, Claudia Román, Julio Schvartzman, and Élida Lois talked about the arc of its arguments and opened my eyes to sources as well as points that needed further consideration or revision. Susana Monreal of the Instituto de Historia at the Universidad Católica in Uruguay and Juan Manuel Palacio of the Centro de Estudios Latinoamericanos at the Universidad Nacional de San Martín in Argentina arranged venues for me to present the research at various stages. Patricia Vargas at the Fulbright Commission in Uruguay and Norma González at the Fulbright Commission in Argentina put me in touch with contacts in Montevideo, Buenos Aires, and across the Uruguayan countryside, and they allowed me to share my work with other Fulbright fellows. Natalie Hartman, Beatriz Riefkohl, and the Consortium in Latin American Studies at UNC Chapel Hill and Duke University offered unique opportunities (in the form of working groups and faculty-student gatherings) to test some of the ideas that I present in these pages.

I am thankful, as well, for the help and goodwill I received from Susana Luzardo and the staff at the Museo Pedagógico José Pedro Varela

(María del Carmen Lema Pensado, María Hortiguera, Graciana Nuñez, Mónica Aguilar, Susana Bertolotti, and Beatriz Ricci); Ariadna Islas and the staff at the Museo Histórico Nacional; Alicia Casas de Barrán and the Archivo General de la Nación in Uruguay; Alicia Brassesco and the Museo del Gaucho y de la Moneda; the library at the Facultad de Humanidades y Ciencias de la Educación in Montevideo; the Museo y Archivo Municipal in Montevideo; Carlos Liscano and the Biblioteca Nacional in Uruguay; the staff at the Museo del Indio y del Gaucho in Tacuarembó; Graciela Perrone, Ana Diamant, and Ariel Fort at the Biblioteca Nacional de Maestros; the Sala del Tesoro staff at the Biblioteca Nacional de Argentina; the Archivo General de la Nación in Argentina; the Complejo Museográfico Enrique Udaondo in Luján; Rubén Cucuzza; the Instituto Bibliográfico Antonio Zinny in Buenos Aires; and April Brewer and the Rare Book Collection at UNC Chapel Hill. I am indebted to philatelists Carlos Hernández Rocha and Marcos Silvera Antúnez in Montevideo and Marcelo Loeb in Buenos Aires, who generously allowed me to sort through and photograph their private collections of stamps, postcards, and *figuritas*.

My family and friends outside of academia helped in ways of which they are perhaps unaware. My mother gave me the gift of her creativity and passion for books, not to mention her unyielding support and encouragement. Her positive spirit and easy smile in the face of life's adversities are constant rays of hope. My brother, sister, and father previously knew little about Uruguay or Argentina—and precisely because of this fact, the questions they posed about this project were challenging and rewarding to try to answer. My grandmother Louise, with her background in journalism and ninety-three years of life to her name, has been one of my staunchest advocates; her wit and sharp questions helped me think differently about this project and the power of storytelling. Ceci, a granddaughter of immigrants and now one herself, has helped me keep things real and shown almost infinite patience with the amazing amount of time this book has required (while never being shy about protecting our time together). Her smile, intelligence, and care have made my life so much richer. And my Uruguayan family (Marta, Andrea, Mirta, and Aurora) have always been eager to help me out any way they can—with good cheer, food, lively conversation, and constant interest.

Thank you all.

Lastly, my great thanks to the Uruguayans and Argentines—aged six to eighty-eight—who opened their homes to me, shared stories and lent materials with heartwarming generosity, and eagerly talked about the meaning of reading and writing for them. To these descendants of yester-year's "everyday readers," and to the readers who continue to marvel at the transformative powers of the written and printed word and of stories read aloud, I dedicate this book.

Introduction

Do you know what PATRIA means? Surely your little ears have heard this word. And on more than one occasion, seeing the enthusiasm with which men pronounce "patria" in the streets, you have felt the urge to join them, to cry out and mix your joy and enthusiasm with that general feeling of happiness.

> —José Manuel Eizaguirre, *La patria: Elementos para estimular en el niño argentino el amor á la patria y el respeto á las tradiciones nacionales* (The patria: Elements for stimulating in the Argentine child love for the patria and national traditions)

■ In these words from his 1895 textbook, addressed to the "niño argentino" (Argentine child), Eizaguirre draws our attention to one of the crucial forces behind the formation of collective identity: print.[1] Eizaguirre promises to satisfy the young reader's curiosity about the meaning of *patria*, or the fatherland. In turn, he humbly requests his audience's attention "so that these pages leave a lasting imprint on your spirit."[2] He goes on to remark that sharing a sense of national pride is every citizen's duty, and that every girl and boy should strive to understand the reasons that inspire the profound love for the patria—something everyone *of course* wanted to feel. All that was needed to achieve this was a little reading.

Making up the region known as the Río de la Plata, Uruguay and Argentina are Latin America's most complete examples of how the intersection between print media and collective identities developed.[3] Today, visitors to the capital cities of Montevideo and Buenos Aires cannot help but notice the deep roots of written culture that are visible in the city centers. Corrientes Street, one of the main thoroughfares in Buenos Aires, is lined for miles with bookstores and bookstalls. In Montevideo, where book-stores abound as well, one can visit a general outdoor market on Sundays where booksellers' tables are spread over more than five blocks. Across both countries, from coastal cities to interior towns, kiosks (the likes of which there is no parallel in the United States) hawk newspapers, magazines, cheap histories, pulp fiction, and even reprints of "classics." With such value placed on the written and printed word, it is no surprise that Uruguay and Argentina had the highest literacy rates in Latin America from the late nineteenth century up through the first years of the twenty-first century.[4] The reach of print culture in the region is a true success story for Latin America. The intriguing questions are these: How did literacy, written cul-ture, and the clear public concern with writing and reading become both so widespread and integral to identity in Uruguay and Argentina? What made Rioplatense print culture unique in the context of Latin America?

This book provides some answers to these questions through a pano-ramic view of the development of this print culture, from the arrival of the first printing presses on the eve of the wars of independence to the first centenary celebration of independence in 1910. *Everyday Reading* is about the special relationship between print, the public sphere, and politics in the Río de la Plata. It connects the many ways of experiencing reading to the activities, festivities, and daily chores and realities of a century that ended with the establishment of Latin America's most successful systems of pub-lic primary education. And it offers a broader understanding of what it meant to read and to be a reader, and how these practices affected identity.

My regional focus is central to my argument and imperative for grasp-ing the full impact of the connections between print and politics, for Uru-guay and Argentina shared a common historical experience up to the early twentieth century. Both were part of the colonial viceroyalty of the Río de la Plata, which fragmented into smaller political units during the wars of independence. The civil wars of the middle 1800s were fought across the Uruguay-Argentina border, with soldiers and military leaders from both countries battling both Uruguayan and Argentine opponents, and their ramifications affected the entire region regardless of topographical divi-sions. The late nineteenth-century push for public education in Uruguay went hand in hand with its development in Argentina. The architects of these systems—Domingo Sarmiento on one side and José Pedro Varela on the other—traveled together, they read each other's writings, and they inspired each other. Teachers and school administrators collaborated with each other and crossed the river to work with their counterparts. Argentine authors of textbooks saw their lessons taught in Uruguayan schools, and vice versa. State formation occurred in similar ways at the same time in both countries, and toward the end of the 1800s, immigrants primarily from Spain and Italy filled the port cities of Montevideo and Buenos Aires and fanned out into the countryside.[5] In Argentina, immigrants accounted for 25 percent of the population by 1895. Similarly, they made up close to 22 percent of Uruguay's population according to the 1900 national census. After 1900, the numbers continued to climb in Argentina, while they declined subtly in Uruguay.[6] Finally, at the turn of the twentieth century, new forms of print media such as illustrated magazines (the best-selling among these was the tremendously successful *Caras y Caretas* [Faces and masks]) and postcards circulated in like fashion on both sides of the Plata River. In short, the forces of modernization touched Uruguayans and Argentines without respect to nationality.

Thus, any study of the development of print culture in Uruguay or Argentina would be only half complete without equal attention to the other side of the Río de la Plata. The examples and focal points may come from either side of the river, but the attachments between readers, print media, and collective identity are characteristic of the region as a whole.

■

Before I outline the three key moments in the story that we will be following, a few conceptual definitions are in order, beginning with a term I have used several times so far: *print culture*. Print culture is formed through the bonds that connect reading publics—both literate and illiterate—to print media and texts, which often go beyond the scope of the written word. More specifically, it is concerned with the relations between the practices of reading and writing, on the one hand, and social behaviors, individual and collective values, economic transactions, political decisions, state institutions, and ideologies, on the other. The study of print culture, whose primary focus is the printed word in all its manifestations, also embraces, for example, the image that appears in a newspaper or magazine, the pasquinade or advertisement posted in the town square, the use of portraits on currencies and postal stamps, the act of reading out loud to a group of *gauchos* (cowboys from the Río de la Plata) at the country store or to illiterate soldiers huddled in trenches, and the embroidered slogans loving wives and mothers sewed into headbands worn by soldiers across Latin America in the 1800s. The terms *reading* and *reading publics* thus take on much deeper, more inclusive meanings.

This broader understanding of what it means to read provides more appropriate tools for studying the effect of print in a region where listening to a text being read aloud—a collective experience in and of itself—was by far the most common form of reading up to the last quarter of the nineteenth century. Print culture takes root where reading practices shape reading publics. This intersection, in turn, allows print media to play a main role in the formation of collective identity, from nationalism to interpretations of gender.

The second concept in need of explanation is that of *everyday reading*, which features both in the sources I study and my methodology for approaching them. In choosing this term for my title, I draw heavily on James C. Scott's pathbreaking interpretation of "everyday resistance" by peasants and Gilbert Joseph's and Daniel Nugent's edited volume on "everyday forms of state formation."[7] At first glance, the idea of everyday reading stands out for being both ordinary and extraordinary. Everyday print culture was largely part of traditional patterns of association, from the newspaper announcements read from pulpits during the period of independence, to the songlike popular poetry of the 1830s, to textbooks read aloud by youth to their families at kitchen tables in the 1890s.[8] These modes of gathering were "normal," insofar as citizens regularly attended mass, often spent time at the dry goods store (which doubled as a bar and social space), and circled around their family tables for conversation. Everyday reading strengthened such forms of sociability; it brought people together more often than before and in greater numbers. That is, people began associating with each other *because* of reading, and reading became the centerpiece of sociability. As a result, it solidified beliefs and forms of behavior. Of course, for these reasons, the role of everyday reading in these actions was extraordinary, too.

Like everyday resistance, everyday forms of reading had unintended consequences. The fury-filled newspaper articles and poetry of the independence wars drove both a printing revolution in the region and a shift to new forms of communication. Popular literature from 1830 to 1880 celebrated rural traditions and modes of behavior, but at the same time it stirred up hatred for the newly formed political parties. The very success of school textbooks and notebooks at instilling gender identity and patriotic spirit on both sides of the river far exceeded the expectations of the authors and the state bureaucrats who supported the publication and use of this type of reading material. The daily reading children did in schools from the early 1880s though the 1910 centenary celebration radically altered the landscape of Rioplatense print culture for the next hundred years.

Everyday reading is also extraordinary for its seeming opposition to the traditional understanding of "literature" still held by some scholars and the general public today. For over one hundred years, scholars from a range of disciplines—most prominently literary studies—and celebrated men (and occasionally women) of letters have considered "literature" to refer to a unique practice and cultural product. A work of literature is something to be admired, goes the thinking, precisely because it is something out of the ordinary—perhaps universal—that transmits fleeting aesthetic value. Literature is *not* part of daily life. Rather, it is the group of writings that certain men (and sometimes women) discuss while sipping tea or brandy, and label as "art" or simply "literature." This notion characterized the scope of the meaning of "literature" throughout the 1800s and much of the twentieth century. It also conditioned the way generations of students have approached the study of the role of writing prior to 1900.

While cultural historians and scholars in literary and cultural studies have done much over the past two decades to modify that image of exclusivity, especially when working with twentieth-century topics, some of its hues still linger when we deal with pre-1900 Latin America, where the sources are much more ephemeral and thus harder to find and access. When I describe the ideas behind this book, one of the most common questions I'm asked by scholars from different fields is, "Which writers or works do you study?" Bartolomé Hidalgo and José Hernández, who figure in this monograph, are among the few writers who are well known today. "Luis Pérez" (an ex-soldier-turned-poet whose fame threatened to overshadow that of prominent intellectuals), *El nene* (an Argentine textbook that went through some 120 editions), "collectible cards" (the ones with stories that were included in cigarette boxes), or "Emma Catalá de Princivalle" (the Uruguayan author of officially selected books on home economics) get far more attention in this book, but far fewer among my colleagues would recognize these references. While less glamour is associated with everyday reading, I hope my focus on it will help transform both how to think about reading and writing and how to study print culture in nineteenth-century Latin America. Put differently, my hope is that we come to understand everyday reading more in line with its pervasive and powerful historical role and function.

We can highlight some general characteristics of everyday reading. To begin, the print media with which readers interact on a daily or at least regular basis are illustrative of this type of reading. Newspapers are a good example. They are produced for sustained and habitual consumption. In the 1800s, copies of newspapers were often passed from one group of readers to another before being used for purposes not related to reading at all, such as wiping up spills. Textbooks of the 1890s offer another example of reading material designed for consistent and repeated interaction, as they were employed in daily lessons in the classroom and in reading time among family members at home.

Popular literature functions in a similar fashion and offers insight into other features of everyday reading: it depends in part on widespread reception, its ability to be communicated orally, its incorporation of certain vocabulary and easily memorized syntax, and its rejection by those who consider themselves arbiters of what is and is not due the title of "literature."[9] Authors of this type of writing aim to insert their work into daily life in ways that, for instance, are not even contemplated by authors of novels who deem their creations appropriate only for society's most "educated" citizens. What popular literature points to more generally are everyday reading's multiple audiences, forms of distribution and circulation, and associated reading practices, with *multiple* being the keyword here.

All these characteristics help distinguish everyday reading from other types of reading and cultural consumption and suggest why it is so important, above all when it comes to understanding the connections between print culture, politics, and identity formation. This brief, general description may suggest notions of "high" and "low" forms of writing or reading publics. While I believe that the very idea of everyday reading embodies something of this dichotomy, my main claim revolves around print culture's impact and reach, which I strive to demonstrate with clear, concrete examples in each of this book's chapters. In Argentina and Uruguay, it was in this shared world of everyday reading where attachments to group identities formed best, and where print media and reading practices inspired behaviors, attitudes, and values that ranged from waging war to educating future citizens. The development of the relationship between politics and writing, and of the increasingly powerful role of reading and writing in shaping individual and group identities, depended on the everyday reading that gradually became a forceful presence in all citizens' lives in the Río de la Plata over the course of the nineteenth century.

Everyday Reading from 1780 to 1910

Three historical moments define the development of print culture in the Río de la Plata and give shape to the chronological arc of this book: the revolutionary moment of independence in the early 1800s, the high point of cattle culture at midcentury, and the establishment and expansion of national public primary schools during the late nineteenth and early twentieth centuries.

We begin by looking at the emerging uses of print and their connections to politics and the public sphere during the revolutionary moment, spanning from the arrival of the first printing presses in the region (the first of which was unpacked in Buenos Aires in 1780) to a short-lived period of peace in the early 1830s. Buenos Aires was a backwater contraband port during most of the colonial period, but it experienced substantial growth after 1780, with its population reaching over forty thousand by 1810. Montevideo—the most densely populated place across the river—grew rapidly too, though it had only a little over a quarter of this number of inhabitants in the early 1800s.[10] It was thus natural enough that the provinces of the Plata did not constitute a market for print media during the colonial period like the more heavily populated urban centers of Lima and Mexico. The lack of a culture of print in the region during the colonial period made the arrival of printing presses and their deployment of texts all the more significant during the wars of independence.

The words these first presses published in newspapers, poems, and official documents sparked a printing revolution that went hand in hand with the wars of independence. The power of the printed word and image underwent further elaboration at public celebrations such as the parties commemorating the 1810 May Revolution and the inaugural festivities for the first public libraries in Buenos Aires (1812) and Montevideo (1816).[11] These events helped create new public meeting places where elites and popular classes communicated in new ways, and where print was crucial. Chapter 1 ends with a view of the role print played in the creation and dissemination of new national symbolic repertoires, including patriotic poetry, coats of arms, declarations of independence, and constitutions. From the outbreak of the wars to the signing of Uruguay's first constitution in 1830, print culture grew into a legitimizing force for republican ideals.

Other regions in Latin America were hosts to similar revolutionary publications. Venezuela had *El Patriota Venezolano* (The Venezuelan patriot; published by the frustrated independence seeker Francisco Miranda) and the *Gaceta de Caracas* (Caracas gazette; a paper that switched ownership repeatedly from the patriot side to that of the royalists). Antonio Nariño gained fame for his work as a newspaper editor and all-around revolutionary kind of guy in what would become Colombia. Mexico had *El Despertador Americano* (American wake-up call), and Chile *La Aurora de Chile* (A new morning in Chile), to name just a few examples.[12] Yet the sheer volume of this type of print media in the Plata made it stand out, as did the fact that the *Gaceta de Buenos Aires* (Buenos Aires gazette) was the longest-lived independence-era newspaper and that it had inspired a flood of like-minded and reactionary papers. Also, public leaders pushed hard for reading to become part of public life, and singular figures such as the Afro-descendant Jacinto Ventura de Molina were writing up a storm in Montevideo. Taken together, the seeds for the unique role of print in this region were sown.

Where the relationship between print and politics really gained traction was in popular, gauchesque writing—both verse and prose—at mid-century. Nowhere else in Latin America was there a similar type of writing that negotiated the meeting of oral and print cultures and that allowed for the popular consumption of print media on the scale seen in the Río de la Plata. Chapter 2 looks at this process through the connections between print culture and cattle civilization.

Around the end of the wars of independence, estate owners teamed up with the proprietors of beef-jerky factories, enjoying enormous profits from the processing and sale of animal products up through the 1860s. The *caudillos* (charismatic leaders) of cattle culture became powerful political actors.[13] This was even more the case during the civil wars that rocked the region up through the 1850s. Almost everything written during this second moment revolved around the politics of cattle culture. This was no laughing matter, at least most of the time, for there was an enormous amount of writing produced in these years, and it was highly provocative in partisan terms.

At the heart of the relationship between print, politics, and power in midcentury Uruguay and Argentina was popular literature—primarily gauchesque verse and prose. The overwhelming majority of gauchesque writing supported the Argentine caudillo and head of the Federalist Party, Juan Manuel de Rosas, his Uruguayan counterpart Manuel Oribe and the Blanco Party, and, following the end of the Rosas years, traditional ways of life related to the countryside. The link between politics and print was also informed by verse in *bozal* (a language that imitated the speech patterns of Afro-descendants), partisan slurs that competed for support from enslaved and free blacks in the region, and compositions that spoke to supposed concerns of African-descended communities.[14] While the authorship of such texts was often anonymous, there is no doubting that Afro-descendants (who made up close to a third of the population in both Montevideo and Buenos Aires around midcentury) and the media that aimed to reach them were central to the development of print culture during these years. Liberal elites based primarily in Montevideo shot back in print against these popular literary currents, but most of their compositions were written for members of their own social class and thus unsuccessful in fostering popular opposition to the cattle-based social order.

Through classroom lessons, textbooks, and student notebooks, the public primary schools continued building the relationship between print, identity, and politics. Examined closely in Chapters 3 and 4, the historical moment not only solidified the uniqueness of this relationship, but also guaranteed the spread of print culture throughout these two countries in ways not seen elsewhere in Latin America, with results felt into the twenty-first century.

Throughout the second half of the nineteenth century, Latin American leaders attempted to develop public education systems. It was widely believed that education was not only central to progress and what it meant to be a "civilized" nation, but also a way to end the civil wars and political infighting that had plagued the region from north to south. Yet in most of Latin America, the efforts to create and implement publicly funded schools—primary or secondary—did not come to fruition until well into the twentieth century. There were several theoretical advances in Mexican education in the 1880s—the beginning of the so-called Golden Age of primary instruction—but there were tremendous difficulties in implementing a uniform system throughout the different states.[15] The number of primary schools more than doubled during the Porfirio Díaz years of the late 1800s and early 1900s, yet only 30 percent of school-age children were attending them in 1907. And in 1910 still close to 70 percent of adults in Mexico could not read.[16] In Chile, where a law calling for compulsory primary education was introduced in 1843 (though not approved until 1860), the education system likewise functioned better in theory than in practice. In 1859, roughly 12 percent of children aged seven to fifteen went to some form of primary school. By 1907, this figure had increased only to around 35 percent, and literacy rates were still low: 42 percent for men and 38 percent for women. Another law requiring children to attend school was passed in 1920.[17] Brazil's fragile legislation regarding public education was annulled in 1891, and the government did not reinstitute it until the 1930s. In 1870, decrees in both Colombia and Venezuela called for the creation of secular, public education systems under the control of the state, and in Ecuador and Guatemala the national governments took over municipal regulation of schools.[18] Yet nowhere did these efforts translate into success stories for public education of the likes experienced in the Plata.

Chapter 3 zooms in on the establishment of public primary education systems in Uruguay and Argentina at the end of the 1800s that really allowed everyday reading to take hold all across the region. Public schools also provided the states with a whole new range of opportunities to regulate print media and messages for very captive and impressionable audiences. In the 1860s and 1870s, Domingo Sarmiento in Argentina and José Pedro Varela in Uruguay set national public education on their shared list of things necessary for successful nations. To achieve this status for the Plata, they needed resources, and schools were key resources for instilling love of country in the youngsters and the tens of thousands of immigrants making their way into the region. Through the textbooks, notebooks, and other forms of print media they selected for use in public schools, the sowers of alphabets held direct influence over the forms of collective identity these texts were designed to inspire. The combination of all these factors made public primary schools sites where print was connected to the formation of collective identities and the project of shaping citizens for their nations like never before.

Chapter 4 considers the textbooks that taught young readers lessons in patriotism and motherhood—or, put differently, lessons in national and gender identity. Beginning around 1880, the national boards of education in Uruguay and Argentina selected the official texts for use in primary schools across both countries. Hundreds of titles were published on national history and geography, moral and civic education, and, specifically for female students, hygiene and home economics. The lessons that ran through these texts were also present in titles not solely devoted to the subjects mentioned.

The authors of these books, along with the bureaucrats who selected them, sought to instill love of country and patriotic spirit in their young readers; they strove to present a shared history that readers could tap into as a source for community; and they intended to shape girls into patriotic mothers who would understand their education as a civic duty. With these lessons for a nation, reading was a practice that occurred beyond the classroom. Children took books home and read them with or to their siblings and parents, and adults learning to read and write often used the same textbooks. In all these instances, the act of reading was one of national importance, in its promotion of community identity and gender roles. The comments students scribbled in their notebooks, the exercises they completed based on the books, and the letters of patriotic devotion they crafted are strong indicators of how children took to heart the lessons they learned. They show how reading became linked to citizenship. And given the numbers of students who had attended primary schools in the Río de la Plata by 1910, and the ways such textbooks were read in the wider community, such lessons clearly allowed for the popular appropriation of official discourses on nationalism and gender identity.

By the 1910 centennial celebration of independence, then, print culture had reshaped forms of communication in Uruguay and Argentina. Reading and writing were the most important components of education; popular novels flourished, as did illustrated magazines for the general public; new national currencies, especially in the form of paper money, circulated symbolically charged images; postcards communicated complex messages about sons going off to battle as well as simple notes about family meals;

tobacco products carried meaningful names and imagery, and some even included prizes such as cards depicting highlights from the poem *Martín Fierro* and popular novels; and in small rural towns and in the capital cities, circuses and theaters performed written culture for large audiences eager to follow the next gauchesque drama or immigrant story. These types of print media, which saw massive distribution beginning around 1890, are the focus of the epilogue, their rightful place in the story. By the time they appeared, the contours of print culture were defined and print media were part of daily life for all Uruguayans and Argentines—even illiterate ones. There was no escaping this fact, and nothing better than the required use of national currencies makes this point.

My broad chronological scope and regional approach are deeply indebted to previous scholarship on questions of reading and identity in Latin America. On the subject of print in nineteenth-century Latin America, Benedict Anderson's model for understanding the connections between "print capitalism" and incipient national communities during the wars of independence has been a constant point of reference for scholars (including me) dealing with this period and beyond. As Anderson rightly asserts, newspapers and other print media did play a significant part in garnering support for the patriot cause and stirring feelings of community, though this occurred only during and after the wars of independence, and through multiple modes of contact with reading.[19]

Others have explored fruitfully the links of writing to identity formation in a variety of contexts. In her often-cited *Foundational Fictions*, Doris Sommer did so with an eye toward novels that speak of erotics and politics—the romance behind the creation of national communities from Cuba to Argentina. Nicolas Shumway teased out the power of literary imagination in the "invention of Argentina." Paula Alonso and Iván Jaksić edited collections of essays that reveal features of the periodical press and oratory in the efforts to build sentiments of nation across Latin America. Fernando Unzueta has braved the murky waters of the affective dimension of reading. And, several studies on the politics of memory in 1800s Uruguay and the book editing industry in nineteenth-century Argentina have appeared in the last decade.[20]

While all this work—in fields spanning from literary studies to cultural and book history—has been crucial in leading to new understand-ings of the roles and impact of writing in Latin American history, three activities merit further sustained attention: (1) focusing consistently on the interactions of readers with print culture; (2) looking more broadly at the landscape of print in the nineteenth century—centering, for example, more on the spectrum of connected print media and reading activities as they were experienced then, and less on treating texts (novels, newspaper publications, poetry, and so on) in isolation; and (3) specifically for the context of the Río de la Plata in the 1800s, framing problems through a regional perspective rather than concentrating on them within strict national confines. I hope that by beginning to address all three of these in the pages that follow, this book will offer a more complete picture of the relationship between print culture and collective identity in the Río de la Plata.

Chapter 1

Words, Wars, and Public Celebrations

The Emergence of Rioplatense Print Culture (1780–1830)

■ By 6 December 1779, the deal had been sealed. After sitting inactive for more than a dozen years in the dark, dank basement of the University of Córdoba, the first and only printing press of the Cordoban Jesuits was ready to make the journey over to Buenos Aires. When the Spanish crown ordered the expulsion of Jesuits from Spanish America in 1767, the press had been in use for only a year, producing materials for the acclaimed Colegio de Monserrat. It had been disassembled and hastily stored in the basement, with no care taken to prevent moisture from penetrating the wood or to package properly the lead type blocks.[1]

Only in 1779 was new interest shown in the press, ironically by a representative of the Spanish crown—the newly appointed Viceroy of the Río de la Plata, Juan José de Vértiz y Salcedo. Vértiz, whom historian and one-time Argentine president Bartolomé Mitre later praised as the most progressive colonial official the colonies had seen, had the notion to create a *casa de niños expósitos*, or orphanage, in Buenos Aires. After all, the city's population—and number of orphans—was rapidly expanding with the growing importance of Buenos Aires as a commercial port. Vértiz recalled that there was a press in storage in Córdoba (confiscated from the "ex-Jesuits," as the viceroy called them), and envisioned financing this humanitarian venture by establishing a print shop in Buenos Aires, in the same locale as the future orphanage.[2]

In mid-September 1779, Vértiz wrote to the rector of the Colegio Convictorio—formerly de Monserrat—in Córdoba to inquire about the condition of the press and to ask what it would be worth. The rector wrote back, humbly stating that Vértiz could of course have the press, paying the Colegio what suited his fancy. The rector added that since there was no inventory detailing the parts of the press, it was hard to tell what was missing. Its condition, however, was not beyond repair, which was what the viceroy was looking for. On 16 October, Vértiz wrote back to say he would pay the Colegio what the ex-Jesuits had spent in the early 1760s, and asked the rector to set things in order for the press's voyage.[3] Finally, in December, wooden boxes packed full of the press's parts were loaded into a covered cart owned by a certain Félix Juárez. Juárez directed his oxen along an old colonial commerce route, traversing the pampas, and arrived in Buenos Aires in February 1780.[4]

There, at the newly created orphanage-print shop named the Casa de Niños Expósitos, the viceroy financed the press's rehabilitation, and before long, it was turning out publications. Vértiz submitted his argument for the shop to Carlos III, albeit nearly a year after the press had arrived in Buenos Aires and printing activity was well under way. In proper formal style, the king dispatched a royal certificate of approval to Vértiz in which he wrote that the press would be "very useful and even necessary in that city," and lavished praise on the official for "all you have done regarding this matter, giving you thanks for the notorious zeal with which you labor in the service of God, and for me."[5] Neither the king nor the viceroy imagined he was laying the foundation for the birthplace of revolutionary print media during the wars of independence.

By 1810, over 1,200 publications had been printed, including letters, official edicts, textbooks, Rousseau's *Social Contract*, bills of sale, and the Río de la Plata's first newspaper, the *Telégrafo Mercantil*.[6] With the May Revolution of 1810, the Niños Expósitos press became an instrument of the patriots. During the next decade, it fired off thousands of circulars, poems, newspapers, official documents, letters, and patriotic songs, all waging rhetorical war on monarchic power. By the early 1820s, the old press's type blocks were well worn. It was time to move on. In 1824, Bernardino Rivadavia, who was then minister of the Buenos Aires provincial government, signed into law the new Imprenta del Estado, which would take over the work and some of the materials of the Niños Expósitos print shop. The old press at the shop was taken by Victorino Solá to Salta, where a remarkable transubstantiation took place: in the late 1860s, the blocks were melted into several hundred bullets that would be used to fight off some of the last bands of gauchos led by Felipe Varela, then wreaking havoc in the northwest.[7] The historian and bibliographer Antonio Zinny lamented the trajectory—literally—of the type blocks of the old Niños Expósitos press. It began with the blocks as messengers of civilization, he wrote, and ended with them piercing the bodies of "barbarians."[8]

■

The "biography" of the Niños Expósitos printing press, its vigorous days of revolutionary youth in Buenos Aires to its old age and death among gauchos in Salta, outlines the two key moments during which Rioplatense print culture emerged, namely the wars for independence and the most profitable years of cattle culture. The revolutionary moment, spanning from the British invasions of the region in 1806–1807 to a time of relative peace in the early 1830s, saw the birth of print culture in the Plata and is the focus of this chapter. Chapter 2 takes on the relationship of writing to cattle culture.

The revolutionary moment of Rioplatense print culture imparted enduring characteristics. First, writing served as a weapon of war to convince and condemn, with words of independence driving a veritable printing revolution and leading to a revolution in forms of communication. Second, the newly sown emphasis on the importance of the printed word—promoted as a tangible sign of legitimacy—began opening up a new public sphere that encouraged greater public interaction between lettered elites (those who could exercise power through the technology of writing) and those (literate or not) who occupied lower positions in the social hierarchy, such as free blacks, women, and slaves. Public libraries and patriotic celebrations are examples of the new meeting places. Lastly, print culture during the revolutionary moment was critical to the elaboration of new symbolic repertoires to accompany the new republics, in poetic military marches, national anthems, coats of arms, and constitutions.

Throughout the wars of independence, lettered elites were the ones who for the most part set the parameters that the budding culture of print would follow. That said, there were literate Latin Americans who were not members of elite groups but could still interpret and manipulate legal, political, religious, and poetic discourses in writing.[9] And, the unlettered interacted closely with new modes of communication by listening to public readings of wartime newspapers, participating in public celebrations where print was central, and by associating with new symbolic icons disseminated through print. Simply put, the revolutionary moment was the beginning of greater contact between people and print—the first stage toward the transformation of print media into everyday reading.

By looking at a sample of oral and written components of print during this period, we will see that the emergence of Rioplatense print culture began with words and wars. Moreover, patriotic celebrations and the creation of repertoires of national symbols were central to this story. If the revolutionary moment defined this emergence, the reach of the wars, the notion of "independence," and the initial efforts to create "national" and "republican" discourses were in turn indebted to the words, celebrations, and symbols that gave life to print culture in the Plata. Certainly much of the fighting broke out not "because" of what was written in a given text, although there are examples of papers (such as the *Southern Star* in Montevideo, covered in this chapter) and loose leaves that led directly to armed conflicts or were tangled in the messy lead-up to insurgent and royalist action (Simón Bolívar's well-known "Proclamation of War to the Death" is a good example from elsewhere). The more interesting and important question is how such print media stoked the flames of revolution, and how they became more pervasive forms of communication.

What we are dealing with here, then, is a moment in literary history that has not received attention proportionate to the impact it had on writing in the region during the rest of the century. Wartime newspapers, state-organized celebrations, and patriotic poetry appeared all across Latin America during the first third of the nineteenth century.[10] But it was in the Río de la Plata that the longest-lived paper of independence spread its messages; it was there that some of the earliest anthologies of "national" literature began to circulate; and it was the region that saw the greatest proliferation of new presses, newspapers, and loose-leaf production from 1810 to 1830. Let us begin with some of these words of independence.

Words and Wars of Independence

The history of Montevideo's first printing press is not as exciting as that of the "ex-Jesuit" press that ended up as bullets in gauchos, but it was a wartime press from the start. When the British invaded the Río de la Plata in 1806 and 1807, they were driven out of Buenos Aires, to the surprise of all. In the rival port city of Montevideo, British soldiers were able to establish a foothold that, while lasting only six months, allowed the occupying forces and merchants to launch a print shop. In his colorful and casual style, the self-taught Uruguayan man of letters Isidoro de María relates "public opinion" toward the press in the early nineteenth century: "Bah! There was no need to speak of that. . . . For some broadsheet or almanac, the *factory* over at the Niños Expósitos in the viceregal capital was more than enough . . . to teach the *Christ* to one or another young fellow."[11] But things changed in 1807. "By chance, or maybe by the luck of the devil," de María tells us, referring to the establishment of the British print shop, "its first birth was a little newspaper titled the *Southern Star.* . . . 23 May 1807 was the day of the birth, but the little fellow was short-lived, because he gave up the ghost in July of the same year."[12] Indeed, the press the English brought was only active for a couple months. Yet, in this short stint, the writers of the *Southern Star* introduced a new liberal, mercantilist attitude toward commerce in the port city and aimed to discredit the Spanish crown's capacity to rule the viceroyalty of the Plata.[13] So effectively incendiary were its pages, published in English and Spanish, that the Audiencia of the Río de la Plata charged Mariano Moreno—one of the intellectual heroes of independence—with the task of writing a refutation of the paper's claims. Given that he agreed with most of them, this put Moreno in a difficult position, which he got out of by advising that silence was the best way to put an end to the spread of the *Southern Star*'s propaganda.[14]

The Audiencia did not leave it at that. In June 1807, it issued an edict—published, of course, by the Niños Expósitos press—that prohibited the sale, possession, or reading in public or private of the *Southern Star*, judged to be the most "pernicious," "seductive," and effective weapon for the achievement of its "evil" designs.[15] Anyone who came into contact with the paper or who had knowledge of others possessing or reading the damned *Southern Star* and did not immediately report this to the proper authorities would be judged a "traitor to king and state, and would face the irreversible punishment corresponding to this atrocious crime."[16] Words of independence were not taken lightly.

With the Niños Expósitos print shop doing a fair amount of business, and with its press in need of spare type blocks, the prospect of acquiring the Southern Star press, which the British had abandoned when they left the Plata, looked attractive to the Audiencia. The war between England and Spain made it impossible for the Audiencia to request the shipment of new parts from Europe to the Plata. More importantly, the Audiencia believed that if it could wrench the press from Montevideo, they could put an end to the threat of malicious propaganda being spread in print in the future. So in September 1807, the Southern Star press, having been disassembled and packed up, was taken by boat across the river to Buenos Aires. There it gave new life to the Niños Expósitos shop, which was soon again printing revolutionary material (not what the Real Audiencia had in mind when it purchased the press) that made its way to the Banda Oriental—the territory that would become Uruguay.[17] Presumably some of the Southern Star type blocks also later became bullets used against gauchos.

Newspapers such as the *Southern Star* constitute our first stop. During the wars, daily, weekly, and monthly newspapers sprang up on both sides of the Plata River, and not just in the port cities of Buenos Aires or Montevideo.[18] Interior provinces acquired printing presses and produced newspapers, broadsheets, and poems.

Before the local *junta provisional* in Buenos Aires declared its representative authority over the provinces of the Plata in May 1810, the Niños Expósitos press had had a monopoly on printing in the viceroyalty. With the English invasions of the Plata and the crisis of the Spanish monarchy, politically charged publications grew in number and severity.[19] It was not difficult, then, for the sole press in Buenos Aires to change from being a royal press to a wartime press and instrument for the new governing junta. Its new role became quickly evident when, on 28 May 1810, it published the announcement of the removal of then-Viceroy Cisneros, along with the junta's first official proclamation.[20] A little over a week later, the liberal-minded Mariano Moreno's *Gaceta de Buenos Aires* entered circulation and served as the mouthpiece of the junta. The *Gaceta* would last until September 1821, though its *printed* version was not very accessible to the masses it hoped to reach.

That is exactly why its messages were publicly pronounced in churches and squares, and often in cafés and *pulperías* (country stores), too. Those who could not read the *Gaceta* in print could listen to it as they would to a sermon or story, which were typical modes of communication in late colonial America. In the same way that citizens in church professed loyalty to their faith and learned religious doctrine, they likewise needed to learn about the junta in order to show due reverence, or so goes the circular sent by the junta to the provincial dioceses. Since many rural inhabitants would be unaware of the changes taking place in Buenos Aires, and since many lived in conditions that did not facilitate reading the paper, the junta ordered priests to "bring together the parishioners after mass and read them the *Gaceta de Buenos Aires*."[21]

This same vein of thought is present in Bernardo Monteagudo's call for "functionaries, enlightened citizens, those of the *delicate sex*, and *americanos todos*" to read the paper to workers, artisans, and soldiers. A leading intellectual figure of the period, Monteagudo served as one of the paper's editors (that is, chief writers). "Arms will not lead the way to improve our situation," pleads Monteagudo in the 27 December 1811 issue. All citizens, he argues, must understand their duties (to the patria) in order to know and exercise their rights, but this hope will not be possible without educating those "whose humiliating heritage has always been ignorance. If only some passionate patriot would devote himself to write a political catechism to be used for general education. Meanwhile, we do not have any other recourse save publicly circulated newspapers." What needs to happen, concludes Monteagudo, is for the central government to impose on local mayors "the strict obligation to bring together on holidays artisans and other workers in a public place known by all in order to read and explain to them the newspapers. Judges, too, should join priests in this commitment to share the papers with workers and people from the countryside."[22] Military leaders should likewise have the papers read to soldiers wherever they are stationed. As a military man himself, Monteagudo knew what he was talking about.

People who did not qualify as "enlightened citizens" but who increasingly counted themselves as *Americanos* also took Monteagudo's call to heart, or at least the spirit of it.[23] This was certainly true of the ex-slave Joaquín Fretes in Mendoza, Argentina, accused of being one of the leaders of a slave rebellion planned for May 1812. Fretes had come to Mendoza from Santiago de Chile and joined forces with an Afro-descendant named Bernardo. In Santiago, Fretes had worked for clergymen, one of whom had granted him his freedom so that he could join the patriot cause in Buenos Aires. What distinguished Fretes from other leaders of the rebellion, especially Bernardo, was that he knew how to read *and* write.[24] In fact, Fretes had read to blacks gathered to plot their course of action an issue of the *Gaceta de Buenos Aires* (giving voice to its fiery liberal rhetoric about doing away with slavery), and he spoke about the Junta de Buenos Aires's plans to prohibit slave ships from entering port in the Plata.[25] He also wrote, circulated, and read aloud pasquinades detailing the goals of the movement. If Fretes was the "intellectual" leader, Bernardo had the personal network of contacts with black communities in and around Mendoza, in particular the cobblers' guild. Bernardo recruited participants for the rebellion, telling them that they were going to achieve their freedom and that he had a copy of the *Gaceta* stating as much.[26]

Public readings of the sort Monteagudo encouraged and the kind Fretes carried out were not entirely new; they had occurred during the colonial era, at times as part of royal spectacles. What was new was their dramatically increased frequency, as well as the *Gaceta's* revolutionary content, the reactions it provoked (specifically in the form of print media), and the *quantity* of similar publications that were following suit and being read publicly. During the wars, the printed word filled the streets and the air of the city and the countryside and was the center of attention at secret gatherings as never before.

One of the earliest of these reactions came from the *Gazeta de Montevideo*, started in October 1810. The royalist holdout of Montevideo had been without a print shop since the Southern Star press's departure to the other side three years earlier. Increasingly threatened both by patriot forces from Buenos Aires and cattle hands led by the caudillo José Artigas (who were fighting as much for independence from Napoleonic Spain as from the influence of Buenos Aires), and confronted with the propaganda filling the pages of the *Gaceta de Buenos Aires* and edicts printed by the Niños Expósitos, the *Cabildo* (town hall) of Montevideo decided that it needed a new press to combat revolutionary words. The government leaders made a plea to Carlota Joaquina, then living in Rio de Janeiro. A sister of the exiled Spanish king, she had been married at age ten to the Portuguese prince João (later João VI as king).

A common feature of many of the period's newspapers was the *prospecto*, which served as a sort of introduction to the writers' purpose. The prospecto of the *Gazeta de Montevideo* sheds light on how Carlota and the Cabildo struck a deal. In view of the recent "popular commotion" across the river, one reads, the residents of Montevideo had demonstrated a level of loyalty to Fernando VII that made them the subject of special recognition by the court of Brazil and Carlota. In order to publicize the laudable character of the Montevideans, Carlota sent to them a new press that they christened "La Carlota."[27] As the prospecto goes on to say, Carlota was "interested in preserving the dominions of her august brother," a sentiment manifest in the epistolary exchanges between Carlota and the Cabildo members reproduced in the 13 October 1810 edition of the paper.[28] Thus, the new press was designed from its beginning to help fight the rebels in Buenos Aires and protect the colonies for the dethroned Spanish monarch.

In this spirit, the prospecto declared that the local government would publish the *Gazeta* every Thursday with news of Spain and its kingdom, royal edicts, and "all that could be of interest to the true Patriots."[29] In an early appropriation of the word *patriotas*—a term that would soon become the code name for those across America opposed to the royalists—the writers of the paper hoped to convince their readers to continue supporting the crown and remain strong in the face of the changing tides coming from across the Plata. The prospecto continues, "This is precisely the goal the Government proposes with the paper that is here introduced to you . . . to gather news on all that occurs until calm is restored in the Viceroyalty, and publish it free from decoration and with the simplicity that characterizes truth, so that you see the outlines of your true Character."[30] If words were capable of causing a big enough stir in Buenos Aires to jeopardize the rule of the king, then words from Montevideo should be capable of quelling the fire.

Words, writing, and print were precisely the themes of a short essay titled "On the Press" that appears in the 6 November 1810 issue of the *Gazeta de Montevideo*. In this piece, a certain "Fileno" argues in a string of syllogisms that the *word* is the greatest form of exercising moral order, that *writing* is a way of fixing words, and that *printing* is the perfection of writing. According to this logic, claims Fileno, printing is a "moral" activity, necessary for the proper maintenance of human societies.[31] Given the importance of words, writing, and print, "we can deduce that writing and the press cannot and should not serve to spread gossip or slander" against a person's moral character or, perhaps more urgently, against one's government. Fileno argues that a free press should exist, but "the press should be free insofar as it is necessary to promote the positive side of our civilization" (that is, the side opposed to the trash emanating from Buenos Aires).

When the free press is employed to speak ill of people, "healthy traditions," or "the decency of government," then it loses its moral character.[32]

Fileno's words, and those of other authors of the *Gazeta de Montevideo*, were part of the project to strike back rhetorically at the news from Buenos Aires and other parts of America on the verge of declaring self-rule. The *Gazeta*, however, was not the only paper in print in Montevideo or Uruguay during the revolutionary moment. From the establishment of the Southern Star press in 1807 to the signing of the constitution in 1830 (a year of short-lived peace in Uruguay), close to sixty different newspapers were published.[33] Most of these lasted only a few months to a year, and it was not until 1826 that printing presses produced newspapers outside of Montevideo, but the proliferation of newspapers was significant for the war-torn Banda Oriental, as was the fact that by 1830 nineteen print shops had been or were still printing newspapers and other print media in Uruguay. Between 1826 and 1830, seven presses sprang up outside the city of Montevideo. The parts and type blocks for these presses, as well as for the new ones appearing across the river, came from a complex combination of sources. Many components were inherited or bought from defunct print shops that had acquired materials from the United States and, after the wars, Europe. Other parts were made from scratch by carpenters and ironworkers.

Meanwhile, back in Buenos Aires, the presses were still hot, and the word *independence* was becoming more present in revolutionary rhetoric. In July 1812, the Niños Expósitos press began printing a new weekly paper—*El Grito del Sud* (Cry of the South). *El Grito* was the creation of the recently founded Patriotic and Literary Society of Buenos Aires (a significant name for a group devoted to joining written culture to patriotic causes). The paper came off the press with guns blazing, with the first page dated "1812, third year of liberty."[34] Opposed to every word printed in "insipid rags" such as the royalist *Gazeta de Montevideo*, and speaking of independence openly and without reservation, the prospecto opens bluntly: "Whoever thinks that human suffering derives from origins other than those of slavery and ignorance is either a stupid imbecile or an impudent impostor."[35] As the prospecto continues, there is no mistaking the target of this statement: the Spanish crown, responsible for bringing slavery, misery, and sadness to America. "But the time has arrived to throw off once and for all the weight of oppression," the writer goes on, "and for us to begin to enjoy and exercise those sacred rights that tyrants so long denied us." These rights are enumerated as property, liberty, and security. If the readers are disposed to make an effort "worthy of Americans" to maintain what had been achieved on 25 May 1810, then the miserable yoke can be cast aside forever.

Of course, reading *El Grito* would be crucial to keeping the May spirit alive, etching its meaning into tradition, and remaining free from misery. After his scathing attack on Spain and what the colonial years have done to America, the writer concludes, "I have thus sketched the plan for a newspaper that some members of the Patriotic Society of the Río de la Plata have pondered sharing with the public, convinced that print is the only means of propagating knowledge among the people."[36]

Like the *Gaceta de Buenos Aires*, which had been started by Mariano Moreno, *El Grito* was written by lettered elites, most likely including the author of the future national anthem, Vicente López y Planes. The epigraph in Latin at the head of every edition suggests that the paper was not entirely for the "average" reader.[37] That said, the authors of *El Grito* were aware of the need to reach those who could not understand the epigraph or, in many instances, even read the paper's contents. It was sold outside the city of Buenos Aires, which allowed its messages to travel a certain distance into the interior provinces. Like the *Gaceta* and the decree announcing the importance of a free press, read publicly on 1 December 1811, *El Grito*, too, was read aloud to crowds in cafés and on occasion in church.[38] In the 21 July 1812 issue, the editors even published a patriotic song titled "*Marcha patriótica* with Notes for the Intelligence of Vulgar People," followed indeed by five pages of notes.[39] How accessible they were to "vulgar people," or the unlettered, is another question. If the masses did not find any of these measures helpful in absorbing *El Grito*'s messages, they could still drink in the patriotic spirit at the Niños Expósitos print shop, where they could check out a portrait of the "republican patriot" and "sage magistrate" Mariano Moreno that was for sale.[40] They might even catch on to the wonders of the printed word while there.

During 1815, a year before independence was formally declared for the provinces that would become Argentina, a handful of short-lived newspapers were started that called for independence once and for all. One of these was the appropriately titled *El Independiente*. Like *El Grito del Sud* and the *Gazeta de Montevideo*, *El Independiente* paid tribute to the power of the printed word in its prospecto, which recognized that the paper's value relied on "the divine art of writing that gives permanent life to human knowledge."[41] Attributed to Mariano Moreno's brother Manuel, the prospecto highlights the importance of this new form of print media: "Newspapers have become the touchstone of the national education of a people. . . . It is not so much the distance separating America from the center of knowledge [Europe] that has been the cause of its overdue enlightenment, as much as its lack of good newspapers."[42] El Independiente lasted only four months, however, despite its editor's goal to write in a style accessible to all types of readers and his claims that the paper would live as long as a free press existed.[43] A similar venture of the same period was the newspaper Los Amigos de la Patria y de la Juventud, a monthly that lasted six months and that, as the title indicates, was a friend of the patria and younger generations. The introduction to the paper stated its main concern to be education. But the editor was more inclined to provide space for (French) literary selections, usually illustrative of some moral point, and for questions dealing with war, even though the paper was an advocate of peace—a presentation aimed at tempering the hot attitudes coming from papers like El Independiente.[44]

The short life span of papers like El Independiente and Los Amigos complicates assessment of their impact on readers. Both papers had emerged from visions of reaching beyond the closed circles of lettered elites, but with few issues in circulation, El Independiente's epigraphs in Latin, and Los Amigos's urban tone, it is hard to imagine their words taking hold in the countryside or among illiterate city dwellers. Nevertheless, these papers, along with scores of others, were central to the spread of information during the revolutionary moment. As such, they were part of print media's first inroads toward opening a new public sphere and weaving their way into traditional patterns of sociability. The sheer quantity of publications that appeared on the public landscape and the multiple ways in which they were read increased the chances of the authors' intended messages being effectively communicated and leading to the desired action on the part of readers and listeners.

Throughout the decade stretching from May 1810 to the defeat of the weak forces of central authority operating in Buenos Aires in 1820, over forty newspapers (printed by the Niños Expósitos and other, newer presses) appeared in the provinces that would form Argentina. In the years leading up to Juan Manuel de Rosas's rise to power in 1829, almost two hundred more newspapers entered the scene, eighty of which were published and circulated outside Buenos Aires.[45] For lettered elites eager to spread republican values, the press became a symbol of liberal progress, with the printed word lending legitimacy to their messages and, hence, their endeavor.

Newspapers were key messengers of words of independence, but they were not the only ones. They had help from new public libraries and patriotic parties where print enjoyed a privileged, public place.

Print Culture, Public Places, and Patriotic Parties

The creation of the Río de la Plata's first public libraries was central to the emergence of a culture of print during the revolutionary moment. After newspapers took the first major step in this process by spreading words of war, libraries broadened the reach of print and cemented its connections to republicanism by opening a new public sphere where greater public interaction could take place between lettered elites and popular classes. Patrick Joyce has studied this process in the case of nineteenth-century England. He stresses that freedom and the success of liberalism rested on the creation of "political legibility and visibility" in which each member of society could see the others.[46] "The idea of the *free* library," he argues, "was central to the creation of a new sort of public, one constituted in a civic, urban public sphere. . . . Open, and therefore transparent. . . . Transparency was also the key to its particular function as one variant of liberal community." Libraries, continues Joyce, extended the culture of self-knowledge and self-help to create liberal citizens—or at least that was one of their main objectives—and thus played into "a liberal ethics of governance."[47] These bonds between the legitimacy of republicanism, public access to knowledge, and a new kind of citizen operated in the creation of libraries in the Plata.

The first of these libraries to appear was the Biblioteca Pública de Buenos Aires, which became the foundation of the future national library. There is debate on whether or not the ubiquitous Mariano Moreno deserves credit as the *founder* of the library, but most scholars of Argentina agree on the simple fact that setting up a public library in a time of war was a significant symbolic event.[48]

Moreno took charge of requesting both donations of items for the library's collection and financial contributions from those who were willing to give to this new cause of "public enlightenment." By the end of 1810, he had raised a considerable sum for librarian salaries and gathered close to four thousand books, maps, and other materials for the initial collection. Thus, while the creation of the library was supported by the junta and organized by its secretary (Moreno), it was in effect a public effort that the donations and contributions of Rioplatense inhabitants (albeit from among the wealthy) had made possible.[49] By buying into the public library, they were taking up stock in the new revolutionary culture of print being advertised on a daily basis in the *Gaceta de Buenos Aires* and other patriot papers. In this sense, the library was a symbol of the May Revolution and of the emergence of a new form of communication. It represented the effort to stake a claim on intellectual independence—a metaphorical imperative to accompany the political independence patriots sought.[50]

After multiple changes to the date for opening the library, things were finally ready by March 1812. A week before the inaugural day, circulars advertising the event were sent to priests, military figures, judges, the administrator of post offices, and other government officials, charging them to notify others and attend the event themselves.[51] The inauguration took place on 16 March 1812, and it was a well-attended public act, complete with a military band, lofty speeches, and the presence of the junta's central political figures, all welcoming the new public place where people could mingle with reading materials. Juan Manuel Beruti, who lived through the English invasions of Buenos Aires, the wars for independence, and the Rosas years, tells us in his memoirs that "an infinite number of citizens" were present at the opening ceremony.[52] News about the event in the *Gaceta* was more reserved. A short note that appeared on 13 March to remind readers of the upcoming celebration was the only mention made of the whole affair.[53] The same brevity characterized the news of the library in the 17 March number of *El Censor*, a weekly offshoot of the *Gaceta*. Curiously, the note announcing the opening of the new library—an institution meant to embody the liberal spirit of May—was paired with an advertisement from the secretary of the Cabildo, seeking to sell a slave who knew "something about cooking."[54]

At first glance, such an advertisement seems out of step with the patriotic rhetoric in the newspapers and on display at the inauguration of the library, but it points to the hard realities of the region's evolving political culture during the 1810s and the contradictory meanings of independence. As Peter Blanchard has demonstrated, at the outset of the wars there was a disconnect between the goal of political liberty and access to personal freedom. The French and American Revolutions had supplied a vocabulary that infused revolutionary rhetoric and philosophies of liberalism and republicanism in Spanish America, but it stopped short of resolving how to deal with the enslaved population. Moreover, personal property, including slaves, was a protected liberal right. Neither property owners who favored the patriot cause nor liberal leaders who needed to maintain support from this social sector were eager to make exceptions to this right. Nevertheless, slaves gradually transformed public calls equating colonialism with the bonds of slavery into powerful appeals for personal liberation.[55] Some signs of this were visible at the festivities surrounding the creation of the public library in Montevideo.

The foundation of the Biblioteca Pública in Montevideo was a much more dramatic affair than that of its counterpart in Buenos Aires. It was celebrated with more pomp and a wealth of symbolic performances, and viewed as inseparable from the 1816 *fiestas mayas* (May celebrations). These fiestas, which were also called *fiestas cívicas*, were modeled on those that had first taken place in Buenos Aires from 23 to 26 May 1813. That May, the General Assembly had declared that the fiestas would become an annual patriotic celebration. The preface to the legislation of the fiestas reveals their intended meaning: "It is the duty of free men to immortalize the day the patria was born and to remind future generations of the joyous moment when the strength of the most intrepid broke the idol and overthrew the altar of tyranny."[56] This held true for the fiestas in Montevideo, too: they were meant to celebrate the *beginning* of the nation's new history, which was in the process of being defined, in part by print and in part by ceremonies. But similar as they were to the 1813 fiestas of Buenos Aires, the fiestas in Montevideo in May 1816 were recorded with more zeal.[57]

The anonymously written description of these events begins by relating the occurrences on 24 May, when patriots decorated their houses and buildings in the city with tricolor flags representing Artigas and the separation of the Banda Oriental from Buenos Aires. Arches made of laurel branches and flowers adorned the four corners of the main town square (what is today the Plaza Matriz). Four broadsheets with patriotic verses hung from these arches. The first two spoke of the valiant efforts of America to end the oppression of the Iberian lion. The third and fourth broadsheets went beyond merely singing the praises of those who have thrown off the colonial yoke, instead dwelling on the importance of recording the incipient collective history of the Banda Oriental. Passersby reading the verses of these last two broadsheets were encouraged to remember "the divine month of May" and consider the feats of soldiers from the Banda Oriental as a beacon for fellow Americans fighting in wars for independence.[58]

These publicly displayed printed verses were not without company that day. From 7:00 a.m. to noon there was music and food, and schoolchildren from Montevideo entered the scene around 8:00 a.m. to sing patriotic tunes. After lunch, prisoners were released from jails, and, partaking in the day's ceremonies, "some black dancers appeared in the plaza . . . emulating each other's good behavior and dancing to express their gratitude for the festive day."[59] Later that afternoon, government officials, soldiers, and denizens of the city attended a church ceremony, and at night they watched fireworks and a good "liberal" tragedy.

There were more printed words the next day, this time engraved on a pyramid rather than impressed on broadsheets. Composed by Bartolomé Hidalgo, who had introduced the voice of the gaucho in print, the pyramid's verses celebrated 25 May as the day that "shackles and tyranny disappeared." Schoolchildren encircled the pyramid at dawn. In proper patriotic spirit, they saluted the sun and intoned a song that vocalized the gist of the monument's verses (thanks to that glorious day in May, oppression has ended for Americans, and since then inhabitants of the Banda Oriental have sung praise to the great patria). The fiesta continued throughout the afternoon and night and into the next morning, with food, dance, and a theater performance of Hidalgo's *Feelings of a Patriot*.[60]

On 26 May, the schoolchildren again huddled around the pyramid and chanted their patriotic songs, from 10:00 a.m. until noon, at which time the Cabildo members augustly announced the inauguration of the Biblioteca Pública. Dámaso Antonio Larrañaga—priest, political representative of Artigas, and newly appointed director of the Biblioteca—gave the inaugural speech, in which he proclaimed that the doors of the library would be open to all who were present: "Every class of people has the right and liberty to learn from all the sciences, no matter how noble they are. All will have access to this august repository of knowledge. Come all, from the most rustic African to the most learned European."[61] Aside from being a place where citizens could "become enlightened," the new library would serve as a bedrock for republican ideals.

That the library offered a new place of learning for citizens was true, but the beginning of the period of Brazilian and Portuguese occupation of the Banda Oriental in 1817 limited access to the library and its function as a new meeting ground. Recent scholarship on Afro-Uruguayans and lettered culture, however, lends weight to the notion that white males were not the only ones who took advantage of the library's collection.[62] One Afro-Uruguayan patron of the Biblioteca was an old classmate of Larrañaga, the prolific shoemaker-soldier-writer Jacinto Ventura de Molina. Women made use of the library, too, or at least demonstrated opposition to what it stood for, as evidenced in a supposed royalist critique of the fiestas from the perspective of a female writer. Expressing her discontent, María Leoncia Pérez Rojo de Aldana proclaimed she had attended them with people she called "miscellaneous country bumpkins."[63]

Both the description of the fiestas and Larrañaga's inaugural speech were published in 1816 and distributed throughout the Banda Oriental. Artigas acknowledged receiving copies of both, musing that the fiestas and the library were means of properly forming men who would bring glory and happiness to the nation.[64] In short, first with words of war and now with words of patriotic celebrations, print was becoming an embedded social practice open to more people than its mere producers. Indeed, textual production of both the poetic and documentary sort was a key part of the fiestas, transforming the momentary celebrations into more permanent symbolic events.[65]

Other patriotic ceremonies and celebrations organized during the revolutionary period further illustrate the role of print culture in constructing a new public sphere. Hidalgo wrote a popular dialogue in which his gaucho characters Chano and Contreras discuss the joys of the May 1822 fiestas in Buenos Aires. Contreras relates what he encountered in the city, including the music and dances, fireworks, patriots, crowds, colors, and games such as the *palo enjabonado* (grease pole). He also tells readers about the "glorious verses" on display in the main square that "a fellow countryman" had read to him, not unlike the way such verses would have been read to other listeners.[66]

José Antonio Wilde provides another valuable example from Buenos Aires. During the fiestas mayas of 1823, the Literary Society, which had been created the previous year, offered a prize to the person with the best responses *in writing* to a set of questions loaded with the society's view of indigenous groups in the Río de la Plata.[67] The compensation for the winner was a mere medallion, but then again, the true reward of the competition would have been the sharing of one's ideas through writing.

Public display of pride through print was also part of the festivities held in Buenos Aires two years later, following the arrival of news on the Battle of Ayacucho. Just as the printed word had been deeply entrenched in the beginnings of the wars for independence, it was part of the fiestas marking their end (at least in most of Spanish America). On the night of 22 January 1825, a "dramatic presentation" took place in the Teatro Argentino, after which the crowds went wild singing the national anthem. Then, in an act meant to lend legitimacy to the news, a certain Colonel Ramírez stood on one of the theater's balconies and read the official report of the battle. Wilde recounts that the crowd applauded this public reading with the same "frenzy" that had filled people's hearts as they sang the national anthem.[68]

Revolutionary Symbolic Repertoires

The floundering new institutions that replaced colonial ones in the government of provincial affairs in the United Provinces and the Banda Oriental required new symbolic representations. Revolutionary print culture made possible the elaboration of symbolic repertoires. Furthermore, it was through print that these symbols reached "official" status and became *national* symbols. In turn, they gave another dimension to Rioplatense print culture in the revolutionary moment. Specifically, the elaboration of symbolic repertoires privileged print media as the premier form of communicating national iconography. These repertoires included poetic compositions and songs as well as *parnasos* (thematic anthologies), national flags and seals, and legal documents such as declarations of independence and constitutions. Whether or not such symbols successfully represented "the nation" and the diverse communities grouped as *Argentinos* or *Orientales*, they were widely disseminated through print.

Loose-leaf poems, publicly posted verses, and thematic tomes such as *La lira argentina, o Colección de las piezas poéticas dadas a luz en Buenos Aires durante la guerra de su independencia* (The Argentine Lyre, or collection of poetic pieces published in Buenos Aires during its war for independence) helped establish a set of dates for the construction of national history and cultivated a symbolic vocabulary to describe oppressive tyrants, valiant military heroes, and reverence for the patria. Patriotic verse was central to what some scholars identify as the first stage on the road to the construction of national symbols in Spanish America. From the outbreak of the May Revolution to the end of the wars, creole elites attempted to put in place a new set of symbols to replace those that accompanied colonial power.[69] Revolutionary newspapers chipped away at the old set of symbols, but they did not provide the necessary material, concisely packaged, to craft new symbols. This is where the verses came into play, occasionally in the very same newspapers—often as loose sheets and sometimes as song.

Independence generated a wealth of verse that went hand in hand with the efforts of new government institutions to develop policies on "national" culture.[70] These poetic constructions both appropriated the colonial past to craft it into a new national story and spoke of the birth of nations during independence, each with its own tabula rasa. Indeed, establishing a national poetic discourse and imaginary was as important to the new republics as drafting laws.[71] This was the case in Argentina, where the massive *Lira argentina* and a constitution were published in 1824. Similarly, in Uruguay, the *Parnaso Oriental* followed the 1830 constitution five years later. Hugo Achugar suggests that these collections were more than just compilations of poems written by compatriots: they constitute an ideological and cultural referent that only lettered elites had the power to shape, yet whose contents were beacons of collective identity for all social sectors.[72]

A case in point comes from the origins of *La lira argentina*. In 1822, Bernardino Rivadavia, a champion of liberalism in all its manifestations and at the time minister of the nascent United Provinces government, issued a decree outlining the government's plans to celebrate independence by publishing a volume of all the patriotic poetry written in the United Provinces since 1810—a year that, thanks to the verses, grew to mark a starting point for referring to "national" history. The goals of this initiative were clear: "Presenting poetic productions under this patriotic light will not only contribute to animating public sentiment, but it will also illustrate the level of good literary taste our country has achieved in its early stages. . . . Such a collection . . . is without doubt a monument of the most appropriate sort to celebrate the anniversary of the declaration of our independence."[73] The decree goes on to say that Rivadavia will be in charge of selecting the poems "worthy" of publication, that the collection will feature a distinguished binding, and that the government will foot the bill for the printing costs.[74] Rivadavia's plan did not come to fruition. However, his idea inspired the supposed editor of *La lira*, Ramón Díaz.

According to the note that opens the anthology, the collection is meant to nourish public spirit with the efforts of the editor's compatriots, and "pay due homage to the decision of a people to remain steadfast in the fight for independence."[75] The editor was serious about paying homage: some two thousand copies of *La lira* were printed in Paris and then shipped to Buenos Aires.[76] All of the compositions had been printed before, many in newspapers or pamphlets put out by the famous Niños Expósitos press, but their collection in book form gave them renewed vigor and raised their status to that of official verses. The authors included Esteban de Luca, who had written the popular patriotic jingle "Canción patriótica" around 1810; Bartolomé Hidalgo, whose dialogue on the fiestas mayas and other gauchesque texts had entertained many; Cayetano Rodríguez, who had been involved with the creation of the public library in Buenos Aires; and Vicente López y Planes, whose "Marcha patriótica" had already become part of the national symbolic repertoire by being declared Argentina's national anthem.

In Susana Poch's formulation, national anthems are more than just military tunes or patriotic poems: they are efforts through writing to develop a set of meanings for a community, and this was certainly true of López's "Marcha."[77] This type of writing often made its debut in fiestas patrias, or as songs in collective ceremonies. Through their written and sung performance—thanks to their messages, and with the force of the law behind them—these songs became sacred tributes to the idea of the nation, providing emotional content for the foundation and maintenance of community. The Niños Expósitos published López y Planes's poem as a loose-leaf with a headline stating it to be the *only* "Marcha Patriótica" for official use in the United Provinces.[78] It was soon performed at the fiestas mayas. From there, as the official anthem (of a nation that did not yet exist), and as a direct way to channel emotional support for the cause of independence, the "Marcha" accompanied José de San Martín as his troops spread to fight royalists throughout what would become Argentina, Chile, and Peru.[79]

1813 was a fruitful year for symbolic production in Buenos Aires, for in addition to the "Marcha Patriótica," the General Assembly ordered up a "national" seal or coat of arms to identify official documents. The seal first replaced the colonial seals, and then it acquired a larger role as the representative emblem of the assembly, which claimed to collectively stand for the new political and community unit taking shape in the region.[80] This seal underwent modifications throughout the nineteenth century, but its initial character is still intact, blending European influence with reference to indigenous American societies. The pike and the Phrygian cap were part of the French Revolution's symbolic repertoire.[81] Worn by freed Roman slaves and representative of liberty, the cap was also used by Masonic lodges operating in Buenos Aires in the early nineteenth century. The laurel branches speak to victory, and the clasped hands (not linked definitively to any established symbolic tradition) represent fraternal union between the provinces of the country. The sun rising behind the laurels is suggestive of Incan mythology.[82] In Estanislao Zeballos's friendly history of the seal, he remarks that "the ideals that were on all our minds were *Liberty*, *Equality*, and *Fraternity*; they inspired the *National Anthem*, and they are embodied in the coat of arms."[83] Though they form an exaggerated statement, Zeballos's words touch on the importance of liberalism as a source of inspiration for both symbolic verses and seals.

The new coat of arms quickly made its way from the assembly's printed communications to the public sphere. Beruti records that in May 1813, a "superior order" called for the removal of all the Castilian coats of arms dotting schools, forts, and government buildings, to be replaced by the "great coat of arms of the nation of the United Provinces of the Río de la Plata."[84] The elements of the new seal were not confined to walls or paper, either: they guided people's mode of dress at the fiestas mayas that year, in effect bringing the seal to life. During the fiestas, members of the Buenos Aires government wore red Phrygian caps, just like the one depicted in the seal. The public joined in the performance too, "donning Phrygian caps for hats. The effect of this on good patriots, men and women alike," noted Beruti, "was that all continue wearing the cap. When not worn on the head,

Figure 1.1. The 1813 Argentine coat of arms. In Zeballos, 46–47.

men use it as a cockade with other hats, and women do the same or pin it to their bosom."[85]

In July of the same year, the assembly printed an edict announcing to the public that the seal would be disseminated through yet another medium—"national" coins. The new coins, minted in the silver town of Potosí, had the seal without the sun on the front side; the sun covered the reverse side and was encircled by the words "In union and liberty."[86] This so-called national currency was short-lived, but it attests to the ways in which print culture was diffused throughout the Plata. What began as a seal to be used

Figure 1.2. The coat of arms of the Provincia Oriental. In Andrés Lamas, 56–57.

on official documents of the General Assembly became a national coat of arms and the basis of a design for a currency, which began putting symbolic content in the hands of people across social sectors, a point we will return to in the Epilogue. By the end of 1815, shortly before independence was officially declared in Argentina, the seal had become one of the defining characteristics of the *Gaceta de Buenos Aires*, appearing at the top of the front page of every issue of the *Gaceta* until its last impressions in 1821.[87]

Similar to the Argentine one, the seal that appeared in the Banda Oriental during Artigas's time also portrayed the rising sun, albeit one presiding over a scale of justice instead of a pike and Phrygian cap. "Provincia Oriental" is inscribed at the top, and encircling the sun and scale is the motto "With liberty I neither offend nor fear." This seal, too, was part of public ceremonies. The schoolchildren who animated with song the fiestas cívicas in 1816 carried the tricolor flag and wore tricolor Phrygian caps.[88] According to the anonymous author of the *Descripción de las fiestas cívicas*, the last night saw the debut of "a first-rate flag, and the coat of arms of the Banda Oriental decorated the main façade" of the Cabildo.[89] The coat of arms was also stamped on documents and circulated through print, like the description of the fiestas and Larrañaga's speech inaugurating the library.

This seal was used on and off from 1816 up to the design and implementation in 1829 of what would become, with few modifications, the current Uruguayan coat of arms.[90] During this period of close to fifteen years, the seal represented provincial independence from Buenos Aires, resistance to and independence from Portugal and Brazil, the celebrated arrival of the Thirty-Three Uruguayans in 1825 (see Chapter 4), and the declaration of independence from Brazilian occupation the same year. In early 1829, in preparation for events to accompany the swearing-in of the constitution, the General Assembly established a special commission to develop a new seal. In a display of the spirit of Uruguay's new national symbolic repertoire, the seal was stamped on copies of the *acta* (declaration) of independence distributed during an "allegorical" performance of the declaration. The production was part of the celebration of the signing of the constitution in 1830.[91]

Declarations and constitutions (both dependent on writing and print) were central to the elaboration of symbolic repertoires, too. These types of legal documents legislated the patriotic fervor expressed in symbolic verse and bound citizens to the written and printed letter of the law. The declarations are unique in this regard. Susana Poch suggests that they serve as the hinge "between the official poetic discourse of national anthems and the judicial discourse of constitutions."[92] Furthermore, declarations of independence were the ultimate line in the sand, so to say, and derived their very legitimacy from being expressions of the new power of print culture. After all, it is the written declaration that is commemorated.

The Argentine declaration, issued in July 1816, was a publishing phenomenon for declarations of independence. The congressional session that drafted the document and signed it into law ordered it to be printed in Spanish (1,500 copies), Quechua (1,000 copies), and Aymara (500 copies)—not a bad run for this period.[93] It is questionable how many Quechua and Aymara speakers could read the versions printed in these languages, but the translations were surely read aloud. Although printing the declaration in indigenous languages did not mean that the incipient government envisioned Indians as equal citizens in the new republic (this was far from being the case), it was an important, symbolically inclusive gesture. Moreover, it points to the fact that the state could not ignore these communities altogether in the configuration of the nation, at least while the fight for independence was incomplete.

In addition to declaring independence from Portugal, Brazil, and any other "tyrant," the Uruguayan declaration called for the destruction of written and printed documents that bore any mention of the occupation of the Banda Oriental from 1817 to 1825. Given how Uruguayans abhor even the memory of the documents that correspond to that period of despotism, states the declaration, government representatives of the towns that have archives of these memories "will gather on the first holiday with the parish priest, residents, and the notary, secretary, or whoever it is that records in writing events for the court, and, following the public reading of this decree, will erase from the first line to the very last signature such documents."[94] After this ceremony was performed, the same representatives were to send to the provincial government proof (written or printed) that they had indeed destroyed the documents. That holidays were chosen for these celebrations to occur is significant, for they were when the largest public could join the representatives, priest, and notary in the collective act of erasing memories and past symbolic repertoires and preparing for new ones to accompany the independent Banda Oriental. Fortunately for scholars today, not all the documents were destroyed. The symbolic copying of this declaration was part of the public ceremonies organized for the 18 July 1830 signing of the constitution.

Isidoro de María, who told us about the first press in Montevideo, was present for the merriment in the Plaza Matriz that July. The plaza was well decorated, with national flags dotting every corner. Foot soldiers and cavalrymen sported uniforms that were color-coded white and blue, like

Figure 1.3. *Jura de la Constitución de 1830* (Swearing in the Constitution, 1830) by Juan Manuel Blanes, 1872. A depiction of the festivities on 18 July 1830. (Courtesy of the Museo Histórico Nacional, Montevideo.)

the flag. Government leaders stood on the balconies of the Cabildo, and onlookers packed the plaza and nearby rooftops, despite the chilliness of mid-July. Religion was also part of the ceremony, with a *Te deum* sung to accompany government members as they walked toward the cathedral. After performing their religious duties, they headed back to the Cabildo to sign the constitution.[95]

What followed was truly a spiritual act, blending religion with a newly established reverence for written culture as the legitimate embodiment of the infant state. After the leaders of the government swore their allegiance to the constitution in the main salon of the Cabildo, soldiers were called in from the plaza, followed by "the sovereign People." They stood in front of a state official who asked them:

> Do you swear to God and promise to the patria that you will fulfill all the obligations that correspond to you as a citizen and on which the constitution of the Uruguayan state depends, sanctioned . . . by the representatives of the nation? Do you swear to uphold and defend the representative republican form of government that the constitution establishes? If you do, God will be on your side; if not, he and the patria will demand as much.[96]

The crowds of people pushed and shoved to have their turns at taking the oath and pronouncing the moving "yes, I swear"—some to demonstrate their faith in God and patria, and others probably out of fear that God and patria would "demand" from them the proper respect should they say no.

The ceremony ended with cannon fire that mightily signaled the power of the printed word as rule of law, but that was not the end of the celebration. That afternoon and night the party continued, and "there was not a soul alive . . . that did not make his way to the plaza to watch the lovely *comparsas* [theatrical groups] . . . on the stage decorated with arches and sky-blue ribbons." One of the participants read a poem by Acuña de Figueroa, author of the future national anthem, admonishing citizens to live by their freshly sworn word to the grave. Some received commemorative medals, and loose leaves with patriotic poetry "were thrown like flowers to that world of spectators bent on catching one."[97] Hundreds of others acquired their very own copies of the constitution or declaration.[98] In the San Felipe theater, which according to de María's description was overflowing, two poets read patriotic verses. Thus, like the morning, the night ended with collective acts of praising the written word, which in turn contributed to solidifying the foundation of print culture in Uruguay.[99]

■

The emergence of Rioplatense print culture dovetails with and is defined by the wars of independence. It is the story of words of independence, patriotic parties, and the creation of new symbolic repertoires that combined to initiate a revolution in forms of communication. Beginning with words as weapons of war printed in revolutionary newspapers, poems, and edicts at the outset of the nineteenth century, presses such as the Niños Expósitos in Buenos Aires and the Southern Star and La Carlota in Montevideo sparked a printing revolution. While these print media presented news on the developments of the wars, they also affected public sentiment and public behaviors by inspiring patriots and condemning royalists, when not the other way around. The press and the printed word represented liberal notions of progress and lent legitimacy to republicanism, too.

Patriotic parties and public ceremonies were sites that further promoted print culture. Whether at the fiestas mayas, the opening of the library in Buenos Aires, or the signing of the constitution in Montevideo, these ceremonies and the events and institutions they celebrated provided new meeting places for citizens across the social spectrum. Print was vital to the creation and spread of new symbolic repertoires as well. Patriotic verse, national symbols (such as the coat of arms), and legal documents (such as declarations of independence and constitutions)—all depended on new printing technologies for their messages to be communicated successfully. By 1830, words, wars, and patriotic parties had laid the foundations for new and much more regular contact between people and print. As we will see in the next chapter, for roughly the next forty years—until state institutions became stable, around 1870—new words, new wars, and gauchos would define Rioplatense print culture and take it in new directions.

Chapter 2

Words, Wars, and Gauchos

Print Culture and Cattle Civilization (1830–1870)

■ Like the strands of a good lasso, Rioplatense print culture and cattle civilization are braided together during the second key moment in the development of our story, spanning from the end of the wars of independence around 1830 roughly up to 1870.[1] The 1820s through the early 1860s were by far the most profitable years for the *estancieros* (owners of large estates) and *saladeristas* (proprietors of beef-jerky factories). The prominent figures of cattle culture—the *caudillos*, who were often also owners of estates or beef-jerky plants—cultivated relationships based on patronage to become powerful figures in new, emerging political parties. As such, they were able to foster attachments to their brands of collective identity and their factions.

In the Plata, the caudillo and *patrón* who stood out from all the others was Juan Manuel de Rosas, a towering figure in the historiography of both Uruguay and Argentina. Depending on the author (and his or her political leanings), Rosas was either a tyrannical dictator or a hero who championed all things American and stood up to the meddling Europeans with imperial designs on the material resources of South America. What is certain for both sides, though, is that Rosas was a product (and a principal promoter) of cattle civilization, and that almost everything written between 1830 and 1870 revolved around him and the politics of cattle culture.

With Rosas's rise to the position of governor of Buenos Aires in 1829, a long war of words began over cattle culture in all its manifestations on both sides of the Plata River. In previous years, revolutionary words in the region's first newspapers, public ceremonies to inaugurate libraries and celebrate independence, and the elaboration of national symbolic repertoires through print media had defined the emergence of a culture of print in the region. There was some hope for calm following the liberation of the Banda Oriental from Brazil in 1828. But the peace was fleeting. The dust on the battlefields of Uruguay and Argentina was about to be stirred again by war, this time between new, opposing political factions—in Argentina, by Rosas-led conservative Federalists on one side and liberal Unitarians on the other, and beginning in the late 1830s the corresponding Blanco and Colorado Parties in Uruguay. Economic and ideological interests tied to a world based on raising cattle and exploiting animal products drove the war, as did those opposed to that world. Simply put, talking about cattle was synonymous with talking about politics, and vice versa.[2] At stake in the battles of the pen, lance (sheep shears tied to the ends of cane poles), and rifle were the ways of life of landowners, gauchos, peasants, Afro-descendants, and urban liberals, as well as the primacy of the combatants' particular vision for the nation.

The focus of this chapter is the continued development of a special relationship between print, politics, and the public sphere in the Plata, though with a distinctive twist. During this second stage, popular literature fueled this relationship, primarily in the form of gauchesque verse and prose appealing to country folk and marginalized urban populations. Since its debut during the wars of independence, the gauchesque writing that appeared in newspapers and on loose leaves had been unique to the Plata. Nowhere else in nineteenth-century Latin America was there a similar type of literature that negotiated the meeting of oral and print cultures and allowed the popular consumption of print media on the scale seen in the Río de la Plata. The *corridos* sung and written across Mexico, the *joropos* that plainsmen improvised throughout the Colombian and Venezuelan llanos, the dueling poetry of Brazilian backlands, and the verses *gaúchos* improvised in southern Brazil—these functioned in similar ways, but their reach and impact was minimal in comparison to gauchesque writing in the Plata.

Aside from the sheer volume of the popular literature of this period, what is crucial about its import in our story is that such writing became part of daily life. It was meant to be exactly that. Popular literature's quotidian character allowed it to influence thoughts and behaviors and to operate in the public sphere in ways writing in Latin America had not previously achieved. Writing as a daily experience was thus able to play a major role in shaping new partisan identities.

The intimacy of the written word with spheres of political power was embodied in employees of the Rosas regime, followers of Manuel Oribe (Rosas's Blanco counterpart in Uruguay), and writers paid on an ad hoc basis for verses promoting the party line. Yet party advocates who were *not* functionaries or freelancers produced an abundance of popular print media whose role was also incredibly powerful. Put differently, at this point in our story, the main protagonists are not the elite intellectuals who wrote for their handful of friends in their literary clubs, but the gauchos and peasants who appeared as characters in popular literature and were occasionally its authors. Of course, the authors of this popular literature were privileged by the very fact that they could write, at a time when the overwhelming majority of Latin Americans were illiterate, though this did not always grant them permission to join elite circles. For the most part, the popular literature of these years was pro-Rosas or pro-Oribe, which meant pro-Federalist or pro-Blanco. This translated loosely into favoring land ownership in the hands of a few—a social order not unlike that of the colonial period—and, seemingly contradictory to the notion of federalism, promoting favorable trade conditions for the province of Buenos Aires. Its authors and their compositions were often dismissed by recognized liberal elites and men of letters as, ironically, "too popular."

These liberals advocated opening up the Río de la Plata to the modernizing powers of free trade and the cultural influences of Europe, and they fought to be the representatives of republicanism, though they were not alone in making this claim. They also shot back at Federalists and Blancos with their own printed creations, some which appropriated popular speech in hopes of reaching a broader public. As we follow the contours of the nexus between print and the political, we will see how such elite creations fared.

■

The larger framework for understanding the special relationship of print to power and the political during this period comes from a handful of key scenes. The first of these corresponds to the years encompassing Rosas's first term in office, which began in 1829, and his return to the governorship with "supreme powers" in 1835. During this short span of time, print became intertwined with the goals of estancieros and saladeristas on their way toward entering the high point of cattle civilization. Print media not only branded property—most notably cattle and employees—but also expressed political affinities and identities and attempted to persuade and politicize those who had yet to declare their partisan loyalties. Rosas's second term in office, from 1835 to 1852, outlines the chronological scope of the second distinct scene. It was rife with the opposition's efforts to unseat the patrón, which exploded into the Guerra Grande (Great War) in Uruguay, and it saw much tighter control of the Rioplatense social order. The result was the militarization of print culture, where partisanship dominated and where persuasion gave way to battling the enemy. The last scene, which takes place following the end of civil war in the region, is marked by Rosas's fall from power in the early 1850s and runs up to the acquisition of political authority and power by liberal elites around 1870. The end of the Rosas years signaled the end of cattle civilization as it was known and gave way to a shift in the concerns expressed through the written and printed word. Following Rosas's ouster, writers began dealing with social concerns and toying with artistic aspirations, a turn that corresponded to readers' interests. The liberal elites at the helm of the state started envisioning new functions for print media. Education would be the most important of these.

It is certainly possible to engage with the evolution of cattle frontiers and the economic and social conditions that revolved around them in the Plata without looking at print, but it was elements of print culture that generated in large measure the party identities formed during this period. Poems in papers for rural inhabitants, songs sung in pulperías and in parades, catchwords such as "Federalist" that appeared in public places, and damning slogans woven into headbands worn by partisans of every color—all were decisive in this respect. Likewise, the efforts to put a stop to a political order based on the cattle industry were made, above all, in writing. One cannot conceive of this period in Latin American history without books like Domingo Sarmiento's *Facundo* or Manuel Herrera y Obes's *El caudillismo y la revolución americana* (loosely, Caudillos, patronage, and American revolutions). Nor is it possible to read *Facundo, El caudillismo*, newspapers published for Federalist/Blanco or Unitarian/Colorado partisans, or poems such as José Hernández's *Martín Fierro* without acknowledging their roots in a world ordered by cattle culture.

With this in mind, let us now turn our attention to the roots of the special relationship between print and daily life during these years.

Branding Property and Political Identity

In 1830, a Swiss printer by the name of César Hipólito Bacle made his mark on the world of printing with the publication of the monumental *Colección general de las marcas del ganado de la Provincia de Buenos Aires* (General collection of branding marks in Buenos Aires Province). Bacle had set up a unique print shop in Buenos Aires back in 1828. It was unique precisely because it was the first of its kind to employ lithographic printing successfully in the region. Other printers had tried their hand at lithography in the mid-1820s, but Bacle's shop was by far the most respected and its productions considered to be of the best quality.[3] For this reason, his business quickly attracted the business of the state and acquired the title of Imprenta Litográfica del Estado. The *Colección general* was divided into sections that corresponded to jurisdictions within Buenos Aires Province. Each section consisted of the names of *estancia* (estate) managers and owners in the given jurisdiction—obtained when they registered with the provincial police—and prints of brand marks. With over nine thousand managers listed and pictures of the corresponding cattle brands for their estancias, the work is invaluable for identifying families involved in cattle culture.

The book is all about establishing in print a practical means of clarifying private property issues—pertaining, in this case, to cattle, which were the source of wealth and, in some instances, political power. In addition to defining personal property for its estancia, each brand created an identity for it distinct from all the others that was recognizable in the figures seared into cattle flesh and printed by Bacle. Though there is no mention of the number of copies of the book then in circulation in the province, it is reasonable to imagine that each jurisdiction had at least one for managers and owners to consult. Lithography was, after all, a way to facilitate larger print runs, and with over nine thousand cattle marks dotting the countryside, ranch hands, owners, and managers had to consult the *Colección general* when they could not recall or did not know whose stamps were branded onto the cattle they came across.

Figure 2.1. A scene of cattle branding on the title page of *Colección general de las marcas del ganado de la Provincia de Buenos Aires*. (From the copy in the UNC Rare Book Collection. Used by permission.)

A look at a page of brands from Bacle's book is enough to give an idea of the confusion that could result from the mess of symbols. They appear as a language of their own, its only use being that of communicating ownership. Juan Manuel de Rosas was serious about this point when he wrote about the practice of branding. In his *Instrucciones a los mayordomos de estancias* (Instructions to estate managers), Rosas insisted that all cattle, donkeys, and female horses should be marked and counted during the annual branding act.[4] Bills of sale for cattle often included brand marks, too.[5] And, given that stealing cattle—a common practice—from someone with greater political power (such as Rosas) could be dangerous, would-be thieves also may have found it handy to consult the brand guide.

The collection of cattle brands supplies a way to begin thinking about the bonds between print, the politics of cattle culture, and the quotidian. The bonds concern political capital (and property), party identity, and human relationships. Branding was not the sole manifestation of these bonds,

Figure 2.2. A page of brand marks in *Colección general de las marcas del ganado de la Provincia de Buenos Aires*. (From the copy in the UNC Rare Book Collection. Used by permission.)

however. One of the main forms of print estancia owners used to manage their property was the *papeleta de conchabo*. The papeleta was an ID card that attested to a worker's status, either naming the estancia (or owner) to which he belonged or explaining his situation if he was not employed.

Papeletas were also used as versions of the *pasaportes* required of citizens following the wars of independence. As José Antonio Wilde relates, citizens needed pasaportes in order to leave their home districts, and the law came down most harshly on poor, rural inhabitants, who often had to travel long distances to obtain permission to visit neighboring towns (even towns just a few blocks from their homes). Wealthy urban dwellers could move about more freely, and if they were caught without their pasaportes or passes from the local justice of the peace or police chief, they sometimes managed to escape punishment. This was much less likely to occur in the cases of poor men from the countryside.[6]

Papeletas and pasaportes were largely standard, preprinted documents with details such as name, date, age, marital status, hair and beard color (always important), skin color, and facial characteristics filled in by hand. Although these documents appear in abundance in different repositories across Uruguay and Argentina, statistical records of papeleta and pasaporte printings are scarce. However, the numbers from Montevideo in the 1830s and 1840s give a sense of the volume the Blanco government produced under Manuel Oribe. In 1838, for instance, close to 1,100 documents were issued. This number grew to more than 1,400 in 1842, and two years later more than 3,000 pasaportes and papeletas were registered for the area around the capital alone.[7]

As with pasaportes, in most cases the bearers of papeletas were not the ones filling in the blanks. Rather, their patrons completed the forms. And, similar to the traveler found without a pasaporte, a gaucho discovered without his papeleta could be imprisoned, thrown into the stocks behind the justice of the peace's house or office, conscripted to fight Indians along the frontier, or compelled to work for an estanciero without his consent. Writing thus bound people in more ways than one.[8]

Conscription was what Pancho Lugares—the fictitious gaucho editor of Luis Pérez's newspaper *El Gaucho*—faced for having left his papeleta at home. Through several of the paper's editions in 1830, Pancho relates his autobiography, explaining that he had learned to read at a young age, but when he turned twelve, he had had to learn to tame horses in order to make a living. A few years later, he had joined the forces of a certain Juan Chano (named after the Chano character in Bartolomé Hidalgo's dialogues) during the wars of independence, and afterward looked for work on estancias. One day, he came across a sergeant who asked him for his papeleta. Like many people in the countryside, Pancho had not caught on to how powerful the little printed card could be and the consequences for not carrying it on his person. Pancho pleaded to the sergeant, but to no avail: he was taken to the city, locked up with other gauchos the military had rounded up from his neighborhood, and then sent to the front lines to fight.[9] Fortunately—for other gauchos thinking of leaving home without their papeletas—Pancho could tell his tale in print.

In short, papeletas served as a means for estancia owners to brand their workers and provided forced labor for the estates and the army. Papeletas were part of the estanciero class's attempt to cement law and order in the countryside through antivagrancy legislation.[10] While the papeletas helped to bring about some sort of order, the estancieros and the Federalist and Blanco Parties that represented their interests owed a great deal more to the popular newspapers and verses that inspired affinity with their party lines.

Between 1830 and 1835, dozens of popular newspapers appeared and disappeared, some lasting longer than others and many dealing with issues that resonated with country residents and poor urban dwellers. That most of these papers are not known today stems largely from their being fragile texts and not ones that many readers or listeners would have preserved. This sort of popular literature was exactly that—"popular" meaning to be enjoyed and then passed on to the next person or group, which resulted in great wear and tear on the documents. Other factors contributing to their lack of recognition include their anonymous authorship and the fact that they have been ignored or written off by literary scholars and historians until relatively recently. Among the many authors of these print media (including Juan Gualberto Godoy, who created a paper with a sharp-witted editor, and Hilario Ascasubi, author of three gauchesque papers published in Montevideo), Luis Pérez was by far the most active, penning loose-leaf verses and the bulk of more than thirty different papers between 1830 and 1834 in support of the Federalists.[11]

There is little available on Pérez's background. He had served as a patriot soldier during the wars of independence and he was known for hanging out in pulperías, garnering a reputation for mixing with mischievous lower-class citizens and criminals. His fame began in 1830 when he started creating papers under the names of characters from the countryside and marginal figures of Buenos Aires.[12] The look of the papers, with sketches of gauchos, horses, and other country adornments on the covers, made them appealing to rural inhabitants, and the language Pérez employed was *their* language. They were sold in public places such as pulperías and mar-

Figure 2.3. A woodcut of a gaucho with pen and paper in hand that appeared on the front pages of *El Gaucho*— presumably the fictitious editor, Pancho Lugares. Note the *rebenque* at his feet.

kets, both of which were rich sites for the creation of popular literature and where hardworking gauchos, simple vagrants, and other "riffraff" spent hours on end listening to readings of their contents.[13]

Such writing was deeply tied to cattle culture—after all, its characters and audience were ranch hands—and it inspired some rural inhabitants to try their hand at letter writing, too. Pérez's *El Gaucho, El Toro de Once* (The neighborhood bull), *La Gaucha, El Torito de los Muchachos* (The little kids' little neighborhood bull), and other papers and loose-leaf sheets featured poor city dwellers, gauchos, and even a "gaucha" serving as editors and soliciting contributions from similar residents. And the contributions came. Pérez invented some himself, while others were genuine. In *El Gaucho, La Negrita,* and *El Negrito* (the latter two titles referring to affectionate

Figure 2.4. A woodcut of *La Gaucha*—Pancho Lugares's wife—surrounded by different breeds of cattle and dogs, at the top of a loose-leaf sheet of gauchesque verse, 25 May 1830. She, too, has pen and paper in hand.

forms of address to members of the black community), blacks and women also acquired a voice, albeit one that was pro-Federalist and aimed toward instilling like-minded partisan sentiments. Indeed, as head of the party, Rosas inspired a wealth of poetic production in print and in song. As a scholar of these rich sources wrote, the Restorer of Laws counted among his followers "people used to wielding fountain pens in their studies" and "popular verse makers who rarely put their compositions to paper."[14]

The anonymous authors of hundreds of loose-leaf poems, the language the authors of such texts employed, and the structures of their compositions—from dialogues to *décimas* (traditional ten-line poetic constructions), comical ads to falsified letters—all contributed to the popularity of gauchesque writing of this period.[15] The texts also dealt with mundane issues and everyday concerns such as rising rent in Buenos Aires, the well-being of women washing clothes for a living, and the price of water. That

Figure 2.5. *Interior de una pulpería, Buenos Aires*, by León Palliere, circa 1860. The *pulpero* doled out products at his dry goods store such as beef jerky, salt, and yerba mate, and also served as a bartender. Here, he reads to an attentive group of customers. (Courtesy of the Museo Nacional de Bellas Artes, Buenos Aires.)

they were so popular made them particularly well suited to branding political identity.

Pérez's papers offer great insight into this point and the role of the author as a mediator between the masses and those with political power in the early 1830s. To begin, his papers circulated in both the city of Buenos Aires and the countryside. Pérez employed special postal services to make sure they made their way to readers in the country.[16] Of course, Pérez's gauchesque productions did not appear out of thin air. They drew heavily on the *cielitos* (dance-based poems) and dialogues of Bartolomé Hidalgo and on the journalism of the anti-Artigas author and priest Francisco de

Figure 2.6. "Interior de una pulpería." Pulperías were common gathering spots and watering holes, and they became sites where many works of popular literature were born. Image no. 1 in Bacle. (Courtesy of the Biblioteca Nacional de la República Argentina, Buenos Aires, Tesoro.)

Paula Castañeda.[17] They were crucial to what Angel Rama has identified as a second major trend in Rioplatense gauchesque writing, the first trend having appeared during the wars of independence with the works of Hidalgo, the compositions of soldiers, popular dance and song, and the incorporation of language of the countryside into the formal system of writing. The wars between political factions set the parameters for new directions in gauchesque writing where "poets joined forces with political parties and served as a link between the party line and the illiterate masses."[18] Though Pérez was not employed in Rosas's service, his compositions (and those by others that his gazetteers published) certainly brought together illiterate readers and ruling estancieros, most commonly around expressions of opposition to the Unitarian Party and praise of Federalism.

This position is clearly outlined in one of his most successful papers, *El Gaucho*, printed during 1830–1833. Pancho Lugares, the editor whose troubles without his papeleta were mentioned earlier in this chapter, tells readers that they must be prepared "to give their last drop of blood" for Rosas.[19] Pérez incorporated additional characters such as "friends of Pancho" to communicate his ideas of party affiliation more forcefully. The 7 August 1830 edition features a cielito composed by one such friend in which Pancho plays the violin and the friend prepares Pancho's lasso.[20] The poem is full of references to tools that were part of cattle culture, such the *rebenque*—a riding crop that often doubled as a weapon—and the lasso. The *rebencazo* the author speaks of was a lash with the rebenque, in this case to be wielded against Unitarians to be tied up with Pancho's lasso like cattle prepared for branding. "Playing the violin" was also a way of referring to the common practice of cutting a throat from one side to the other—something every gaucho was accustomed to doing with cattle as well as a form of killing one's enemy. The discourse of violence that appears in this and Pérez's other papers held a certain attraction for his reading public, given that they lived and worked daily with violence.

Pérez took care to include words attributed to women and blacks in his papers, too. The companion paper to *El Gaucho* was *La Gaucha*, edited by none other than Pancho Lugares's wife. She drummed up support among female readers, though her target audience was mixed. The authorship of the voices of blacks—like those of the gauchos and gauchas—is uncertain: it is probable that Pérez himself created the poems, but he may have also collected loose-leaf compositions by blacks to include in his papers, or even written down poetic verses he had heard recited among blacks in Buenos Aires Province. In any case, the voices of the black editors in *La Negrita* and *El Negrito*, those of the contributors to Pérez's many other papers, and the strong will of Pérez's Federalist women characters were all efforts to reach these groups and establish among them seeds of political identity.[21]

A letter from "La morena Catalina" (A black woman named Catalina) to Pancho Lugares is a case in point. Catalina apologizes for her rough written Spanish and tells Lugares that her husband wants to learn to write. He does not know Spanish very well either, but "he's a black felelist, and greaful to da Patria dat freed'em. Every night he be dreamin' 'bout Jua Manue [Rosas], and den in da mornin' talkin' 'bout him again."[22] Writing and Rosas go hand in hand. Catalina's husband may not know Spanish, but he is always thinking of Rosas, which should be reason enough for him to learn to write—one more person to compose words in praise of the patrón.

Rosas himself spoke to the success of Pérez's papers. In a letter to Felipe Arana, dated 26 August 1833, he commented that "peasants and similar folk like verse," and mentioned the impact of the paper *El Negrito* among them: "They gathered in throngs to read the issues of *El Negrito*, fighting for a space. . . . It is necessary to have similar verses, but it is more worthwhile to ensure that if there are few they be good."[23] The effectiveness of such writing in instilling everyday partisan identity shines through as well in the condemnations of Pérez's detractors and enemies, in which they label him a measly "tavern orator," attack his patriotism, complain of the bad influence his papers and characters exercise on "the masses," and question his character for hanging out with people at pulperías (even accusing him of scheming with criminals).

Political identity also showed in one's manner of dress, in garments and in *divisas* (ribbons) attached to hats and lapels or worn as armbands, above all with the color red. The red divisa became an obligatory ornament in February 1832, but even from the first years of Rosas's governorship there is evidence of red taking hold as an expression of one's affinity for Federalism.[24] Take the meaning of the color for a Buenos Aires water seller whose exposition appeared in *El Gaucho* on 6 October 1830: Though poor, he is a good Federalist whose cart is pulled by red oxen. Each ox wears a golden head ornament that reads, "FEDERATION." Combined with the red of the oxen, the ornament may even convince doubters who see him pass or who purchase from him to side with the Federalists. His strategy for selling water is designed for this purpose, too: "One *real* per barrel is the price I give to Federalists, and to Unitarians, well, I charge them double."[25]

Pérez was unmatched in the Plata in his production of popular literature, and to our knowledge the same holds true for the rest of Latin America. In Montevideo, Argentine exile Hilario Ascasubi began a gauchesque paper with liberal characters specifically to combat those of Pérez. Yet while Ascasubi was incredibly prolific in the production of gauchesque writing, his main contributions did not circulate until the late 1830s and early 1840s. Other popular texts were rare in Uruguay during the first half of the 1830s. *El Domador* (The horse tamer) used rural speech to critique the liberal state and its officials, but only two *galopes* (dashes; i.e., numbers) were printed. Popular literary production increased dramatically in the Banda Oriental starting in the late 1830s, as we will later see.

During Rosas's period out of office in 1833 and 1834, the fervor of his Buenos Aires supporters grew stronger and the branding iron hotter. Verses celebrating Rosas's efforts in wars against Indians along the southern frontier were posted on city walls. But some of the most loyal Federalists became the focus of scrutiny, especially following the return of Rosas in April 1835 with "supreme powers." Back in 1831, Luis Pérez had been imprisoned for apparently "offensive" passages in one of his papers.[26] Rosas ordered his release shortly thereafter, and Pérez continued publishing his verses. In 1834, however, he ran into problems with Pedro de Angelis— soon to be Rosas's right-hand man for controlling the press—and then with the minister of the Buenos Aires government. The minister declared that politics could only be treated seriously, which meant not the subject of jokes or of verses like those of Pérez, and he insulted the popular author as a mere "tavern bard" (though one too influential to ignore). In April, the gazetteer was imprisoned again as a result of an increasingly heated series of exchanges in print between him and Pedro de Angelis. Nothing is known of what happened to him afterward. Ironically, Rosas had locked up one of his most faithful and talented soldiers of the pen.

César Hipólito Bacle—the state lithographer—also met an unhappy end. In February 1832, Rosas had signed a decree that cracked down on the freedom of the press and on what printers could safely produce.[27] The new resolutions regarding printing and printers did not sit well with Bacle, and he asked for them not to apply to his business. After all, his print shop was the Imprenta Litográfica del Estado. After repeated attempts to clarify whether lithographs were included in the decree (since it appeared in Bacle's eyes to deal with newspapers above all), Bacle got a definitive answer from Rosas's minister of war: "Keep your most recent letter," began the note, in reference to Bacle's last petition. "No future correspondence or presentation dealing with the matter will be entertained. By this office you have been informed where your current request will be archived."[28] Bacle accepted the new rules, and his press published multiple official newspapers throughout the 1830s.[29]

But the cordial business relationship with the Rosas regime did not save Bacle from perils of a shaky political one. His success came to an end when he challenged Rosas's rules again by taking a trip to Chile to explore the possibility of continuing his work there. He was offered the position of state lithographer, which he chose to accept, but on his return to Buenos Aires to gather his belongings and prepare the shop for the move, his conversations with exiled Unitarians were brought to Rosas's attention. Rosas had been suspicious since the start of the trip, given the dangerous possibility of Bacle communicating with exiled Argentines such as Domingo Sarmiento in Chile or Bernardino Rivadavia in Brazil, or even helping them. Moreover, Bacle had written several letters to enemies of the Federation that were intercepted. Along with Rosas's suspicions, these led to the imprisonment of the lithographer for over seven months. Throughout his stay in jail, Bacle professed his innocence. His trip to Chile had been approved, in fact, by several of Rosas's ministers. However, collaborating with the enemy—whether true or merely perceived—could not be left unpunished, especially if the printed word, capable of being distributed and with a certain permanence, was involved. Bacle died of tuberculosis in 1838, shortly after being released from his dark and damp cell, emphasizing to the last that he was innocent.[30]

Such actions against printers and writers were part of Rosas's second term in office. On both sides of the Plata River, they reflected a militarization of print culture and an even starker political divide. If persuasion had been the key to linking print to the political during the first stage, the second scene revolved around defining one's position in order to fight the enemy—in print as much as on the battlefield.

Long Live the Argentine Confederation!
Long Live Our Illustrious Restorer of Law!
Death to the Savage, Filthy Unitarians!

So goes the *lema* (slogan) of Rosas and his supporters, required on official documents and all correspondence with the government after his return to the governorship in 1835.[31] Across the river, Rosas's ally Manuel Oribe adopted a variation of the lema that read, "Oribe, Law or Death! Death to the savage Unitarians!"[32] As during the wars of independence, print culture from the mid-1830s to the fall of Rosas in 1852 was entrenched on the front lines of the rhetorical and civil wars that engulfed the Plata. Federalist and Blanco sympathizers were by far more successful than their enemies

Figure 2.7. The top of a pasaporte, dated 23 February 1846, with the Blanco slogan and the Uruguayan coat of arms. (Courtesy of the Archivo General de la Nación, Montevideo; Archivos Particulares, caja 320, carpeta 3.)

at getting out the message. This was evident in the rise of nativist sentiment, which stemmed from the same roots (many of them emotional) as nationalism. Opponents of the Rosas-Oribe regime, so active in the press during these years, failed to motivate popular resistance. However weak the opposition was, it was clear by the time Rosas left office and Uruguay's Guerra Grande came to an end that print culture in the Plata had become militarized and that writing was a partisan activity more than anything else.

It was largely through writing that the codes of behavior that fed popular support—or the Cult of Rosas, as John Lynch calls it—took shape. The standard Federalist and Blanco lemas were more than a few words decorating the tops of pages: they were part of a symbolic system that "was a form of coercion and conformity." Lynch argues that following such codes of behavior resulted in thoughts occupied by the color red, and forced people to contemplate whether or not they were wearing the proper dress and using appropriate official language, especially in written documents and public places: "To adopt the federal look and the federal language took the place of security checks and oaths of allegiance."[33] How far Rosas's rule and these slogans' messages penetrated people's lives is hard to gauge and depends on which group of followers one observes. The more thoughtful supporters of Rosas and Oribe questioned the propaganda machine, while their other admirers took up the messages and modes of behavior with enthusiasm.[34] Even the Unitarian and Colorado opponents were in daily dialogue with Rosas's government, especially in their written condemnations of the complete control Rosas had over the articulation of its messages.

There was no escaping the lema. In 1840, an employee in Rosas's service by the name of Casto Caceres forgot (perhaps on purpose) to include the catchphrase "Savage Unitarians" among the other epithets at the start of a decree he drafted. He subsequently wrote a drawn-out letter to Rosas begging forgiveness and attempting to prove that the mistake was not committed by choice. Caceres claimed to be a most faithful admirer of the patrón "in public and in private, in conversation and in writing."[35] Rosas's response to the note of apology is unknown, but the mere fact that such things were written reinforced the relationship between print and the political.

In his memoirs, José Antonio Wilde tells readers of a similar scenario, in which a schoolteacher had to petition Rosas for permission to continue working. In 1844, the teacher had been accused of not showing enough faith in the federation or the Federalist party. Wilde reproduces the petition, showing the numerous signatures and written declarations of loyalty to Rosas. The episode is curious in itself; what is important is that the process had to take place through writing. That is, the state required the teacher to make his case in writing, and it was in writing that the judgment was rendered. Sure enough, the teacher's petition begins with the Federal lema.[36] The same was true of José María de Uriarte's 1851 university thesis, in which Rosas's enemy, the Entre Ríos caudillo Justo José de Urquiza, was called a "crazy savage."[37] Even some private communications began with the slogans venerating Oribe or Rosas, such as the letter from an Uruguayan named Ventura Coronel to his uncle in October 1844.[38]

Dress codes, along with and through writing, contributed to shaping codes of uniform behavior and support for the regime.[39] During Rosas's second term, use of the red ribbon was no longer a simple expression of opinion. In a circular from 1837, a bishop by the name of Mariano advises a priest in Santos Lugares (on the outskirts of what was then the center of Buenos Aires) to predicate to women and children the use of the red ribbon, "informing them that proper use of the divisa is a sign of distinguished service to the patria, to their families, and to themselves." Those who did not take care to wear the red ribbon should, after multiple warn-

ings, be prohibited from entering the church.[40] The lema and required use
of personal adornments, as Jorge Myers argues, were methods of facilitating identification with the regime and pointing out its opponents.[41] Political affiliation had to be visible, as did opposition to the enemy.

Official documents from the Rosas and Oribe governments likewise
employed variations of the slogans. Documents to foreign dignitaries bore
the words pronouncing death to the opposition party members, which left
more than one diplomat wondering about the violence expressed in the
header. Papeletas and pasaportes from 1835 to 1850 carried slogans at the
top; so did a vacation permit to a Blanco solider dated 9 October 1848,
as did bills of sale of animals from the Uruguayan countryside.[42] Hand-
written correspondence between government officials sported the words,
and even exchanges between Rosas and Oribe contained the phrases (as if
either of them would forget the message).[43] The harsh words made their
way into other records, too, such as annual patent reports, as well as a note
from a ship captain in Montevideo detailing passengers he'd seen entering a
French vessel: "Family of the Savage Unitarian Fraga, two people; Family of
the Savage Unitarian Fructuoso Rivera and washerwomen, ten people."[44]

Much of this process of militarization, however, took place through
other forms of print media, which were often connected indirectly to the
Rosas government or his Uruguayan counterpart. Anonymity was important to the regime, especially in the newspapers, pamphlets, and loose-leaf
publications it ordered—or, more often, appropriated. Most of the anonymous compositions, whether cheering for Rosas and condemning Unitarians, or pulling for Oribe and damning the Colorados, dwell on a limited
set of themes: patriotism, criminal opponents, cowardice, bravery, loyalty,
triumph in battle, and party values as patriotic and national ones. These
values permeate a series of décimas composed by one of Oribe's female followers, Fortunata Fajardo de Monegal, who wrote them from Maldonado,
Uruguay, in December 1849, and they inform an anonymous chronicle
of the patriotic July celebrations in the town of Guadalupe, not far from
Montevideo. Not surprisingly, both compositions carry Oribe's lema.[45]

The umbrella of Rosismo was large and inclusive, but the varied group
of opponents to the regime was excluded totally. There was no room for
rhetorical reconciliation, either. According to one unknown writer, women
who did not wear the red hairpin or ornamental hair ribbon appeared to
favor the Unitarians and should be "punished" for such lack of respect.[46]

Figure 2.8. *Divisas* featuring the profile of Rosas and the Federalist slogan: "F o M (Federation or Death [*Muerte*])! Long live the Federalists! Death to the savage, filthy, scoundrel Unitarians!" These were usually worn on hats or pinned to lapels. (Courtesy of the Complejo Museográfico Enrique Udaondo [Luján, Argentina], Sala Federal.)

Voices in the officialist paper *La Gaceta Mercantil* called for "eternal revenge, without pity, war to the death against the vile Unitarian."[47] Writers for the regime, often under the guise of anonymity, followed orders and shot back at Unitarians in prose and verse, belittling especially those in exile as traitors. An illustrative example comes from a "Letrilla Federal" responding to a "Letrilla Unitaria" published in December 1839 in Montevideo. "Whoever wants to read lies," begins the response, "and grow akin to falsifying, / Whoever wants to live in a web of ill designs / and in religion follow the atheist way / Should go to Montevideo today." Another letrilla summed up the importance of defeating Unitarians in print (or in battle) for the continued independence of the patria.[48]

Anonymity not only allowed the writers to get away with outright threats of violence, it also gave them the chance to take on the voice of the enemy in order to carry out a sort of self-slander. This was the case with a curious letter printed in the Uruguayan paper *El Republicano* (The republican) on 17 August 1836, supposedly from Fructuoso Rivera to Juan Lavalle, his Argentine Unitarian companion and a Federalist nuisance. The anonymous author claims that he had found it among some of Rivera's papers. In what is a clear effort to defame Rivera, the author cleverly employs the unseated president's voice to damn Uruguayans and Montevideo: "Can you believe, my good friend, that there is hardly a soul in Montevideo who has not barked at me in the manner of the most ferocious dog. . . . And all for what purpose?" The answers that follow lend strong support to the Blanco Party: a tired Rivera tells Lavalle that he had wanted to retire to simple country life where he could brand his newborn cattle (and those stolen from other owners), but now Oribe has managed to gather public support to start a revolution. The letter concludes with Rivera forecasting his own downfall and how he and Lavalle should continue to rob from others in order to deal with their sad situation.[49]

The militarization of print culture also revolved around questions of race and racialization. Racial identity was conflated with the enemy. Unitarians and Colorados were described as a vile race that had to be eliminated not only from cities and the countryside but also from memory. Verses in a cielito written by a "Federal peasant" read: "Oh deep blue sky / Canopy of our victory, / Nothing shall remain of that race / Not even its memory."[50] The same spirit made Fructuoso Rivera a constant target of Federalist and Blanco verse, mainly because he was on the "wrong" side. Thus, in 1838 and 1839, the editors of the Paysandú paper *El Oriental en Campaña* waged relentless attacks on Rivera's political treason and "banditry."[51] Writers in other venues took the attacks to another level, giving him the titles of "pardo" (a person of African and European ancestry), "pardejón" (a more disparaging form of the term), and "mulato," all used not as ethnic descriptions but as slurs applied because of the party he represented.[52] The legacy of the epithet "Rivera the pardo" lasted through the rest of the century.

Making sense of these racialized references is difficult, because Rosas's support base included many blacks and official discourse advertised their support as an example of the regime's success in connecting to "the people," themes that George Reid Andrews has thoroughly studied.[53] There were many black bards who sang the praises of Rosas, and poems such as the "Hymn to Doña Manuela Rosas Sung by Black Women on a Day of Celebration," which Rosas's daughter herself preserved, shows that the regime had no problem at all with blacks.[54]

On the opposite side of the political spectrum, Colorado forces recruited large numbers of free blacks and slaves to fight against Oribe and Rosas's invading troops. In Montevideo, several Colorado newspapers hoped to solidify the support of black communities by incorporating engravings of black soldiers and conversations in bozal.[55] And on the front page of *El Tambor de la Línea* (The frontline drummer), another Colorado paper "written and published on the days we don't kill *Rosines* [supporters of Oribe and Rosas]," readers could see a proud black soldier drummer. In the second issue of this paper, images of country dancing and *candombe* (gatherings of Afro-descendants in the region, where drumming was an important component) appear, with accompanying verse in bozal celebrating Rivera and the constitution. The editor followed the verse with a note directed to Oribe, telling him that soon these black soldiers "fueled by republicanism" will head his way and that he should "hold on to his underwear, for when you see these forces it will be as my two-year old says: 'Papa, that one did it in his pants.'"[56] What we can conclude from the slippery use of race is that it was another means of denigrating one's enemy, whether Blanco or Colorado, Federalist or Unitarian, and that there was little fear that racializing the other would upset black supporters of one party or another. That is, race was subordinate to party identity, which was exactly the goal of the creators of partisan propaganda.

The militarization of print culture also had its positive, less explicitly violent side, evident in publications glorifying the military and political victories of the patrón and his partisan supporters. One of these was a collection of documents regarding Rosas and his relations with the Argentine Sala de Representantes (House of Representatives) and fellow citizens. The collection carried the lengthy title of *Rasgos de la vida pública de S. E. el Sr. Brigadier General D. Juan Manuel de Rosas, Ilustre Restaurador de las Leyes, Héroe del Desierto, Defensor Heroico de la Independencia Americana, Gobernador y Capitan General de la Provincia de Buenos Aires* (Features of the public life of Brigadier General Don Juan Manuel de Rosas, Illustrious Restorer of Law, Hero of the Desert Campaign, Heroic Defender of American Independence, and Governor of Buenos Aires Province), appropriate for its emphasis on Rosas as a heroic figure battling to preserve the independence of America. One of the documents representative of the spirit of the collection relates the desire of some citizens from both the city and the countryside to make Rosas's birthday a national holiday. The number of citizens who subscribed to the idea was relatively small in terms of the total population of the city and province (around 3,000 and 5,800 respectively), but the Sala took the numbers and the written petitions seriously as signs of deeper popular support. On 23 March 1841 ("the month of Rosas"), the representatives called for a law declaring 30 March a holiday. The numbers were a clear indicator of fervent patriotism, wrote members of the Sala, and the law was drafted.[57] Writing was behind the push for the holiday, and writing gave it legitimate force in the form of law.

Rosas, however, was less inclined to support the project. In a note to the members of the Sala, he modestly and skillfully requested that they merely archive the petitions. His love of republicanism and his faith in his fellow citizens would not allow him to have such a noble day, since it would imply inequality between Rosas and the plebe. The Sala responded to the note on 4 November 1841, claiming that it understood clearly Rosas's reasons for not wanting to accept the grand birthday honor and would duly archive the petitions. But since it still thought it appropriate to recognize the vote of confidence from the public, the Sala proposed the compilation and publication of documents that illustrated the "honors and distinctions awarded to His Excellency in remuneration for his selfless service . . . as a model of sublime patriotism and love of liberty." The publication that resulted was the very *Rasgos de la vida pública*, distributed by justices of the peace in Buenos Aires Province and the interior.[58]

A similar work of positive propaganda was *La rosa de marzo* (The March rose), published in 1843. Little is known about this curious book, aside from the fact that some copies were printed on pink (i.e., rose-colored) paper and that it was one of a limited number of bound book volumes published during the Rosas years. It was not Federalist red, but the symbolism was still clearly present in the lighter shade of the pages. The number of copies printed remains a mystery, but the book was devised for a "popular" audience rather than the small circle of Rosas's confidants.

This is most evident in the way the text is organized, the book consisting of reader-friendly vignettes composed by "Federalist citizens." According to Victoriano Aguilar, the editor of the book, Rosas's birthday party in 1843 was the inspiration for the civic compositions, which flow chronologically and correspond to a month and year when Rosas had performed some valiant act of manliness or made a significant political decision. What makes them particularly well suited for the larger reading public—of literates *and* illiterates—is their attempt to narrate a history of Rosas that caters to notions of a shared past for all (Federalist) citizens of the region.[59]

Of particular importance was getting across the notion of Rosas as the champion of America, always ready to fight for independence (although he had opposed independence) and defend Americans from imperial foreigners (whom the Unitarians represented). So goes the logic of *La rosa de marzo*. A handful of compositions, including the "Canción al triunfo de las armas federales sobre las hordas del inmundo salvaje unitario incendiario pardejón Rivera, en las puntas del Arroyo Grande" (Song relating the triumph of Federalist might over the hordes led by the filthy, savage provocateur and pardejón Rivera on the edge of Arroyo Grande), deal with the connections between Rosas and Uruguay. There are a number of other songs, their music included, for the avid Federalist who wants to express party sentiment with a tune. And like official documents and all other publications siding with Rosas, the title page struts the Federalist lema.

While these two books help us understand the positive propaganda that constituted a dimension of the militarization of print during the Rosas years, they were exceptions in terms of publication. Newspapers, looseleaf sheets, broadsheets, and pasquinades were by far the most prominent forms of print media during this period. Newspapers were especially well suited to partisan warfare in print, in part because they were fairly easy to start, provided one had the financial resources to do so, and in part because they had potentially large readerships.[60]

Under Rosas's second term, control of the press was tight in Argentina and Uruguay, except in the city of Montevideo. Strict regulations and censorship over what was published were implemented. There were, however, different degrees of restriction from the time Rosas stepped into the position of governor. From 1829 to roughly 1835, the Buenos Aires government allowed the publication only of papers that did not publish in favor of Unitarian policies. Unitarian authors operated in exile, primarily in Montevideo and Santiago, which partly explains the large quantity of publications in Buenos Aires supporting Rosas and Federalism. Federalist enthusiasts were not altogether free, though. Those who exercised their supposed right to opine on political questions in ways that could compromise the government were dealt with, usually by seeing their papers shut down or facing time in prison, as described earlier in the case of Luis Pérez. On the whole, though, the press functioned at a high level of production during Rosas's first term in office, during which over one hundred different newspapers were printed in Argentina. That said, the year he was out of office—1833— saw the greatest number of papers published.[61]

Harsher treatment of newspapers (and their authors) was implemented in the late 1830s, above all following the beginning of the French blockade of the Río de la Plata in 1838. After Rosas's return in 1835, the Federalist and Blanco lemas began appearing on newspapers on both sides of the river. Three officialist papers in Argentina—*La Gaceta Mercantil, El Diario de la Tarde*, and the *Archivo Americano*—became the big guns of the press, and they were made available for free by the Buenos Aires provincial treasury.[62] Rosas's confidants managed the propaganda machine, though in the case of the *Archivo Americano*, whose chief editor was Italian immigrant Pedro de Angelis, Rosas took a hands-on approach, organizing the subjects for the paper into folders that passed between his house and that of de Angelis, as well as editing articles.[63] It was in these three papers, and in ones such as *El Republicano* and *El Defensor de las Leyes* (The defender of laws) across the river on the outskirts of Montevideo, where much Federalist and Blanco verse was printed or reprinted. Public readings of the papers played right into Rosista discourse, as did more importantly the widespread distribution of print media such as pasquinades and loose-leaves that were not put out by the government but supported the great caudillo.[64] Publications that did not serve to disseminate appropriate propaganda were short-lived if they even saw light to begin with. The numbers are telling: from 1836 to 1851—a period lasting three times as long as Rosas's first term—only around sixty different papers were published in all Argentina.[65] In contrast, the liberal holdout of Montevideo escaped the crackdown on the press during the Rosas years: over one hundred publications were printed in Uruguay during Rosas's second term, most of these in Montevideo.[66]

Print was critical to public ceremonies during this period, too. The activities of April 1836, marking a year since Rosas's return to power, bore this out. On the edge of Buenos Aires's city limits, where pulperías flourished, peasants sang their written and improvised compositions in honor of Rosas. Back in the city center, pasquinades and announcements were posted in the main square, along house walls, and throughout the streets. One of these that spoke the patriot fire in Rosas's heart was pinned to the wall of San Ignacio Church on Potosí Street and surrounded by Federalist flags. Another set of verses were visible near the university: they, too, spoke of a patriotic Rosas putting an end to tyranny. The words of a popular song for the celebration also spoke of the patria being saved from tyrants, thanks to the Federalists. With lines such as "Death to all those who aren't Federalists!," the song helped remind those who thought twice about party identity to shape up.[67]

Similar public parties took place in October of the same year, this time celebrating the anniversary of the beginning of Rosas's political career. Portraits of Rosas and his wife decorated the city center. Anonymous authors contributed their poetry to the festive spirit. At least one of these authors wrote a poem to the "Heroine of the Desert Campaign," Rosas's wife: as a beacon of pure patriotism, went the poem, she deserved to be as much the center of attention as the patrón himself.[68] Myers observes that, as a good politician, Rosas maintained that such assertions were "the free expression of popular sentiment."[69]

This, of course, did not keep Unitarians and Colorados from contesting the social order that Rosas, Oribe, and the estanciero class defended so fiercely. But despite the enormous quantity of writing these opponents produced, they could not rival the success of Federalist authors. Quite simply, the Unitarian and Colorado parties failed to inspire popular support through print.

An Unsuccessful Opposition

The strongest band of Unitarian opponents came together in meetings at the last bookstore of Marcos Sastre, a Uruguayan who had immigrated to Buenos Aires in 1833.[70] From the time he arrived, Sastre had owned and operated numerous bookstores, and each had provided a reading room of sorts, lent books to subscribed members, and served as a gathering place for intellectuals. He opened his last store in 1837, and it was here that a literary salon and the so-called generation of 1837 were formed. Participation in the salon, however, was not as flexible as joining the previous reading clubs had been. Interested individuals had to subscribe for a period of one year, which cost sixty pesos—an amount that limited access to the group. Members could bring guests on occasion, but the agreement was set up to preserve the boundaries of the salon.[71] This was an exclusive club where members such as Domingo Sarmiento, Juan María Gutiérrez, Vicente López y Planes, Esteban Echeverría, and Juan Bautista Alberdi were bound together by liberalism, class, and most importantly, opposition to Federalists and Blancos.

It was the group's focus on political questions that led to its downfall. Some claim that Echeverría's readings, concerned with the road Argentina was going down with Rosas, sparked official opposition. Perhaps it was the emphasis the salon placed on works by French authors—in particular those who dealt with republicanism and equality—and how such writings were in line with the political objectives of the members. The end result was that the young intellectuals fell out of favor with Rosas, which made subsequent relationships between the salon and government difficult and dangerous, and led to divisions among these intellectuals. In January 1838, Sastre published a note in *El Diario de la Tarde* announcing that it was necessary to stop the salon's activities. A few weeks later, he began auctioning off books, and by May the bookstore had closed.[72]

The members went their various ways—Echeverría to Montevideo, Sarmiento to Santiago, and so on—and they continued waging their war against cattle civilization through print. Gutiérrez called for the creation of a "national" literary tradition that could respond to events of the day and be wielded in political battles.[73] Echeverría would go on to criticize the power of estancieros in his now-canonical story *El matadero* (The slaughterhouse; not published until 1871), which described events at a Buenos Aires slaughterhouse. And Sarmiento would author what has become the definitive contemporary critique of cattle culture, *Facundo*. But these authors wrote for a small reading public to which they belonged in hopes of expanding that group to include "others." Unitarians in exile were constant contributors and chief editors of newspapers from the time Rosas took office to 1852, but these papers were unable to compete with the popular Federalist and Blanco papers. What they did share was the partisan motivation behind almost every word written and printed. Artistic aspirations took a back seat to political concerns. Unitarian and Colorado partisans wrote for their social class, and it was their social class that they envisioned leading the fight against estancieros and constructing a republic founded on liberal principles.

One of the most notable efforts of liberal intellectuals was *El Comercio del Plata*, printed daily in Montevideo between 1845 and 1852. Designed from its inception to combat Rosas and Oribe, the paper had average print runs of over four hundred copies a day, distributed mainly to elites who held subscriptions.[74] But its intellectual tone limited its accessibility and did not make it popular outside small circles. The paper's founder, Argentine exile Florencio Varela, was aware of this and recognized the importance of popular, gauchesque papers that would be of greater interest and availability to rural inhabitants. On 16 November 1846, he recommended to readers the work of his compatriot in exile in Montevideo, Hilario Ascasubi, and commented in *El Comercio del Plata* that "if the press is going to exercise any influence over our residents in the countryside, it will only be through those picturesque and animated forms of writing that they can identify with because of the language, characters, and a class of verse that makes them laugh. It is this type of writing that makes them happy when they sing it to the sound of their guitars in pulperías and sitting around campfires."[75] Valentín Alsina echoed Florencio Varela's amazement at the reach of popular literature and subscribed to the idea of using it to "instruct the masses."[76] Ironically, even Manuel Oribe recommended Ascasubi's creations to a friend, asking the friend to facilitate contacts for the poet.[77] Writing for gauchos was precisely what Ascasubi did.

Exiled in Montevideo from the early 1830s to the end of the Rosas years, Ascasubi was the only writer on the side of the Unitarians and Colorados who enjoyed veritable success in the venture to wage war through print *and* to reach a large public.[78] Ascasubi was a rival of the Federalist gazetteer Luis Pérez.[79] Like Pérez, Ascasubi drafted gauchesque verses and dialogues that appeared as loose leaves and in newspapers. Like Pérez, he wrote for his party, though he collected sums for the things he produced for leaders such as Rivera and Urquiza. And like Pérez, Ascasubi was a soldier-poet. His papers had titles in the same spirit as those of Pérez: *El*

Figure 2.9. The liberal gaucho Jacinto Cielo whirls his *boleadoras* (a hunting weapon consisting of stones tethered together with braided colt skin or leather) on the front page of an Ascasubi newspaper. Ascasubi's verses harkened back to those of Bartolomé Hidalgo, which were in circulation during the wars of independence. Even the names of some of the paper's main characters—Jacinto and Chano—were references to characters in Hidalgo's poems. In this sense, Ascasubi, Pérez, and other authors of gauchesque verse tapped into a common set of popular cultural referents rooted in Hidalgo's verses. *El Gaucho Jacinto Cielo*, 11 August 1843 (No. 9).

Arriero Argentino (The Argentine herdsman, 1830), *El Gaucho en Campaña* (The gaucho on the trail to save the patria, 1839), and *El Gaucho Jacinto Cielo* (1843). These all presented ruffian gaucho editors and were published in Montevideo. He collected his loose publications of poetry into a volume titled *Paulino* that he dedicated to Urquiza. The definitive version of this collection, which did not include his gauchesque newspapers, was published in 1872 with the revealing title of *Paulino Lucero, ó Los gauchos del Río de la Plata: Cantando y combatiendo contra los tiranos de las repúblicas*

EL GAUCHO.

No tiene dia fijo
para su publicacion,
por lo tanto no se ad-
miten suscripciones.
Se anunciará el dia
antes de su salida.

PRECIO.
6 vintenes número

LUGARES DE LA VENT.
Libreria de Hernan-
dez, almacen de Va-
rela, en la Plaza y en
lo del Sr. Domenech.

EL GAUCHO EN CAMPAÑA.

POR LA PATRIA Y EL AMOR.

MONTEVIDEO, LUNES 30 DE SETIEMBRE DE 1839.   NUM. 1.º

INTRODUCCION.

Soy Ciudadano Gaucho Oriental y pa-
yador que aunque me he criado entre los car-

Y que defiiendan tan lindo
La patria y su libertad
Para cautivar mi agrado
Y mi cariño *cabal.*

Figure 2.10. *El Gaucho en Campaña*, another of Ascasubi's papers, sporting a character similar to Jacinto Cielo on its front page, 30 September 1839. (Courtesy of the Biblioteca Nacional, Montevideo, Materiales Especiales.)

Argentina y Oriental de Uruguay (1839–1851) (Paulino Lucero, or The gauchos of the Río de la Plata singing and fighting the tyrants of the Argentine and Uruguayan Republics).

In *Paulino Lucero* and his gauchesque papers, Ascasubi's war against Rosas and Oribe is waged by a *liberal* gaucho who appropriates the nativist attraction of the figure of the gaucho to change the minds of rural and urban followers of Oribe and Rosas. The compositions are as much about strategy as they are about entertaining rural readers. Take, for example, the poem "The Card Game," supposedly by a soldier under Rivera's command. It appeared in *El Gaucho en Campaña* in late 1839, and at the head of the poem is a note to the editor in which the author (Ascasubi) tells how he will relate the valiant resistance of the Uruguayan troops against Rosas's invaders. In what comes close to mirroring the language used by Federalist supporters to talk about Unitarians and Colorados, the author speaks of

Rosas as a coward, thief, and traitor: "That Rosas—come on, damn it! If he comes . . . if he so dares / Although we have to go after him, all the way to Buenos Ayres / We'll give that feisty gaucho a good scare." The heated words continue, rounding off the poem with the idea of relaxing on Rosas's estancias and roasting up a fine *asado* (barbecue) cut from among Rosas's cattle with General Rivera.[80]

Ascasubi was a master at composing cielitos in which he narrated battles won against Rosas and Oribe, creating letters purportedly from frightened Federalist generals to their leader, imitating the language of Blanco supporters, and giving comical voices to some of the leading figures of the Rosas regime, including Rosas himself. One of his inventions consists of a summary of military action from General Pascual Echagüe to Rosas. Ascasubi claimed the document had been found in a trunk that the general had lost in Entre Ríos after his defeat in the battle of Cagancha in 1839. As can be expected, the general laments his loss in the Banda Oriental, and then advises Rosas that it would take resources beyond their reach for them to stand a chance in another fight. Rosas's reply—also invented by Ascasubi—is a furious one, but no less comical than the blunders of battle confessed by Echagüe. Writing as both men, Ascasubi skillfully depicts them as eager to praise their Unitarian and Colorado enemies for their valor and skill in battle and as representatives of a group lacking cohesion.[81]

Like many of the Federalist poets, with the works of the revolutionary writer Bartolomé Hidalgo as his models, Ascasubi wrote lively dialogues between peasants. One of these is a conversation held by Norberto Flores and Ramón Guevara, two Uruguayan gauchos who discuss the invasion of the Banda Oriental and how it was necessary to join the ranks of those fighting to preserve the patria. At the high point of the chat, the two men speak of the dark prospect of Rosas ordering people around in Uruguay, which would equal a total loss of independence. Flores asks Guevara what he thinks, and Guevara responds in a way that sheds light on how party affiliation casually became imbedded in one's identity: he cannot contemplate not taking sides. This is the very idea Ascasubi hoped to get across to his readers—that they had to take sides. Of course, the only viable option was to oppose Rosas and Oribe. Guevara hopes this idea is clearly expressed by the words embroidered on the headband he asks Flores to buy: "Long live

Figure 2.11. A peasant greets a friend on horseback on the front page of Isidoro de María's gauchesque paper. The byline reads, "Swallow this pill!" *El Gaucho Oriental,* 7 October 1839 (nos. 6–7).

the constitution and free Orientales! Death to the invading Echagua!"[82] *Echagua* was a play on words, poking fun of General Echagüe as well as loosely meaning "water thrower." The headband would have amused Ascasubi's country audience, who at least could "read" the image of the words, while reinforcing the dialogue's blend of party line and patriotic sentiment.

The militarization of print culture was about fighting the enemy and defining one's own position. It was almost never about persuasion, which made this second stage sharply distinct from the partisan efforts in print to gain followers during Rosas's first term. Linked to the rural-urban divide so pronounced at midcentury were nativism and liberalism. When it came to the effectiveness of print, nativism and Rosas's particular brand of nationalism came out on top, evident in the popular support he received during his years in office.[83] The connection of nativism to the rural, patriotic, and anticosmopolitan image of the regime came with the hope of defining a party identity that could at the same time be transferred to the republic, or even the nation. Ironically, the Rosas years were brought to an end by the rival estanciero Justo José de Urquiza. The end result was the unraveling of the lasso that had print culture intertwined with the politics of cattle civilization. But by the time this happened, writing—especially forms of popular literature—had infiltrated successfully patterns of daily life.

Undoing the Lasso: A Culture of Print at the Crossroads

The end of the Rosas years essentially marked the end of cattle civilization, at least as it had functioned up to 1850. The long years of civil war had sent Uruguayan cattle production back to levels lower than those seen during the late colonial period.[84] Rosas's exile (which began in 1852) also had a major impact on the goals of authors, the functions and types of writing, and the makeup of reading publics. Rioplatense print culture was at a crossroads.

In this last scene, liberal elites were cultivating a coherent program for the future, and the social order that was part and parcel of cattle culture was not in their plans. Between 1852 and 1870, they would take over state administration in Uruguay and Argentina, finally acquiring the political authority and political power that had eluded them for half a century. Throughout this short period, there was a gradual unraveling of the connections binding the printed word to a world that revolved around cattle. By 1870, there was a marked turn among authors toward social concerns, especially those related to the consequences of political action, such as the decimation of indigenous populations and the attempts to rid the countryside of gauchos. The social twist of the last period was still a political statement. What vanished was partisan coloring.[85]

Gauchesque writing changed significantly during the second half of the century, above all because the lives of the rural inhabitants who were its characters were changing. With Rosas out of power, rapid evolution in agricultural practice, and the rise of sheepherding (which would eventually overshadow cattle culture), gauchesque authors turned their attention and the focus of their writing to social conditions, almost with an eye toward the past, looking nostalgically to the days of old. It was during this period that the myth of the gaucho as a noble citizen and protector of a cultural heritage started taking shape (later to be deployed as a nationalist icon).

Authors also began searching for ways to bring country gauchos and urban dwellers closer together.[86] This is what the Argentine writer and Unitarian politician Estanislao del Campo had in mind with his verses.

Del Campo began his writing career as an admirer of Hilario Ascasubi. He was also a supporter of *mitrismo*, the spirit of liberalism promoted by Bartolomé Mitre, president of Argentina in the 1860s. In the end, mitrismo was very much in line with the Unitarian Party, so del Campo's alliance with the ideology meant that he addressed an elite urban audience as well as the rural one that was Ascasubi's prime readership. This difference came out clearly in del Campo's *Fausto: Impresiones del gaucho Anastasio el Pollo en la representación de esta ópera* (*Faust*: Impressions of the gaucho Anastasio el Pollo at the performance of this opera).

Fausto is a landmark publication, in part because of its commercial success—rare for a celebrated man of letters—and in part because of the portrait it paints of gauchos. After its first publication in the newspaper *Correo del Domingo* in September 1866, *Fausto* was reprinted in a number of forms. The popular paper *La Tribuna* published it in October of the same year. In November it was put out as a *folleto* (pamphlet), with the revenue from sales collected for the wounded in the War of the Triple Alliance, and with commentaries by several members of Buenos Aires's literary elite.[87] And in 1870 del Campo published the poem again, this time in book form with other verses.[88] The newspaper *El Pueblo* commented on the new pamphlet version the day it hit the streets: "The author of this poem is sure to sell a great number of copies, especially in the countryside, where the work has generated enormous enthusiasm."[89] In the following day's issue, dated 9 November 1866, the same paper announced that many requests for the folleto had come from the countryside and that copies of it would be distributed that night in Buenos Aires at the operatic presentation of *Fausto*. The folleto came with a detailed lithographic image of Anastasio relating the story of the opera to his pal Laguna on the banks of the Río de la Plata. The image was a portrait of sorts of del Campo and one of his close friends, but rural inhabitants could nevertheless identify with it as a scene of two peasants conversing. The success of the poem aside, the characters del Campo masterfully depicts are *unarmed* gauchos, which reflect the emerging myth of the gaucho. They make no mention of savage Unitarians or Federalists. Rather, their jovial nature makes it easy for the traditionally rebellious persona of the gaucho to be absent from the scene.[90] This new representation was in sync with one of del Campo's goals: to assimilate the gaucho into the ways of urban liberals, a notion appealing to del Campo's audience.

Along with the changing motivations of writers, the nature of the audience or reading public was a key factor in the culture of print reaching a crossroads. After the Rosas years, liberal writers became gradually more concerned with a reading public that wanted texts to aspire to be "literary" as well as political. This change was evident in the foundation of literary societies that often brought political enemies together with the common goal of forging a national literary project and a community of writers. Women were becoming increasingly a part of this new reading public, and it was women, many of these writers thought, who could help shift literature away from rough partisan discourse.[91] But with the exception of del Campo's *Fausto*, liberal print media struggled to gain a substantial readership. The most significant audience for print media during these years continued following popular verse. This phenomenon can be attributed both to the primarily rural demographic character of the Río de la Plata, as well as to the ways such verse tapped into the hearts of those associated with a dying cattle culture and suffering the accompanying vicissitudes.

Formed by rural inhabitants and lower-class urban residents of the Plata, one of the most important characteristics of this new community of readers—possibly even *the* most important characteristic—is that it did not exist before the appearance of gauchesque writing. The people who were doing the reading—or, as more often was the case, were being read to—had been around, of course, but it was thanks to the works of authors such as Hidalgo, Pérez, Ascasubi, and del Campo that a new popular readership had come into existence. What's more, as Angel Rama has pointed out, "we are dealing with the broadest and most active literary audience in all the nineteenth century, by far much bigger than any audience addressed by elite authors during the same period."[92] The best-selling works of close friends Antonio Lussich and José Hernández bear witness to the size of this readership as well as the new issues on the table in popular poetry.

Lussich wrote *Los tres gauchos orientales* (The three Uruguayan gauchos), a dialogue that chronicles the battle led by the Blanco general Timoteo Aparicio against the Colorado president Lorenzo Batlle. The poem was extremely well received upon its publication in 1872. A second edition came out a year later, a third in 1877, and then a fourth edition in 1883. In a letter he directed to the publisher of the fourth edition, Lussich remarked on the social concern at the heart of the book: "The reception this book has had is truly flattering for me. I have tried to paint examples of what we could call a legendary race—one that, as the overwhelming law of progress would have it, is tending to disappear. What is left for future generations, however, is the memory of this race's virility, intelligence, and patriotic self-sacrifice."[93] In contrast to the gauchos in Federalist papers and the early writings of Ascasubi, who were writers waging a war between supporters and opponents of cattle culture, Lussich's gauchos aim to draw attention to a sector of Rioplatense society that was in danger of disappearing. To put it simply, social justice had replaced flag waving for a party as a matter of national importance. And Lussich's remarks shed light on another component of the myth of the gaucho: race.

The fourth edition of *Los tres gauchos* brought the total number of official copies in circulation to at least sixteen thousand. While the editorial success was a source of pride for Lussich, he was most proud of his effort to defend "those disgraced pariahs, victims of the neglect they live with, stripped of all the promises and guarantees to which they have rights as free citizens."[94] These pariahs were peasants who had so inspired Lussich as a soldier with General Aparicio. For him, they were the most sincere patriots—always the first to defend the notion of liberty and eager to sacrifice everything to preserve the patria. This was reason enough to put into print for posterity the ways of a lifestyle on the verge of disappearing.

This was the point expressed by his character Luciano Santos, the scribe of sorts of the conversation the three gauchos held. Santos overheard the three from behind a patch of bushes and decided to record what they said as a "national story." This story, or one aspect of it, tells of the war. The characters Julián and Baliente lament that war has shut the doors of the patria to patriots of the countryside—doors that had been opened only by the revolution they had fought alongside General Aparicio. There is talk about emigrating, and both recall all the things they once had but have since lost: flocks of sheep, a small piece of land, horses, a house, and beloved sweethearts who either died of sorrow or joined hands with another man. This is the luck of the draw, Julián notes.[95] The real story comes with Santos's closing words about a remedy for the degenerating social situation of gauchos. "The faithful native son," writes Santos, "will learn education." Indeed, he goes on, gauchos may be ignorant, but they are still vessels in which knowledge may accumulate; wise people are just vessels with a fine finish. "Even the fiercest gaucho will be a useful citizen. . . . Set up once and for all the school / Instead of buying so many arms / That only give rise to more alarm. . . . And into a doctor the gaucho will be transformed." While not many gauchos earned the formal title of "doctor," education was the remedy in Santos's (and Lussich's) eyes.[96]

Education was a motivating factor behind José Hernández's now mythic gauchesque poem *Martín Fierro*, which also appeared in 1872. By the mid-1870s, the publishing success of Hernández's poem had overshadowed that of *Los tres gauchos orientales*, del Campo's *Fausto*, and many liberal writers' works combined. This did not stop Sarmiento's liberal government from chasing after Hernández (one of its most outspoken critics) to the point of forcing him into exile. This experience, however, surely reinforced his perspective on the sad situation of rural residents. In the revealing "A Few Words with My Readers" that opens *La vuelta de Martín Fierro* (The return of Martín Fierro, 1879), Hernández comments on the success of the poem and offers ideas on the act of reading and how the language of the poem imitates the language of so many who have not read before. The goal is that "readers identify closely and intimately with the poem, and that reading it be a natural continuation of daily existence." Here again we find the power of popular writing tapping into daily life. Hernández knew the value of this mundane, ordinary literary presence: "Only in this manner will my readers pass from the rigors of a day's work to the book, and only in this way will its reading be amenable, interesting, and useful for them."[97] He goes on to say that if a book could teach readers how to live upright lives, be noble and productive citizens, to respect their parents and fellow paisanos, to foment love among spouses, and, among other things, to love freedom while respecting law, then it would be a good book, notwithstanding the spelling errors contained within. *La vuelta* is such a book, he argues, and many more need to take up where it leaves off, teaching its lessons in a way that is barely or not at all perceptible so that they can be absorbed without confusion.[98]

Hernández's educational project, and that of other authors who also appealed to the power of education, was not meant to be carried out in the classroom. It aimed to help peasants deal with the problems they faced, such as conscription, the constant search for work that took them away from home, an unfair legal system that stripped them of property and dignity, and political retribution for any number of reasons. In the scheme of the changing character of print culture, *Martín Fierro* was a leading example of the turn toward social concerns. Though the poem was all about gauchos, its publication, like that of Lussich's *Los tres gauchos orientales*, reflected the undoing of the lasso, with the threads of print and cattle cultures going in different directions.

Hernández's call for creating similar texts was not in vain. Through the 1870s, 1880s, and 1890s in both Uruguay and Argentina, hundreds of folletos and loose-leaf gauchesque poems, plays, and novels were printed, performed by traveling circus troupes, and presented in theaters in Buenos Aires, Montevideo, and small towns throughout the Uruguayan and Argentine countryside and along the Uruguay-Brazil border.[99] Titles such as *La fiesta de los ruriales* (The fiesta of us country folk), *Poesías campestres* (Rural poetry) by the "soldier and gaucho oriental" Calistro Fuente, the random *Carta del gaucho Cipriano relatando sus amores con una coqueta* (Letter from the gaucho Cipriano relating his amorous encounters with a coquette), and Eduardo Gutiérrez's *Juan Moreira* told similar stories.[100] They were all part of a larger vein of *criollista* literature, much of which was a variation on the Moreira and Fierro story lines of good gauchos (read *criollos*, or native sons) gone bad as a result of a corrupt system of justice.[101] Some titles were more serious than others, yet all aimed to fit in with the quotidian, a goal that *Martín Fierro* achieved remarkably well.[102]

■

From 1830 to 1870, an evolving culture of print in the Plata was braided to an economy based on exploiting cattle products and the politics of estancieros and saladeristas. Almost everything written during these years engaged this reality in one way or another. The rule of the patrón and estate owner Juan Manuel de Rosas corresponded to the most profitable years of cattle civilization. During his first term in office, writing branded political property and party identity. In a second distinct stage, factions competing for party loyalty militarized print culture. As a component of the civil wars being fought in the region, popular verse printed in newspapers and on loose leaves and posted in public spaces led a rhetorical war against a "savage" enemy. In spite of the many fronts on which the Unitarians and Colorados challenged Federalist and Blanco propaganda, gauchesque writing, and the politics of cattle culture, they were unsuccessful in comparison to their opponents when it came to inserting themselves into traditional modes of association and garnering popular support. After all, for most of the readers they were attempting to reach, siding with Rosas or Oribe would have been much more emotionally satisfying than lining up with a group of elites who were fans of the foreign. Beginning in the 1850s, a broader range of concerns, such as those dealing with aesthetic aspirations and social conditions, gradually replaced fighting to promote party affiliation and identity through print.

Focusing on words, wars, and gauchos allows us to draw some important conclusions regarding the second period of print culture's development in the Río de la Plata. To begin, distinct forms of popular literary production, with gauchesque poetry and papers at the forefront, led not only to new roles for writing in the public sphere, but also secured a place for literature as a practice that was often part of everyday life. This new role gave writing significant power to influence the formation of party affiliation and identity, whether the act of reading occurred in silence or out loud in a group setting as a collective mode of entertainment.

Unlike anywhere else in nineteenth-century Latin America, this popular literature negotiated the meeting of oral and print cultures and allowed for the large-scale consumption of print media. That Rosas and Oribe were good gauchos themselves made state appropriation of popular discourse seem completely natural. The state and its functionaries, however, did not have a monopoly on the written word. Foot soldier of the press Pérez was an ardent Federalist whose papers were all the rage, but he was not on the government payroll. When opposition author Ascasubi tapped into the power of gauchesque writing from the liberal stronghold of Montevideo, he enjoyed substantial readership. The very popular quality that made gauchesque writing such an effective form of inspiring and reaffirming affinity for a political party thus limited the ways in which the state could appropriate it.

In sum, the formation of political (and party) identity through print depended on the ability to engage popular sentiment in order to get the message across. This was a lesson learned the hard way by Unitarians and Colorados who cared nothing about writing things that could be read, discussed, and sung at the local pulpería or around the campfire at night. This did not stop such writers from engaging in political debate in print. It just meant that their words were ineffective.

By the 1870s, the ties between print and cattle cultures had unraveled. How to integrate the rural majority of the Uruguayan and Argentine countrysides with their urban fellow citizens turned into a priority for not only sympathizers with the disappearing way of life, but also liberal elites thinking about how to harness progress to their nation's future. The key for both groups resided in education. And with the first big waves of immigrants settling in the port cities of Buenos Aires and Montevideo, it was education liberal-style that would play the next and definitive role in orienting Rioplatense print culture.

Chapter 3

Sowers of Alphabets
(1870–1910)

■ With the advent of public primary education around 1880, the relationship between print, the state, and the public sphere would change entirely. Education opened the gateway to much greater public interaction with print culture. After all, primary education, by far more important than secondary education, was now *compulsory*, and the numbers of students attending school rose quickly.[1] One of the results was a rapid rise in literacy rates. Though attempts were made to promote public education in places such as Chile and Mexico, it was in Uruguay and Argentina where education was most successful, which solidified the unique relationship between print and the public in the region. In a word, the establishment of public education systems in the Río de la Plata between 1870 and 1910 was the keystone to converting reading and writing into public concerns.[2] Education allowed print to spread throughout these two countries to an extent unlike anywhere else in Latin America. It also provided the state with a whole new range of opportunities to regulate print media and messages, and for a captive and very impressionable audience. Through textbooks, notebooks, and other print media selected for use in public schools, state functionaries exercised direct influence over the forms of collective identity these texts aimed to inspire. All these factors made public primary schools sites of everyday reading where print was connected to the formation of collective identities like never before.

Our tour of the sowers of alphabets whose educational systems reconfigured the landscape of Rioplatense print culture will assess how effective they were, but we will first look at the motivations behind the creation of public education systems at the end of the nineteenth century. After considering education as a solution to a moment of social crisis, we will move on to the bureaucratic framework of learning the ABCs, focusing on textbook selection committees and time allotted to reading and writing in the classroom. Lastly, we will see how some students used and interacted with these new forms of everyday print media.

■

José Pedro Varela passed away on 24 October 1879, at the young age of thirty-four.[3] Yet, as the lyrics of Victor Lima's song "Sembrador de abecedario" (Sower of the alphabet) tell us, the "shepherd" of the school "will never die."[4] Indeed, Varela's death occurred at the beginning of the long life (or immortality) of his ideas, which still thrive today. These ideas constituted the *Reforma Vareliana* and would serve as the foundation of the public education system in Uruguay, but the reformer had not lived to see their success.

Almost all Uruguayan newspapers lamented the passing of the young director of schools. One of his biographers wrote that the news resounded in the soul of the republic.[5] On 25 October, the government issued a call for Varela to be honored as one of the great citizens of the nation. The sad day in October had come, wrote Uruguayan president Lorenzo Latorre, "when the seeds he planted in our patria's soil were just beginning to bear fruit." According to a decree issued on the same date, all government offices would be closed the day of Varela's interment.[6]

Varela's burial was accompanied by widespread public recognition. His fellow champion of education Orestes Araújo tells us that no fewer than twenty thousand people showed up for the services on 28 October.[7] The paper *La France* remarked that Montevideo had never seen such an outpouring of public sentiment. "An immense crowd," noted the paper, "in which all classes, all nationalities, all ages . . . combined and formed a human wave that grew street corner by street corner. It is fair to say that the entire city was on foot to follow the procession of the great man who will be from here on immortal."[8] *El Siglo* described the day's events with similar awe.

The grand gestures that accompany the burial of national heroes were not lacking, either. "The Government has fulfilled its obligation," stated *El Siglo*. "The cannon let loose sorrowful reverberations; the national flag flapped in the wind as on days when the nation mourns; authorities paid their respects to Varela's body. . . . Everybody was there, and everybody lamented the great loss the country had suffered. Everybody cried and sang Varela's praises."[9] The coffin was adorned with flowers and placed in a chariot pulled by six horses and flanked by the highest government officials. Throughout the day politicians spoke, as did colleagues from the Society of Friends of Public Education and the administrative body of public education (the Dirección General de Instrucción Pública, or DGIP). Notably absent from the apotheosizing event were clergymen, church officials, and advocates of preserving the teaching of Catholicism in the classroom—Varela's enemies.

The following years saw commemorations that contributed to solidifying the legend of Varela. His portrait began to appear in classrooms across the country. In 1880, the DGIP declared that from then on, schools would close on 24 October to pay tribute to Varela. In 1881, the anniversary of the reformer's death was an even bigger event. Perhaps because of its popularity, it also generated some controversy. Varela's connection to president (and military strongman) Lorenzo Latorre sparked a divide among members of El Ateneo (The Athenaeum), a group of intellectuals who contributed to public debate in newspapers and political circles. The row started when the group's followers of Varela planned to hold a literary gathering in order to commemorate his work on the second anniversary of his death. Other Ateneo members were strongly opposed to the idea, claiming that Varela had made the wrong move when he collaborated with Latorre, an enemy of liberalism, and thus deserved no such recognition. Volleys were exchanged in the press in July 1881. One author defended Varela by writing, "Varela's work is immortal. . . . He sowed the seed that is going to produce citizens yearning to carry out their duties, citizens who understand their rights; meanwhile, the dictatorship of Latorre will naturally disappear."[10] The bond between the memory of the sower and his seeds was growing stronger.

After months of debate in the press, the literary gathering took place in Montevideo's premier theater, the Teatro Solís. More people turned out for this day, in fact, than for his burial two years before. After lofty speeches by lettered elites, young schoolchildren passed by Varela's grave, leaving flowers and other adornments that ended up covering the tomb.[11] Seven years later, the dispute over Varela had cooled. In fact, there was now a certain unified voice that praised him for fighting the "dictator" from within. The manifesto of the Liga Patriótica de la Enseñanza (Patriotic League of Education), formed in 1888, summed up the new reverence for the reformer: "From a carefree society—one indifferent to questions of education; racked by hatred, partisan resentment, and doctrinal worries; and subjugated by a dictator—Varela began creating a community that fell in love with the cause of education."[12] In the spirit of unity behind education, some of those who had opposed recognizing Varela in 1881 now signed on to the Liga's words of praise.

By the turn of the century, Varela was assured of his place in the national pantheon, and his myth was becoming more and more ingrained in Uruguayan history, thanks largely to the thousands of children who were attending public schools and learning to love the *fundador de la escuela* (founder of the schools). Second grader Carmen Biasotti wrote affectionately of Varela in her class notebooks: "He loved us [children] a lot and worked for our happiness and that of the patria. All Uruguayans should ...respect his memory."[13] In December 1918, politicians and schoolteachers inaugurated the Plaza José Pedro Varela, gathering around a sculpted monument to the reformer. The hymn composed for the event spoke of harboring for eternity the memory of Varela. Fit for the day's proceedings, the hymn sang of Varela as a national hero to be considered alongside José Artigas, and it ended with a line admonishing Uruguayans to cherish the fruits of education and proclaim them in order to keep the spirit of Varela's reform alive. The sculpture depicts schoolchildren circled around a seated Varela who, not by chance, holds a book in hand.

Since the inauguration of the plaza, Varela has continued to represent something unique about what it means to be Uruguayan. This idea is visible on Uruguayan paper currency, where his image—as well as that of his plaza—has appeared since 1975. A stamp issued in 1995 to mark his 150th birthday conveys a similar meaning. Songs to Varela are still sung in schools today, and his portrait continues to preside over young students in the classroom. The Colegio José Pedro Varela, a landmark on the Avenida 18 de Julio in the center of Montevideo, is passed by thousands every day. The Museo Pedagógico José Pedro Varela (The José Pedro Varela Pedagogical Museum), also in the heart of the city, pays homage to him, introducing visitors to the world of education in the late nineteenth century. In short, his status as a national hero is still alive and well.

Varela's plans for reforming the system of public education in Uruguay consisted of a handful of basic but significant changes, spanning from making primary education compulsory and free to opening coeducational schools, establishing "normal" schools (for training elementary school teachers), and building an administrative bureaucracy to oversee all aspects of public education. He lived to see these backed by law, but his plans did not begin to bear fruit until after he died. The same is true of a man he admired who was his counterpart across the Río de la Plata: Domingo F. Sarmiento. While he was no longer a key player on the educational scene in his older years, Sarmiento was (and is) considered the architect of Argentine public education. Though he lived much longer than Varela, he, like the younger Uruguayan, passed away just as public primary education was gathering steam. Since his death in 1888, Sarmiento has been apotheosized, although his legacy has been much more polemical than Varela's (the latter a veritable unifying force).

What is it that has made these two men the stuff of legend and myth? What is it that led the writer and musician Alfredo Zitarrosa to proclaim that all Uruguayans are *Varelianos* (followers of Varela)? Put differently, what makes Varela and Sarmiento national heroes? The answer lies in their being sowers of alphabets. Both José Pedro Varela and Domingo Sarmiento considered education necessary for the formation of well-behaved, hardworking, and loyal citizens, and for future national prosperity. Moreover, for both men, as well as for the bureaucrats who carried out their educational programs, reading and writing were *the* most important tools for making education effective.

Education, Social Crisis, and the Need for Literate Citizens

Following the end of the decades-long civil war in the region in the 1850s, intellectuals such as Varela and Sarmiento proclaimed that they and their fellow citizens were suffering from a period of social crisis.[14] In their eyes, "lawless" gauchos continued to control the sparsely populated countryside. In Uruguay, rural inhabitants launched a string of civil wars with government troops and got into trouble on a regular basis, as good gauchos do, in pulperías. One of the greatest fears expressed by those who thought it imperative to tame the Rioplatense countryside was that the children of the ruffian gauchos would follow in their footsteps, perpetuating the cycle of violence and prolonging the social crisis. On the Argentine Pampa, there was the additional element of Indians raiding settlements and contributing to the urbanites' heightened sense of the necessity to instill order. During the 1860s and 1870s, the Argentine government experimented with the temporary and tragic solution of war in order to exterminate gauchos and Indians. José Hernández tells of this persecution in *Martín Fierro*. As we saw in Chapter 2, he also remarks on the need for education to help rural inhabitants avoid being targets of the national army. Ultimately, though, the war waged by state armies in Uruguay and Argentina did not end social crisis, and it was a vision of education different than Hernández's that became lauded as a cure for social problems.

Putting an end to crime in the cities and sowing order in the countryside began with the establishment of strong systems of public primary education that would spread alphabets. Another solution promoted concurrently with the founding of public schools was immigration. Hardworking Europeans, went the argument, would help cement progress in the region. It was only a matter of replacing the dark stock of gauchos and Indians with the lighter-toned Europeans. Immigrants, though, would soon be viewed as part of the problem, because they formed their own communities, spoke their own language, and harbored patriotic feelings for their former homelands. The arrival of massive waves of immigrants from the 1870s into the second decade of the twentieth century inspired a surge in nationalist sentiment. If gauchos were one sector of Rioplatense society targeted by the revolution of education, Italian and Spanish immigrants and their children were another. These newcomers—and, more importantly, their children—had to be integrated and "nationalized." The public primary school was a perfect place to start this endeavor.[15]

The lettered elites who were forming the educational bureaucracies thought literate citizens would be citizens who knew how to behave well and harbor the correct patriotic sentiments. Such ideas had been floating around since the Rosas years, but they gained in popularity during the 1860s and 1870s. In the late 1860s, for example, after returning from a tour of Europe and the United States, Varela wrote that "the great mission of the public school is to lift up our rough, scraggly compatriots [*el populacho*] to the level of dignified people [*el pueblo*]; it is to make out of disorder and loss elements of order and progress."[16] His words echoed an earlier analysis that the Uruguayan José Palomeque had conveyed in his 1855 report on the state of education. Palomeque had decried facts such as there being only thirty schools for a country of 129,000 citizens, and he told of young boys becoming gauchos instead of educated gentlemen: "Painful is the scene of what happens in the small towns across our countryside: by age *five* a young boy is already riding around on horseback and can be seen hanging around cafés and pulperías, *at the dreadful horse races*, and in places where cattle are slaughtered and processed. . . . It's in places such as these where the most powerful vices of our country are acquired."[17] Palomeque called for a series of reforms in order to create a viable public education system. These were not heeded, but they served as the base for Varela's reform in the late 1870s.

The Argentine sower of alphabets Onésimo Leguizamón shared Palomeque's sense of urgency. In his official memoirs, Leguizamón stated boldly that "free and compulsory education is simply a question of national security." Those unwilling to require parents to send their children to school, he continued, should be ready to see jails fill up. And there was more: "The absence of education is not an innocent fact. It breeds dangers to society; the ignorance of the people is *the most threatening of these dangers to the nation*."[18] Like Varela with the Palomeque report, Leguizamón found inspiration in the earlier writings of a fellow educator: Sarmiento.

Sarmiento's interests in education stretch back to his years as a primary school student in San Juan, and they would pervade his writing until his last day. His experiences with the rewards of reading as a young boy (his reading skills won him the respect of adults, and he was paraded around town as an exemplary student) shaped his understanding of reading as a tool to help citizens move from the uneducated countryside to the enlightened realm of letters.[19] His career as an educator began while he was in exile in Chile in the 1840s. The Chilean minister of education sent him on a tour of Europe and the United States to explore educational systems. On his return, he published two book-length studies on public education based on his observations while traveling, *Educación popular* (Popular education) and *Educación común* (loosely, Public education). In both works, he makes the case for why education is needed in Latin America and argues for the values and social change it will inspire. He put forward these arguments repeatedly throughout his life as a writer of hundreds of newspaper articles and as an educator in various administrative positions. In addition to being named the first director of the Comisión Nacional de Educación (National Commission of Education), created in 1875, he served as the director of schools in Buenos Aires Province in the late 1870s, advocating the creation of schools for adults as well as children.[20] These schools were mainly night schools, with schedules to accommodate the workday of adults.

Night schools (generally for those older than fifteen) and military schools were considered imperative to reducing illiteracy in the Río de la Plata. In Argentina, José Ramos Mejía, one of Sarmiento's successors, was one of the strongest supporters of night schools, and the highest-level educational bureaucrats at the turn of the century devoted attention to them. Interestingly, the curriculum at night schools and some military schools was similar to that of primary schools, and the textbooks used were primary school textbooks that appeared in the 1880s, 1890s, and the first decade of the twentieth century (more on these textbooks later). Military schools in Argentina—those set up for conscripted soldiers and immigrants—doubled in number in 1908, as did their number of students, which reached close to five thousand that year. These schools were designed to be on the front lines of nationalizing the immigrant population.

The establishment of military schools was part of the campaign to modernize the Argentine national army at the turn of the century.[21] Across South America during the late nineteenth century, contact between local and European militaries increased. This was in line with the process of modernization that was changing the urban landscape and the economies in Argentina, Uruguay, and elsewhere in the Americas. European officers traveled to South America on "missions" to train forces, and soldiers from Peru to Argentina spent time in Europe learning about military professionalism and professional militarism. Questions such as what militaries do in peacetime, the social role of soldiers, and the "civilizing mission" that military forces can have, all were central to the developing relations between civilian politicians and military officers and the type of military education that they would design.[22] Thanks to these exchanges, which instilled in them European-style military thinking, the Europeanized officers in Argentina as well as elsewhere in South America saw their roles in a clear, nationalistic light. As Frederick Nunn argues, they preserved the past and its traditions, and at the same time saw themselves as builders and shapers of the nation's future. These politicians and officers considered the army "the bridge uniting past and present, material and spiritual, peasants and workers, professionals and oligarchs."[23]

Military schools held daily seminars where eager adult learners could find additional instruction in subjects ranging from history to reading and writing. Soldiers who aspired to move up in rank were required to attend these extracurricular sessions.[24] Despite the fact that adult education grew rapidly around 1900, public primary schools would still be the main sites where the majority of citizens acquired the skills to read and write and learned about work ethic and patriotism. And while Sarmiento's influence on adult education of this sort was strong (after all, he founded the first real military school in Argentina in 1870, the Colegio Militar), his greatest impact was felt in primary education.[25]

The names making up the Argentine educational bureaucracy changed from 1880 to 1910, but the overall policies determining the course of education remained constant, and the driving force behind these was Sarmiento's vision of public education. One historian of education sums up this point: "All the Argentine educators and bureaucrats involved in educational policy at the end of the nineteenth century and beginning of the twentieth inherited Sarmiento's pedagogical discourse."[26] The pervasiveness of Sarmiento's influence stemmed from more than just his overpowering personality and flood of writings. He founded the first normal school in Argentina in 1870, and generations of teachers trained there then "normalized" his teachings in their classrooms, by incorporating them into the lessons assigned daily to young Argentines and immigrants. Sarmiento's work also had a bearing on the shape of Uruguayan public education, though indirectly, being a source of inspiration for José Pedro Varela and his fellow pedagogues.

Varela met Sarmiento in the United States, where the much older Argentine took him under his wing, and where both had been in conversation with the educator Horace Mann from Massachusetts. Varela admired Sarmiento's educational ideas, and on his return to Montevideo, he began elaborating on them in newspaper articles and speeches. In 1868, he and fellow advocates for public education founded la Sociedad de Amigos de la Educación Popular (the Society of Friends of Public Education). The society established a school named after the group's first president (Elbio Fernández), created public libraries, and started the publication titled *La Educación Popular*.[27] In 1870, Varela began writing regular editorial pieces

in the newspaper *La Paz* (Peace). The general idea of these was to promote the exchange of the sharp point of a lance for the nurturing skills of a
teacher. In the following years, he wrote editorials against caudillismo that
would ultimately form the basis of *La legislación escolar* (Legislation and
the public school), one of his two lengthy studies on education.[28]

A glance at the chapter titles and subtitles of these studies gives the
reader a clear sense of the value the reformer saw in education. His massive
La educación del pueblo (Education of a nation), published by the society in
1874, was the first of these large-scale approaches to public education.[29] In
a section on the benefits and goals of public schools, Varela deals with topics such as "education augments fortune" and "education lessens crime and
vice." Another major section of the work is dedicated to the connections between democracy and education. In times of social crisis, Varela and many
others in both Uruguay and Argentina considered the classroom's power to
impart orderly behavior a key to establishing stable democracies. He further elaborated on this thread of thought in *La legislación escolar*, published
in 1876. Like the first work, it begins with an assessment of the current
state of education in Uruguay and the problems posing hurdles on the way
to a better future. Varela maps the principles of a public primary education
system and details how it should work, from inspections on the departmental level to the number of students that should attend each school and
what schoolhouses should cost. *La educación del pueblo* and *La legislación
escolar* would constitute the underpinning of the new legal framework for
public education in Uruguay, and they would have a lasting imprint on the
shape education would take in the country.

But it was not so much what Sarmiento and Varela wrote that had
such a mythic impact. Their books were read and debated by fellow intellectuals, of course, in the meetings of the Society of Friends of Public
Education and other literary groups. Yet such works were not widely disseminated, at least not directly. Where their ideas really came to fruition
was in public debates on the curriculum, as well as in the system of school
inspections and the overall general workings of public primary education
that were implemented after both Varela and Sarmiento had died. Official
state backing of projects for public education in Uruguay and Argentina
arrived with the "laws of public education." The first of these was passed
in Uruguay in 1877, two years before Varela's death. Varela's *La legislación*

escolar had served as the blueprint for the new law, and he had led the effort to get it passed. Heading up the law was the stipulation that public primary education would be compulsory and free. Varela's hope that it would also be secular was slightly modified: the final version of the law promoted the teaching of Catholicism in schools, but it made clear that no student was required to attend classes or other presentations on religion. It was not until 1909 that the proposal to make schools secular became law.[30] Parents whose children did not attend school (public or private) would face fines. Immigrants who allowed their children to miss class on a regular basis risked having their Uruguayan citizenship suspended. Article 15 specified that at least one primary school should exist in every part of the republic where there were fifty or more children to attend classes. Two other salient articles, 20 and 45, stipulated that public education would be mandatory in barracks, jails, and hospices, and that school libraries would double as public libraries.[31]

The passing of the law put the state in control over a wealth of print media, as we will see shortly. Of course, there were opponents of the reform. Administrators of interior and rural departments protested the centralization of school administration in Montevideo. Teachers who disagreed with components of the new curriculum disregarded them in their classes. And a number of liberals in the capital criticized Varela for what they viewed as his collaboration with and support for Latorre. Varela's enemies pushed for public education to have a more Catholic and less positivist tint, for the schools to remain sexually segregated, and for a different curriculum. However, even they shared the belief that education was necessary to bring order to the countryside. This common understanding of the role of education was derived in large measure from what Jaime Monestier claims were principles of "a collective spirit" among Uruguayans, a spirit that had its roots in Artigas's struggles during the wars of independence. Varela gave the educational reform a moral character that linked it to Artigas and the realization of the republic, which in turn allowed citizens to identify with the reform program as a patriotic initiative. If it were not for Varela and the public support he inspired for the development of national education, Monestier argues, José Battle y Ordóñez would not have been able to carry out the program that turned Uruguay into "the model country" at the beginning of the twentieth century.[32]

The Uruguayan law of public education and Varela's reform fueled debates at the 1882 Pedagogical Congress, held in Buenos Aires as part of the Continental Exposition. It was at the congress where debate over how best to implement a program of civic education resulted in the proposal of the so-called citizen's curriculum. This program would consist of lessons in the Spanish language, national history and geography, and civics. The main mode of engaging these subjects would be through reading, specifically through the *libro de lectura*—a form of textbook organized as a narrative or series of narratives meant to entertain in order to disseminate a particular message.[33] Libros de lectura became best sellers from the late 1880s on.

The Argentine law of public education was passed two years later, in 1884. It reiterated much of the Uruguayan law and the final resolutions of the congress.[34] As was the case in Uruguay, much of the debate about the law was concerned with the role of religion in public schools, though the secular component remained part of the legislation. And, like the Uruguayan law, the Argentine reform resulted in an immediate reorientation of course content across the board, with lessons on reading and writing serving as the keys to other subjects in the curriculum: national history and geography, calligraphy, morals, civics, and, especially for girls, hygiene and home economics.[35]

In sum, the reformers' motivations for establishing public systems of education on national scales in Uruguay and Argentina were rooted in putting an end to a period of social crisis. Between 1880 and 1910, the foundations of the public education systems were laid, and these foundations would orient education in both countries throughout the twentieth century. During these years, bureaucrats formulated rituals, refined curricula, and put into place the administrative structures of these new state institutions.

The primary school was not meant to maintain class distinctions. The greater priorities were establishing order, instilling sentiments of loyalty toward the nation, and inspiring citizens to consider education as a matter of public concern.[36] Schools were workshops for building the social skills that children would later practice outside the classroom. Therefore, it was important that students left their social backgrounds at the door, so to speak, in order to effectively feel part of a community.

The Bureaucratic Framework of Education and the ABCs

Educational architects and administrators argued that what students read was critical to the effectiveness of schools in the Plata. Moreover, the children, their families, and the state interacted through reading activities in the private space of the home and the public space of the school. These ideas were built into the bureaucratic framework of public education; they were behind the print media schoolchildren could get their hands on; and they configured the new widespread, daily contact of residents with a variety of reading practices.

The laws of public education also sanctioned the creation of central administrative bodies or national school boards to oversee the educational endeavor. In Uruguay, the directing body was the DGIP, and the law centralized its operations in Montevideo. Departmental school commissions had to report back to the DGIP. These commissions carried out the work of the DGIP in the interior and were crucial to the success of education in Uruguay, as well as to the maintenance of the authority of the national school board.[37] The members of the DGIP held weekly meetings and had their work cut out for them. According to the 1877 law, their tasks included—to name just a few—overseeing public education throughout the republic, hiring and firing teachers, selecting books to be used uniformly throughout the nation, selecting the books that would make up the collections in school and public libraries, editing a periodical dedicated to educational issues, and awarding diplomas.

The DGIP's counterpart in Argentina was the Consejo Nacional de Educación (CNE), or National Council of Education. Created in 1881, the CNE was a massive bureaucratic agency, and it stood as the staunchest advocate of the 1884 law of public education.[38] Like the DGIP, the CNE allocated funds to provincial school districts, deployed inspectors to observe how its mandates were being carried out, developed the curricula of primary and secondary schools, and organized committees to review and select textbooks for use in schools. Just about everything that had to do with public education on the primary and secondary level passed through or was generated by the CNE. There were also provincial boards of education in Argentina. They were in charge of holding schools up to expected standards of hygiene, discipline, and morality. They encouraged kids to go to class, developed courses for adults, and promoted the creation of public libraries. These provincial boards carried out the work of the CNE on the regional level, and they had to report back to its seat in Buenos Aires.[39]

For both boards, textbooks were a top priority. One of the first measures the CNE carried out following the passage of the law of public education in Argentina was to ensure the free distribution of textbooks and other print media and necessary school materials to students whose families could certify that purchasing these things was beyond their means.[40] If the CNE wanted to produce literate citizens, then it had to take the lead in providing students with the *right* texts. The idea was that school was a microcosm of society where reading was an important practice that shaped interactions. In Uruguay, the DGIP was even more progressive about the distribution of textbooks, supplying them free of charge to all public schools. It was up to departmental administrators on both sides of the Plata to guarantee that only official texts were being used in the classroom. Determining which textbooks would receive official endorsement, however, was the work of committees centrally based in Montevideo and Buenos Aires.

The informal roots of textbook selection committees can be found in the administrative bodies that preceded the national boards of education in Uruguay and Argentina.[41] The first sets of formal rules regarding textbooks, though, came with the laws of public education. In the late 1870s, the original members of the Uruguayan DGIP composed the first list of recommended texts for use on a national scale.[42] As the educational bureaucracy added more sowers of alphabets, a commission within the national board gradually took responsibility for this task. In Argentina, the formal beginning of the rules for deciding on textbooks came in 1887, when the CNE held the first textbook competition.[43] Like the CNE, the selection committee that grew out of this event and organized future annual competitions was a large administrative affair.

The way textbook competitions worked in Buenos Aires was straightforward. Authors had to submit copies of their texts to the textbook selection committee, which in turn directed texts to be reviewed by divisions corresponding to classroom subjects. There were several "staple" divisions: reading and writing, civic and moral instruction, grammar and foreign languages, history and geography, mathematics, natural sciences, and drawing and music. Once the list of approved texts was published, teachers could choose the most appropriate from those named for each subject.[44]

Through the implementation of rules that resulted in some texts being discarded and certain qualities of others being praised, the selection competition slowly defined a new type of genre—the textbook, ranging from books on national history and hygiene to the libro de lectura.[45] The textbook genre formed the heart of what would become one of the most profitable sectors of the publishing world.

The textbook selection committee members changed from year to year, but they were publicly named and almost always linked to the bureaucratic framework. In principle, committee members were supposed to be teachers or individuals associated with the administration of public education. In many instances, authors of textbooks (many of whom were teachers, such as the ubiquitous Isidoro de María in Uruguay and Joaquín González in Argentina), sat on the selection committees. The state approval of textbooks demonstrated support for the formation of certain forms of collective identity, which we will see up close in the next chapter. The stamp of the DGIP or the CNE also guaranteed the commercial success of texts, for those that made the official list sold thousands of copies to the school boards, libraries, and individual readers and students. Not surprisingly, intimate connections developed between the boards and the publishing industry. The relationship was symbiotic: publishers whose works were approved made out like bandits, gaining access to a large market of readers for multiyear periods, while educational administrators locked in good prices for the books they purchased and were asking families to buy.[46]

Argentina's CNE offers a good example of how the relationships between the boards and the publishing industry functioned. Publishers were occasionally tapped to serve in administrative positions or on textbook selection committees. This was the case of Jacobo Peuser, a member of the provincial school board in Buenos Aires and one of Argentina's most successful publishers at the turn of the century.[47] The same was true of Angel Estrada, a friend of Sarmiento and founder of the publishing firm Angel Estrada y Compañía (Angel Estrada and Company). He was also a founding partner of the Fundición Nacional de Tipos de Imprenta (National Foundry of Type Blocks). Estrada had been in the business of selling imported wines and papers, but he later went on to make education his focus. His press became one of the largest producers of textbooks.[48] Among the most successful of Estrada's publications was Andrés Ferreyra's *El nene* (roughly, *The little lad*). Ferreyra wrote many textbooks, but none had the commercial appeal of *El nene*. It went through 120 editions from its debut in 1895 to the publication of the last edition in 1959. Needless to say, the book was highly profitable for the publisher.

Of course, Estrada's relationship with Sarmiento did not hurt his ability to acquire textbook contracts, but this connection was not his only one. Estrada himself was a member of various provincial boards of education in Buenos Aires during the 1870s, which placed him at the center of the state initiative to expand public education, and he maintained close relationships with authors who wrote texts and were functionaries in the new educational bureaucracy. His brother José Manuel served as a high-ranking administrator of public education and, not surprisingly, often recommended textbooks published by Angel Estrada y Compañía.[49] There were similar, tightly knit contacts between Uruguay's DGIP and the publisher A. Barreiro y Ramos. From the 1890s on, A. Barreiro y Ramos enjoyed contracts for the printing of notebooks, textbooks, lists of approved texts, and memoirs of national and departmental inspectors. Printing the memoirs made good economic sense. In 1903, for instance, the DGIP paid A. Barreiro y Ramos to publish 1,800 copies of the national inspector's memoir (a hefty tome), which was subsequently distributed to educational administrators in Montevideo and the interior.[50]

All of this publishing corresponded to—and facilitated—a new stage in the popularization of Rioplatense print culture. In the last decades of the nineteenth century, and up through the 1910 centenary celebration of independence, there was an enormous upswing in readership in the Plata. Throughout the 1870s, the number of public libraries and so-called circulating libraries grew in Uruguay, thanks to the efforts of Varela and the Society of Friends of Public Education. Learning the ABCs, after all, was becoming a serious matter. The increase in the amount of print media available and the numbers of readers getting their hands on a host of different types of texts ruffled the feathers of some at the beginning—most notably the clergy.[51] Public and circulating libraries in Argentina had similar support (in the figure of Sarmiento) and opposition (in the members of the clergy) during the 1870s. But the real explosion in readership came with the expansion of primary education, for there was no stopping the influence of education on the public's understanding of the importance of reading. Methods for teaching reading and writing were a constant thread running through the pages of *El Monitor de la Educación Común* (The public education monitor, the publication of the Argentine board), and they were discussed regularly at pedagogical conferences. Members of the educational bureaucracy presented papers with titles such "The Necessity of Establishing Cosmopolitan Circulating Libraries" and "National Texts," and the guiding themes of the 1900 pedagogical conference included "Literary Education" and "Texts."[52]

The multiple target audiences of textbooks were also connected to the rise in readership. Authors of books for children attending primary school dedicated the texts to the young students, but they often addressed parents in prefaces, proclaiming that the whole family could benefit from reading the lessons, together or individually. The national inspector of public education in Uruguay highlighted these audiences in a circular he sent out in March 1901. Given that books evoked ideas of patria, the home, hard work, and values, he wrote, and in light of print being the most fecund messenger of progress in young nations aspiring to educate their citizens, the DGIP needed to promote wide support for school libraries. More than merely repositories of materials for teachers, school libraries would "provide encouragement to those students who distinguish themselves during the week through their hard word and good conduct. These students will be able to take books to their houses, thus allowing students from our public schools to contribute to the spirit of education in our rural homes."[53] With these multiple readers in mind, it is no surprise that sales of textbooks skyrocketed in the Río de la Plata. What is surprising is that, at least according to one tally, at the end of the century the textbook market accounted for more than 50 percent of all book sales in Argentina.[54]

Of course, the sowers of alphabets faced an uphill battle. The selection and effectiveness of textbooks was critical to achieving their goals of winning the hearts of children in the countryside and "nationalizing" the children of immigrants flooding into the Río de la Plata at the turn of the century. History texts were considered particularly well suited to the task of shaping identity, for not only could they impart an idea of collective values, but they also created a story of the origins of the nation. The need for "national" texts led bureaucrats and publishers to support a national textbook industry, replacing works in translation and those used in Spain with books written about Uruguay and Argentina by Uruguayans and Argentines. This new appreciation for homegrown authors was clearly illustrated in the criteria used by the division of moral and civic instruction to evaluate textbooks submitted to the CNE's 1902 competition. Texts worthy of the official stamp of approval should, "by means of observation of facts and a clear, scientific method, impress in the child reader what is and should be the conduct of man in the home, in society, and toward the patria."[55]

The same spirit infused the development of schools along the Uruguay-Brazil border and the creation of normal schools in Uruguay and Argentina. Some of the first schools along the border opened their doors in the early 1890s. Orestes Araújo, himself a prolific author of textbooks, tells us that these schools were intended to "contain the advancing influence of Brazil on [Uruguayan] language and national traditions and customs, a goal as patriotic as it was ultimately unattainable."[56] The children who attended these schools, then as well as today, spoke Spanish and Portuguese, and they shared much in common with residents on the other side of the line. Loyalties to the patria, however, ran deep in the borderland (sometimes even dividing families), thanks in part to the new schools.

Normal schools played their part, too, in spreading a uniform program of education and in sowing the seeds that would grow into loyalty to the nation. Because they were designed to serve as training academies for teachers, normal schools attracted far more female students than male. The bureaucrats believed that women were much more naturally inclined to be teachers and that their soothing voices and motherly appearance would maintain order in the classroom. In fact, thanks to recruitment efforts and curricular design for female students, women made up 85 percent of the teachers in Argentina by 1910.[57]

Like their models in the United States, normal schools enacted a scientific discourse that outlined teaching methods considered "objective" and thus measurable in concrete terms. The objective character of normalist pedagogy could be extended to the practice of reading. Strict, scientific application of a method of reading in the classroom, went the idea, would help quell whatever forms of resistance to reading the instructor faced and inspire children to pursue reading activities outside the school, in the home.[58]

The story of one normal school student in Buenos Aires at the turn of the century gives a sense of how effective this pedagogical approach was in transforming a young girl who did not care much for reading into a sower of alphabets bent on teaching her students to read and write.[59] Rosita del Río, as the student was named, was initially not sure if she liked all the reading she had to do in the normal school: "I preferred sewing and drawing, I think because I was better at those things." Little by little, though, Rosita grew more fond of reading. After she started attending the normal school, she recited poems at home to her brothers and sisters, not for their meaning (which she claims she did not much understand), but for how they sounded. Reciting poetry was a sort of game that encouraged her to read more and more, eventually leading to the opinion of reading she held as a teacher: "I always believed that we had to produce students who could read well, even if that was the only thing they could do."[60] Normal schools were a sort of factory of sowers of alphabets, but their work would

Figure 3.1. Female students reading in the Galería de Lectura y Descanso (Hall for Recess and Reading), Internato Normal de Señoritas, Montevideo, 1893. (Courtesy of the Museo Pedagógico José Pedro Varela, Montevideo, Photography Collection.)

not have been valuable if it had not been complemented by rural schools and, of course, teachers willing to make their lives along the border, in the countryside, and among the "riffraff" of urban slums.

Despite the spread of normal schools in the 1890s and 1900s, teachers still had a certain amount of room in selecting the textbooks they felt were most appropriate for their students. The 1902 Uruguayan list of official textbooks, for example, named multiple texts that could be used for lessons on geography and national history, with a note specifying that teachers could "use one of the above." At the end of the list, though, another note qualified the use of textbooks: "The selection of a textbook for a subject does not mean it is obligatory for the teacher to use a book for that class, but rather that if the subject requires a textbook, then only the designated text should be used."[61] The same options and restrictions appear throughout the decade in the other lists of officially approved textbooks for Uruguayan schools. Teachers, however, used some books that had not been approved at all, in spite of the directive stated on the lists.[62] The same held true for the ways teachers used textbooks in Argentina, though in both countries there were incentives to use the official texts, which were inexpensive—if not free—for instructors and students. Also, school inspectors in the cities and in the countryside cracked down on the use of "unofficial" books in the classroom.

Enforcing the use of approved textbooks factored into the greater charge to school inspectors, outlined in the Uruguayan law of public education to be that of using "all means available to foment in the department [under the inspector's jurisdiction] public zeal for the improvement and spread of public education."[63] The inspectors carried out their tasks rigorously, manifest in records of the sheer numbers of visits and hours they put in each year observing classes and school buildings.[64] Inspections were performed in Argentina to a similar degree.

In the end, the bureaucratic framework of teaching the ABCs led to educational reform being carried out in a uniform way in schools throughout the region. The centralization of administration, the adoption of the same pedagogical methods across all classrooms, and the use of similar (if not the same) textbooks in urban and rural schools all contributed to providing students with a shared understanding of the nation. Monestier sums up this point for the case of Uruguay: "The reform contributed in large measure to students—and later a significant portion of the population—

sharing a strong sense of their rights and duties as citizens."[65] Once the CNE and DGIP began dealing in textbooks, a whole new market niche opened up for printers in the Plata, stimulating the practices of reading and writing in the classroom and beyond. Education thus became central to what it meant to be Uruguayan or Argentine.

Reading and Writing in the Classroom and Beyond

That the number of students attending Uruguayan and Argentine public schools rose each year certainly gave educators plenty of fertile ground to cultivate. But making sure every student had access to reading materials meant developing a range of other types of print media—such as reading charts and, more importantly, *cuadernos* (notebooks)—to supplement books. After all, reading and writing were the heart of education, necessary to the study of all other subjects. A look at some of the source materials used to impart the ABCs, particularly in Uruguay, will make this point clear.

Children got started with reading and writing exercises at a young age—in kindergarten, to be precise. There they followed a neatly defined set of lessons elaborated by Enriqueta Compte y Riqué, one of the first and most celebrated Uruguayan female educators.[66] The time students were to spend on these exercises gradually increased from one grade level to the next, and in each successive grade the reading level of their assignments grew progressively more complex. Following the 1877 law, the typical day of class included one and a half to two hours focused exclusively on reading and writing exercises. Other areas of study, such as morals and religion, geography and history, and grammar, were reading and writing intensive. In fact, in almost every subject, students practiced reading and writing, including in math and in lessons on objects.[67] Administrators tailored the division of class time through the 1890s and early 1900s in order to be in line with the latest pedagogical strategies, which meant devoting more time to reading and writing.

In the public schools of both Uruguay and Argentina, reading and writing were diverse activities. "Reading" involved reading aloud syllables, words, phrases, and paragraphs, as well as repetition of what a teacher read and moments of reading in silence. There were various types of reading

Figure 3.2. Male students at the Escuela de Artes y Oficios (Arts and Trades School) in Montevideo, circa 1895, painting the Argentine coat of arms and preparing chalkboards with alphabets for use in school. (Courtesy of the Biblioteca Nacional, Montevideo; Materiales Especiales, ABN 1817.)

aloud, too. One was reading aloud as a class a passage that the teacher had chosen that the students had first read individually in silence. Another allowed a student to select the passage he or she wanted to read to the others. A third type was known as "improvised reading," where the teacher selected a passage to read aloud that the students had not seen before. These different exercises were meant to make reading fun and to help students improve their skills and confidence. "Writing" was also a varied practice, ranging from drawing letters (for students in kindergarten or first grade) to jotting down words and phrases dictated by a teacher and learning how to write properly in cursive and compose meaningful paragraphs. The students did these things occasionally on loose-leaf sheets, but by far the most common media used for writing practice were personal chalkboards (tens of thousands of these were distributed free of charge to Uruguayan students each year) and notebooks (which were used even more than chalkboards).

Numerous series of notebooks were used systematically in Uruguayan and Argentine schools, and they were printed in such large quantities that

Figure 3.3. Students at School 34 in Peñarol (outside Montevideo) learning to write in cursive with fountain pens, August 1912. (Courtesy of the Museo Pedagógico José Pedro Varela, Montevideo, Photography Collection.)

each student usually received two or three per year. The presses that published textbooks printed the most widely used notebooks. Furthermore, many notebook series boasted of following a certain methodology for the instruction of writing, when not claiming that they had been "written" by a well-known teacher or textbook author. What is most interesting to note about these receptacles of student writing is that they convey complex moral and civic messages similar to those learned in books. From those whose covers display detailed lessons about national heroes and historic events to others whose pages share simple guidelines and phrases to trace in order to perfect writing technique, notebooks of all sorts served as direct links between students and the messages of the sowers of alphabets.

Take, for example, the Vázquez Cores series issued as a "practical and theoretical writing course" (as it was titled), which consisted of twenty-one different notebooks. Teachers could find all these available for free at the bookstore and print shop of Vázquez Cores in the heart of Montevideo. Of course, the free notebooks were a way of enticing teachers to consider purchasing other materials at the bookstore where, as advertised on the covers, one could "stock an entire school in twenty-four hours."[68] Author of numerous geography books, Francisco Vázquez Cores designed his notebooks around the fairly straightforward principle of tracing over sample sentences at the top of the pages and then rewriting these between the lines below, or crafting new sentences with the letters and words the student had learned to write. The *Letra inglesa* (English letters) series forms the largest set of notebooks and the one with the most obvious messages. At the bottom of most pages, Vázquez Cores has noted that students will engage in writing exercises that trace the general outlines of Uruguayan history. Notebooks 6 and 7 of the series have particularly concentrated lessons on *historia patria* (patriotic history) to 1830, in which students have to rewrite sentences such as "In the department of Florida on 25 August 1825 the Banda Oriental proclaimed its independence from Brazil," "Montevideo is a beautiful city," and "At long last I have returned to you, my beloved patria!"—this last sentence to practice exclamation marks.[69]

Other important notebooks in Uruguay include the Barreiro y Ramos series; the set produced by the DGIP and its successor in the 1900s, the Consejo Nacional de Instrucción Primaria y Normal (National Council of Primary and Normal Instruction); and the Cuadernos Nacionales (National notebooks), a particularly patriotic set that we will see more of in the next chapter.[70] The Barreiro y Ramos notebooks follow the same method as those of Vázquez Cores, though the sentences to be rewritten by the students have a stronger moral and political imprint. In notebook 6, for example, the student was to trace expressions such as "Flies do not enter a closed mouth," "Not everything that shines is gold," and "Artigas was the founder of the Uruguayan republic."[71] Antonio Barreiro y Ramos did not miss out on the opportunity to advertise the textbooks he published, either, printing on the back covers of the notebooks a list of recent, officially approved textbooks for sale at his bookstore. The DGIP notebooks were slightly more discreet in their presentation of symbolic content. Their pages are blank, with only lines for writing. It is on the covers where students met the messages. Some covers have drawings of historic figures— Artigas, Rivera, and of course Varela—and others go into more detail, with a portrait of the figure on the front and a biography on the back. This format of drawings on the front and text on the back characterized the Cuadernos Nacionales series.

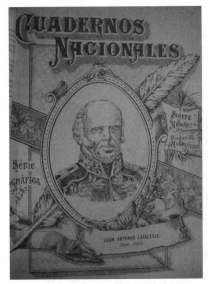

Figure 3.4. The covers of two notebooks widely distributed in Uruguay circa 1900: on the left, a Cuadernos Nacionales cover with the bust of Juan Antonio Lavalleja; on the right, Fructuoso Rivera appears on a notebook bearing the imprint of the DGIP (National Board of Education). (Courtesy of the Museo Pedagógico José Pedro Varela, Montevideo.)

The popular notebooks in Argentina were designed in the same way as the Uruguayan ones, they were meant to function in the same way, and many were printed by the savvy textbook publisher Angel Estrada.

The numbers of notebooks that were distributed to students on a yearly basis following the Reforma Vareliana made them particularly well suited to deploying moral and civic ideas. In 1879, some 51,500 notebooks were sent out to less than half as many enrolled students across Uruguay. By 1887, this number had risen to over 80,000 for a school population of just over 30,000, and by 1895 close to 170,000 notebooks were being distributed to 50,000 students.[72] This trend would continue into the 1900s and solidify the importance of notebooks. Of course, school notebooks went hand in hand with textbooks. And it was in textbooks, too, where students and their families had crucial contact with the ABCs—in libros de lectura, progressive readers, and content-based texts, to be exact.[73]

Many titles vied for a spot in the new textbook market in the Plata, but only a handful were selected to serve as official texts. These saw astound-

Figure 3.5. The cover of notebook 1 (of 5) in J. V. Olivera's *Método de Caligrafía*, used in both Argentina and Uruguay. (Courtesy of the Museo Pedagógico José Pedro Varela, Montevideo.)

ing print runs and made lasting impressions in the region.[74] Like the notebooks, the lessons in books for helping students learn to read and write were full of moral, patriotic, and civic messages. In Uruguay, pedagogues such as A. Vásquez Acevedo, Julián Miranda, Francisco Berra (who was very active in Buenos Aires, too), and Orestes Araújo became successful authors whose works continually made the lists of official texts. Throughout the 1890s and 1900s, the DGIP purchased tens of thousands of copies of their books. These were housed at the agency's depot, and then sent out to departmental school administrators around the country.

A few numbers give an idea of the sales volume of the texts in question. In 1890, the DGIP distributed over 2,100 copies of Araújo's *Lecturas ejemplares* (Exemplary stories, songs, and poems); 5,000 copies of Vásquez Acevedo's first volume of *Libros de lectura* were sent out in 1896; and from 1900 to 1903, schools received some 4,700 copies of Araújo's *Perfiles biográficos* (Biographical sketches).[75] The DGIP's goal, after all, was to provide every student with copies of the necessary textbooks for the school year.[76] Students did not own the copies, but they were certainly encouraged to take them home and work on their reading lessons with family members. By comparing the numbers of textbooks distributed in a given year with the numbers of students who attended school on a regular basis that same year, it is clear that in contrast to what we saw with the notebooks, not every student had his or her own copy of a textbook. The ratio was closer to one book for every two or three students. However, those who wanted to take a book home could check out a classroom text or library copy, provided it was available. This is exactly what authors and teachers encouraged students to do in both Uruguay and Argentina. The DGIP pronounced libraries with the appropriate collection of texts to be "an indispensable component of the elementary school, for they complete the child's education and take the beneficial influence of healthy readings to the heart of the home."[77]

Aside from the pure economic gain associated with large print runs, there were other important reasons that accompanied the goal of addressing students and their parents. One of these was the fact that children who were acquiring the skill at school would introduce many family members to reading for the first time. Parents who knew how to read were asked to play a role in the educational process by reading textbook lessons with their children. This is the idea the Argentine educator Pablo Pizzurno summed up in the note to teachers and parents that opens his *El libro del escolar* (Every schoolkid's book), and features in the first lesson.[78] Here we meet the young student Federico, who reads to his younger sisters and parents. After Federico is finished, the parents ask their daughters to recount what they heard, making the lesson truly a family affair. A similar example comes from the preface of Amelia Palma's *El hogar modelo* (The model home), a textbook on home economics used in Argentine schools. The author of the preface writes that this new "interesting" book responds to the needs of both the family and the school, and thus asks "madres" (mothers) and "maestras" (teachers) to put it in the hands of their daughters and students "with the security that they will soon have the satisfaction of harvesting the most valuable fruits."[79] Other authors addressed their multiple reading audiences in a slightly different way, knowing their books would be used in adult schools and sold to a general public. Araújo, for instance, spoke to the readers of his best-selling *Episodios históricos* (Lessons from our past) as "la juventud" (youth) and "las clases populares" (the wider reading public).[80]

The state, the school, and the larger public also intersected during the end-of-year exam period and at ceremonies for the distribution of prizes to students who had performed particularly well in a subject. Exams were

Figure 3.6. A young student shares a book with his mother on the cover of Emma Catalá de Princivalle's *Ejercicios progresivos de lectura, ortología y ortografía, primer libro.* (Courtesy of the Museo Pedagógico José Pedro Varela, Montevideo.)

Figure 3.7. A scene of reading in the home. In Vásquez Acevedo, 109.

public events where, in some instances, community members participated on examination committees.[81] Both teachers and students invited parents to these events. This was the case with the exams in 1891 in Cerro Largo, along the Uruguay-Brazil border.[82] The neighbors at the exams drew attention to the school and helped both to publicize its mission and to make the school a public space, with parents partaking in the year-end recognition of the students' advancements. It was critical that parents were invited into the classroom, for it allowed them to feel proud of their children and at the same time exercise their parental influence, all while celebrating the youth's achievements. Exams gave teachers and parents the chance to meet each other and discuss the students' progress, as well as a way to introduce many parents to reading, writing, and the benefits of public school. This was not a matter of little importance, especially in the countryside where children—especially boys—often needed to work to contribute to supporting the family, and where many parents did not see much value in schools.[83]

Like exams, the distribution of prizes was a public event, usually led by the national inspector of public education and held in a premier location such as a theater. Up to the mid-1870s, students were rewarded with medals. In the 1880s and 1890s, little cards replaced medals, partly because they were more economical for boards of education to purchase, and largely because boards awarded prizes to more and more students in order to encourage hard work. Rewards were divided by subject: grammar, writing, reading, home economics, merit, and several others. To give an idea of the quantity awarded, in 1887, in Montevideo alone, primary school students were the recipients of twelve thousand cards.[84] In addition to providing positive reinforcement, the awards ceremonies showcased schools as institutions deserving community pride.

In class, at libraries, during exams, and in the home, students and their family members definitely spent much time with the work of José H. Figueira, by far the best-selling author of textbooks in Uruguay. He wrote a set of five books that were selected as official texts when they were first published in the 1890s and then reedited and used consistently in primary schools up through the 1950s—a phenomenon similar to that of *El nene* in Argentina. The titles of the texts—*¿Quieres leer?* (Do you want to read?), *Adelante* (Come on!), *Un buen amigo* (A good friend), *Trabajo* (Work), and *Vida* (Life)—reveal the intimate connection between reading and everyday reality. Both Figueira and educational administrators envisioned a progressive learning process: learning to read would lead to the influence of reading on one's work, which would then pave the way for reading as an integral component of a rewarding life.

The different editions have slight modifications (most notably the covers), but the emphasis on specific values, modes of behavior, beliefs, and the importance of reading remained intact through the years.[85] This continuity guaranteed Figueira praise from the DGIP, as well as a lucrative business deal. In 1901, the national inspector Abel Pérez wrote that Figueira's texts were largely responsible for the advances made in the teaching of reading, writing, and grammar. They had also succeeded in capturing young readers' attention—an honorable feat for any writer.[86] It is no surprise, then, that his five-volume set was purchased in large quantities for distribution to Uruguayan students. In 1895, 3,500 copies of *¿Quieres leer?* were supplied

Figure 3.8. An invitation to read, on the cover of Figueira's *¿Quieres leer?* (Courtesy of the Museo Pedagógico José Pedro Varela, Montevideo.)

to schools, and that was just the beginning. Five years later, the DGIP sent students 5,632 copies of the same book, 5,373 of *Adelante*, and 3,590 copies of *Trabajo*. As the numbers of enrolled students rose, so did the volume of sales of Figueira's texts. In 1901, over thirteen thousand copies of *¿Quieres leer?* and almost six thousand copies of *Un buen amigo*, to name just two of the books, were purchased and distributed among yearning readers.[87] Interestingly, in the early editions of the books, a note was included after the title page stating that all copies not bearing the author's signature would be deemed pirated, which suggests that there was a market for unofficial versions of the books, too.[88]

So what was it that made Figueira's books so popular? Though the DGIP certainly played a part in the success of these books, credit goes to the author for their design. In the eyes of the DGIP and teachers, they were a group of books based on a sound methodology, well balanced in the subjects of lessons covered, and full of helpful advice to teachers for every lesson.[89] They connected learning the ABCs to powerful moral directives, principles of patriotism, and work ethics. In a word, Figueira's texts were the best the textbook commission had seen, and it was not until 1904 that the commission began to recommend conditionally a similarly progressive series of books—what would become a six-volume set by Emma Catalá de Princivalle.[90] Second, the Figueira series had attractive images and narratives that distinguished the books from other libros de lectura where the narratives were not as exciting and images had not been integrated into the reading lessons. This may sound like a trivial point to us now, but for new readers at the turn of the twentieth century, these aspects of Figueira's books contributed to making them revolutionary among school texts and other books published around the same period. Lastly, the five texts were right in step with the pace of students as they moved from one year to the next. Moreover, all the books, including the most elementary, ¿Quieres leer?, were suitable for use in classes for adults and by children reading at home with their parents.

Print media for learning the ABCs, with short narratives that contained moral lessons, were not the only ones making their ways into the hands of schoolchildren. Texts devoted to lessons in patriotism and books written exclusively for female students were among the most widely distributed reading materials in the Río de la Plata. As we will see in the next chapter, they were some of the most effective at instilling in young readers a sense of group identity. While most of the examples of reading materials in this section have come from the educational success story of Uruguay, they shed light on the relationship between students, parents, and the state in Argentina, too. The same types and numbers of texts were used in Argentina, and these were vetted through the same bureaucratic process. Likewise, reading materials were made available to provincial school districts in a similar way. And most significantly, the interaction of students and parents with seeds sown by the state was the same. This is evident in the numbers of schools and students attending schools on both sides of the Plata River, as well as in the rise in literacy rates.

Just how effective was the new school system in the region? Though not an exhaustive statistical portrait, a look at the numbers of schools and enrolled students over the period 1880–1910 illustrates the expansion of the public primary school system and provides an index to measure its effectiveness.[91] In Uruguay, 24,785 students were enrolled in 310 public schools throughout the country in 1880. By 1890, the number of public schools had risen to 470, and enrollment to 38,747, and in 1900, 571 schools served 52,474 students. Finally, in 1910, there were close to seventy-five thousand children attending almost eight hundred public primary schools.[92] An estimated 40 percent of school-age children still did not attend any sort of school—public or private—or receive instruction in the home in 1910, but this was the lowest percentage within all Latin America, and a drastic improvement from the first days of the reform's implementation. In 1878, for instance, over 80 percent of the school-age population did not attend school.[93] Noteworthy, too, about the statistics on schools in Uruguay is that the majority of public schools were in the countryside, opposite the case with schools in Argentina where the majority were concentrated in Buenos Aires and the province of Buenos Aires. In Argentina in 1890, there were roughly 2,400 schools throughout the republic and an enrollment of some 203,700 students in public schools. By 1900, there were eight hundred new schools operating, and the number of students had risen to close to 369,000, largely as a result of the arrival of massive numbers of immigrants. And in 1910 over 600,000 students registered to attend around 5,400 public schools.[94] Approximately half of school-age children, however, did not attend schools in this same year, but like Uruguay, this figure had decreased notably since the passage of the 1884 law of public education. These numbers help us to see the broader picture of how public education successfully spread across the Río de la Plata.

It was thanks to schools and sowers of alphabets that literacy rates among Uruguayans and Argentines rose, too. Measures of literacy in Latin America in the late nineteenth and early twentieth centuries are often part of census reports. These, however, must be considered with caution. First, the numbers were compiled by government agencies that may have been inclined to shape them in a way that corresponded to their interests. Second, significant sectors of a nation's population were, in some cases, not factored into the census report. That said, some numbers can give us a sense of literacy rates. In Argentina, for example, the percentage of *analfabetos* (illiterate citizens) among those age fourteen and above throughout the country went from 78 in 1869 to 54 in 1895, and then to 35 in 1914 (years of national census reports). The figures vary widely when broken down according to province and the city of Buenos Aires. To take just one year, 1914, illiteracy in the capital measured 9 percent, compared with 27 percent for the province of Buenos Aires and 64 percent for the remote northwestern province of Jujuy.[95] Literacy in Uruguay followed a similar pattern, with rates much higher in Montevideo than in other areas. In 1900, just under 54 percent of the country's 755,000 people older than age six were literate. Literacy for the same age group in Montevideo, meanwhile, measured 66 percent, in contrast to 38 and 39 percent for the interior departments of Artigas and Tacuarembó.[96] The figures steadily rose, though. According to the 1908 national census, 58 percent of people age five and older were literate, and the literacy rate for the same age group in Montevideo measured 75 percent.[97]

Other indicators of literacy can be found in student compositions. These are much more fragile than records of statistics, given that they were often written in notebooks that were not kept or that have not survived well the passage of time, but a few examples make the point. Nine-year-old students of Enriqueta Compte y Riqué's class wrote glowing letters (probably with the help of the teacher) to the director of the Museo y Biblioteca Pedagógicos (now the Museo Pedagógico José Pedro Varela) of a visit they made to the Museo in November 1901. Students claimed that the experience at this institution paying tribute to the public education system was "unforgettable" and an excellent way for them to end the school year.[98]

Another example comes from the notebook of Raudelinda Pereda, a student in Tacuarembó in 1898. The notebook is one of the few with student writing that has been preserved. Its appearance is delicate: a sky-blue paper cover with fraying edges encloses the browning pages that contain Pereda's writings. The image on the cover portrays a young female student perched over her writing desk, plume in hand and pondering what to write. In the background, a book sits next to an inkwell. It is easy to imagine Pereda as the girl in this scene as she crafted her compositions, one of which praises the school: "Is there any rational being so unhappy as to ignore what the school is and its value? . . . The school is that sub-

Figure 3.9. The poetic cover of a notebook belonging to Raudelinda Pereda, from Tacuarembó, 1898. (Courtesy of the Museo Pedagógico José Pedro Varela, Montevideo.)

lime educational center in which people learn with ease," she writes. "It is where one studies with joy; it is where you find a friendly teacher who is dedicated to the education of the kids. In sum, it is the place where the best moments of childhood occur." She ends her tribute by saying that it is the school that "instills respect and affection in the tender hearts of children." It is clear that the school inspired affection and respect in Pereda's heart. The students may have been instructed to write a paean to the benefits of the school, but Pereda's words come across as her own, especially given her teacher's response, in a note at the end of the composition: "Make sure you use commas, and don't doodle!"[99] The point is that the practices of reading and writing were taking hold, and with them came the messages sowers of alphabets hoped to instill in young hearts.

■

The advent of public primary education in the Río de la Plata put into progress a cultural revolution whose results, like the presence of Varela and Sarmiento, are still palpable today. Between 1870 and 1910, schools were established throughout Uruguay and Argentina, enrollments and literacy rates rapidly rose, and the state began to regulate print media like never before. This period also solidified the relationship between print, the public, and politics; it was when print media really became "popular" with state backing and officially part of daily life. The agricultural metaphors involving seeds sprouting, blossoming fruit, harvesting benefits, and the like, that educators, authors, and bureaucrats employed were plentiful, even perhaps too often cited. Yet they were apt descriptors of the process and results of creating solid public education systems, for the future of both Uruguay and Argentina would subsequently be based on generations who had learned to read and write.

Being the sowers of alphabets and architects of public schools in the Plata certainly guaranteed Varela and Sarmiento privileged places in the history of the region. Both dreamed of a success story for education, but neither could have imagined that the system of public education in the Río de la Plata would become the most successful and effective in all Latin America. Nor could they have imagined that in the short span of a little over thirty years—from the time of the Uruguayan law of public education up to the first centenary celebration of independence in 1910—Uruguayans and Argentines would become the most literate Latin Americans.

What really solidified their entrance into the pantheon of national heroes, though, was their vision of and contribution to shaping citizens for the new national community through lessons rich in civic and moral content. These daily lessons for a nation are what immortalized the sowers of alphabets and, as we will see in the next chapter, the ones young students felt most deeply.

Chapter 4

Lessons for a Nation

(1880–1910)

■ In the naturalist W. H. Hudson's novel *The Purple Land*, the self-styled explorer Richard Lamb traversed the rural interior of Uruguay during the early 1870s. One of the many adventures Lamb experienced in *The Purple Land* found him resting in a wooded area one afternoon before continuing his journey on horseback toward Montevideo. His peaceful nap was startled by the horrific spectacle of young boys engaged in what appeared to be partisan warfare. They lined up, red *divisas* (ribbons) facing white, drew their knives, and charged at each other. Three from the Colorado side were left standing. When a lone Blanco mustered the energy to make one last attack on the victors, Lamb rushed toward the boys to protect him. With the exception of this boy, whom the three Colorados had been about to finish off, all the combatants (including those on the ground, who quickly sprang back to life) ran off into the woods. Only then did Lamb realize that they had been playing at Reds and Whites, "a mimic war . . . manoeuvres, surprises, skirmishes, throat-cutting, and all."[1]

Deep signs of party affiliation were still starkly visible some thirty years later to the Uruguayan journalist José Virginio Díaz as he traveled throughout the countryside. One female teacher from the department of Durazno lamented the political affinities of the children who divided themselves up into Blancos and Colorados, according to the partisan colors of their parents. She complained to Díaz that during recess these kids "pull out their knives and turn the playground into a battleground. They only cut each other's clothes—their *bombachas* (loose-fitting pants) and coats—but any day now they'll get fired up and stab each other."[2] This teacher went on to say that she had to get out of the little town and that she couldn't deal with the situation anymore.

Later, the *maestro* who took her place also grumbled about the partisan playground battles. Where things really got out of hand was when the parents got involved. The children are "devils" and pass their time in shenanigans, he huffed. "If you reprimand them or give them a whipping with the ruler, then the whole family shows up, *faca* (a long knife for daily chores) or pistol in hand." He went on to tell Díaz, "It's wonderful to be a teacher in the pastoral Uruguayan countryside!"[3]

Children in other schools behaved differently, although there was no getting around the fact that a large number of Uruguay's rural citizens, young and old, already held some party affiliation. Turning this party identity into a more inclusive national one where partisan conflict could be less explosive (or at least not result in knife fights and ruined clothes at recess) was one of public education's most difficult challenges. According to Díaz and the teachers, what was needed was national unity—a spirit of national community that transcended party divisions and offered a sense of collective identity that both Reds and Whites could share. This was exactly what inspired Uruguay's best-selling authors of books on national history to write textbooks with lessons for a nation. It also inspired state officials to prohibit teachers and students from any open manifestations of partisan loyalty.[4]

Across the Río de la Plata, in Argentina, there were no Blancos and Colorados engaging in civil war, but similar political feuds between liberals and conservatives were simmering during these years as well. Immigration fueled the debate and, as we saw in the last chapter, set educational bureaucrats on the road to developing a national public education system with the aim of shaping future citizens who would make for a more unified nation. On both sides of the river, the end of the Paraguayan War in 1870 meant the beginning of the process of consolidating state institutions. In Uruguay, this process was plagued by tensions between Blancos and Colorados that seethed through some moments, and during others boiled over into full-scale civil war, up to the early 1900s. The school and its lessons for a nation were going to be the way forward.

My argument in this chapter is that textbooks on national history and books written expressly for female students were some of the most powerful texts affecting the formation of national and gender identities in the Río de la Plata. In both Uruguay and Argentina, textbooks with lessons for a nation allowed for the popular appropriation of official discourses on nationalism and gender identity. These daily lessons were on the leading edge of a culture of print that was rapidly spreading throughout Rioplatense society, and they fundamentally altered how cultural codes and codes of behavior were transmitted. Whereas gauchos were the protagonists in the development of print culture at midcentury, children had taken over this responsibility at the end of the century. This is what allowed textbooks to play such a prominent role in the popular dissemination and appropriation of nationalist sentiments.

■

From the time Lamb crisscrossed Uruguay in the 1870s to the centenary celebration of the May Revolution (the latter held shortly after Díaz's encounters with the teachers), literary production in the Río de la Plata skyrocketed, driving a second printing revolution in the region. These were years that saw the rise of writers such as Eugenio Cambaceres, whose naturalist novels and stories about dandies have made their way onto "official" lists of Argentine literature, and the Uruguayan Eduardo Acevedo Díaz, whose historical novels helped solidify José Artigas's status as Uruguay's first national hero. The literary historians Ricardo Rojas and Manuel Gálvez, both from Argentina, appeared on the scene around 1900, as did the highly successful Uruguayan playwright Florencio Sánchez. This period also framed the *modernismo* movement in the Plata, with an active Rubén Darío in Buenos Aires during the 1890s, and José Enrique Rodó across the river in Montevideo. Rodo's antimaterialist treatise *Ariel* was published in 1900.

The turn of the century was a moment when access to the limited world of writing started to open up, and when being an author began its transformation into a viable profession. Eduardo Gutiérrez's immensely popular gauchesque novels were a prime example of the changing position of the author. Characterized as "the most pernicious and unhealthy literature ever produced in Argentina," Gutiérrez's mythic *Juan Moreira* and similar novels sold enough for him to become one of the first writers to make a living solely off writing.[5] Other authors who irritated lettered elites and challenged their stronghold on print media during these years included

Julio Figueroa, a name behind carnival songs and gauchesque pamphlets in Uruguay, and people such as Elías Regules and Orosmán Moratorio, as well as Abdón Arostegui, who composed criollo dramas for circus performances that captivated Uruguayan and Argentine audiences. As with the late nineteenth-century popular literature we observed in Chapter 2, these dramas were short plays that put the growing nativist, criollo spirit on display, and they were successful beyond anyone's imagination, thanks largely to their thematic content and integration of quotidian concerns.[6] Circus characters often represented rural types and acted out conflicts between different social sectors; horses and campfires livened up the scenes in which they appeared; and acts of injustice, lasting friendship, and tender love riled up crowds throughout the region who eagerly waited for the next drama, novel, or pamphlet.

These various writers played a major part in this second printing revolution, as did the new, professional journalists who produced a flood of newspaper and magazine publications. There is much more to the story, though. Certainly it was a moment when the outlines of "national" literatures were being defined more clearly, albeit by a select group of men who believed they were the best judges of what real "literature" was. Their definitions became gradually more tinged with nationalist sentiment toward 1910. After all, an anniversary—especially a centenary—is always a good time to sound the nationalist note. But when it came down to print media affecting the formation of collective identities in this stage of the development of Rioplatense print culture, all this new literary production was overshadowed by textbooks that presented young readers and future citizens with lessons in patriotism and lessons in motherhood.

As we covered in Chapter 3, textbooks were the closest link between print, power, and collective identity during the 1890s and the first decade of the twentieth century. Toward 1910, newspapers and forms of literature such as the magazine Caras y Caretas and gauchesque poetry sold in pamphlets rivaled textbooks in quantity. As the centenary celebration approached, the official visions of national and gender identity advocated by textbooks were challenged by popular plays written by and for immigrants and migrants, as well as the very real task of integrating millions of newcomers into the national social fabric. Some immigrant communities even set up private schools where Spanish was not the language of choice, and where "patria" referred to the place the children's parents had left behind.

But overall, the public school, the home, and the government-endorsed lessons for a nation were extremely effective in instilling affection for the national community and specific gender roles within this community—a result the sowers of alphabets had dreamed of. In fact, these lessons secured the bonds between reading and the public sphere as well as the importance of print in everyday life.

Textbooks on national history and women's social roles were not unique to the Plata. From the 1850s on, similar works were published in Mexico, Colombia, Venezuela, and Chile, although the real publishing push of textbooks in these other countries did not take place until the early twentieth century, mainly after 1910.[7] Likewise, as Adolfo Prieto points out, in both the Plata and other regions of Latin America, the lessons students learned in schools created a reading public and fit right into the larger process of modernization that was being carried out around the turn of the century.[8] What stands out about the case of the Río de la Plata, aside from the unmatched quantity of textbooks published and when they appeared, is how widespread these texts were—they were read by children and parents alike—and how deep they reached into not only the minds and hearts of young students but also Rioplatense society at large. These books often included passages from canonical authors, telling stories with young protagonists and strong moral messages. In some cases, the lessons were presented entirely in verse. The fact that they were among the most widely read texts by far at the end of the nineteenth century and the beginning of the twentieth gives them a major part in our story.

Lessons in Patriotism

Patriotism and how to love the patria formed the backbone of texts on national history and civics, and they were themes that ran through textbooks on subjects ranging from calligraphy to home economics.[9] What the lessons in patriotism aimed to do was to create an *emotional bond* with young readers, be it through the books specializing in national history and geography or those that incorporated the patria into other subjects. Patriotic spirit, identification with the idea of nation, and nationalism, after all, are rooted in feelings, and it is through a look at how lessons interacted with feelings that we will better understand the role of textbooks in instilling affection for the nation. Love of the patria was conveyed with characteristics of both familial and romantic love. It was familial in that it was unconditional and cast in the light of parents loving their children, and vice versa. The romantic side of love for the nation came with the passion patria inspired. In both instances, this love was supposed to trump other affiliations.

While educational administrators and textbook authors attempted to rise above partisan divisions, lessons were not neutral. A good test of this is simply looking at how Juan Manuel de Rosas is mentioned in history books, if at all. Book after book leaves him out of both the Uruguayan and Argentine collective past. When he receives mention, it is negative: Rosas the tyrant, the years of tyranny, a period of violence and shame. The periodization of historical moments and the treatment of blacks and indigenous groups in the Plata are other good indexes for approaching official historiographical perspectives. The majority of history books on both sides of the river date the beginning of national history with the May Revolution of 1810. Colonial history appears in some texts. Indians are presented as savages. Blacks rate better portrayals, with some stories lamenting slavery and others praising the loyalty of black soldiers during independence. That said, the presentation of liberal elites' understanding of history did manage to leave out petty partisan politics, at least from the narratives, in hopes of constructing a unified story line.[10]

Crafting *national* histories—albeit ones without Rosas—was clearly the goal. Achieving this goal depended in large measure on the creation of a pantheon of heroes who would fit into a common shared past and act as tour guides and role models for those learning the story. Figures who acquired mythic status in the case of Argentina included José de San Martín, Manuel Belgrano, Mariano Moreno, and the polarizing figure of Sarmiento. In the case of Uruguay, they included José Artigas, Fructuoso Rivera, and Dámaso Larrañaga, as well as Juan Antonio Lavalleja, commander of the group of Uruguayans who had led the charge to liberate the Banda Oriental from Brazilian occupation in the mid-1820s. This group had become famous as the Thirty-Three Orientales (although in reality they had been more than thirty-three in number), and they got plenty of patriotic mention in textbooks.

Some of these men even saw their status rise to that of national hero largely as a result of textbooks. Such figures had to fulfill several standard expectations: inspire national unity, represent both a valiant past and hope for a bright future, and serve as a model citizen.[11] As the names illustrate, new heroes tended to come from the moment of independence, rather than from more contemporary political situations. Independence and its actors were safer bets for rallying people of divergent political colors around the nation.

A good illustration of this point comes from Petronila Wagner Sosa's *Patria, hogar y fraternidad* (Patria, home, and brotherhood), where a lesson presents Pepito, a young boy who collected stamps with images of national heroes (more on such stamps in the Epilogue). What is interesting in this story is that the boy did not tolerate any of his friends joking about the heroes represented—a detail that might seem hard to swallow were we not aware of the author's agenda. Pepito's little sister Luisita often pulled his leg, but she was also "filled with the love that her brother felt for these heroes and she always enjoyed listening to her brother recount the feats of these men." Then something tragic happened. Luisita unintentionally tore the corner of a stamp bearing San Martín's portrait, which led Pepito to lament that his stamp collection was no longer complete and that somehow the character of San Martín had been disrespected. Luisita then decided to purchase a nice new stamp of San Martín for Pepito. The moral of the story, as summed up at the end, is that love for the patria is unconditional and contagious, and that those who harbor this feeling deserve to be held in high esteem by their compatriots.[12]

Independence heroes played a foundational role in lessons in patriotism for another reason, too: educational administrators considered public education a continuation of the work of independence. In their time, the heroes of independence had fought to liberate the country from colonial power. The school's patriotic task was to educate youth, carrying out Artigas's dream (and often quoted statement) of Uruguayans being "as educated as they were brave." This is how Varela understood the role of the school, and it was an argument bureaucrats used to persuade parents and rural inhabitants who questioned the new institution of the school.[13]

Even if the military and political figures who were the subjects of so many lessons in patriotism did not reach the status of "hero" in the eyes of the student, these characters had nevertheless become cultural referents. If all a young student learned was to associate the name Rosas with the idea of tyranny, as presented by so many textbooks, and the names of Belgrano, Moreno, and Artigas with independence, then opposite or different interpretations would have been much more difficult for that student to ponder. Thus, in 1909, one young student wrote with ease that "Tyrant Rosas . . . was very bad for Argentines."[14] Simply put, lessons in patriotism had a type of fail-safe guarantee. If they did not inspire students to become proud patriots, at least they could fall back on the backdoor method and establish the cultural referents for future generations, which in itself was half the battle.

A last general consideration must be taken into account before we look at some concrete examples. Lessons in patriotism were distinctly connected to the home: they fostered the idea of the school as a public home, or as a public extension of the private world of the home. How children behaved at home, the values they learned there, and exercises that required students to think ahead to when they would be homemakers themselves were all subjects that textbooks covered. The idea was that what youngsters learned at home could be carried on in school, and what was learned at school could be taken back to the family abode. That students took home the lessons they learned and shared them with their parents and siblings meant that the stories and morals studied in textbooks mixed with oral culture, especially when the parents or brothers and sisters were illiterate. As was the case with popular gauchesque literature, this meeting of oral and print cultures is critical to understanding how the popular classes integrated into their lives the messages state officials promoted in schools. Of course, how good a read the book was also influenced its success in reaching large reading publics.

Among the hundreds of titles containing lessons in patriotism published between 1880 and 1910 were civics books and civic catechisms. The textbooks on civics aimed to educate students in the art of government, usually by going through the definitions of nation and then explaining the branches of government and the general principles of the constitution.[15] A copy of the constitution was normally a standard feature, too. As this simplified description may suggest, these texts were not the most engaging, despite many of them being on official lists of textbooks year after year, especially when compared to a book on national history narrated by a young boy or girl with whom the young reader could identify. However, these books still dealt in love for the patria, some more effectively than others. Julián Miranda's best-selling *Educación cívica* (Civic education), for example, consistently employs the first person plural to get across the notion of community—one connecting him to his readers, the readers to each other, and all readers to the daily reality of other Uruguayans. He hoped to encourage children to love the patria, its history, and its symbols like they loved their homes. "The well-being of our patria," wrote Miranda, "is our own well-being."[16]

There are many general national histories as well. While their narrative techniques are often of the same poor quality as those of civics texts, these histories do lay out periodizations for history and often present a catalog of historical heroes, or figures children would come to know as heroes.[17] Some textbooks were like *La patria en la escuela* (La patria in the classroom), used in Uruguayan schools to introduce national symbols. Its author argued that the communication of patriotic symbols through verse would make the idea of the patria tangible, which would help root affection for the nation in young readers' hearts.[18] A trilogy of history books saw above-average success and multiple editions: Orestes Araújo's *Perfiles biográficos* (Biographical sketches), *Episodios históricos* (Lessons from our past), and *Lecturas ejemplares* (Exemplary stories, songs, and poems). All three were repeatedly selected as official texts for use across Uruguay, due in part to innovations Araújo introduced (his position in the educational bureaucracy probably did not hurt, either). *Perfiles biográficos* was one of the first books with illustrations. Each lesson is headed by a portrait of the figure or hero in focus. Presenting biographies was also a departure from dull narrative; these biographical profiles were profiles in civic education and were meant to serve as models to follow. *Episodios históricos* follows the same format, although events replace the biographical portraits, accompanied by accounts of the behavior of the figures in *Perfiles biográficos*. The goal of these texts was noble: to help students acquire the building blocks for thinking of a collective past. Moreover, these compilations were on the leading edge of the campaign to consolidate a group of national heroes in Uruguayan history. But there were books with other lessons in patriotism that were, simply put, a lot more fun and engaging than those found in civics texts or the more bland general histories.

One of these was José Manuel Eizaguirre's revealingly titled *La patria: Elementos para estimular en el niño argentino el amor á la patria y el respeto á las tradiciones nacionales* (The patria: Elements for stimulating in the Argentine child love for the patria and respect for national traditions), approved by the Argentine board of education three years in a row. It begins with a note to teachers and parents in which Eizaguirre explains that he has put together a group of readings to serve multiple audiences: "School-children, parents lacking a complete education, workers, and the over-whelming majority of citizens that, even knowing how to read and write, do not understand the idea of patria or know their own patria." With the changes immigrants are bringing, he writes, it is imperative that children and their parents learn about what the patria means. Eizaguirre also in-cludes a note to the "niño argentino," where he asks his readers—boys *and* girls—to lend him their undivided attention so that the pages of *La patria* leave an indelible mark on their souls. The logic was simple: "Today you are just a child, but think about tomorrow when you will be a grown-up. If from childhood you begin learning about the patria, then you will grow from being a good son or daughter, sister or brother today to a good par-ent tomorrow, and always a good ARGENTINE."[19] What Eizaguirre was referring to was the role of everyday reading in everyday reality.

La patria is divided into two parts. Book 1 presents short chapters on the meaning of patria and the importance of venerating its values, with the lessons moving from interactions in the home as the root of the na-tional community to people connecting in town, then to people joining to-gether in the department, next in the province, and finally to fraternity in the patria—the national community. Book 2 deals with national history and geography in lessons addressed to "my compatriot," one of Eizaguirre's narrative strategies for maintaining a constant dialogue with the reader throughout the text. At the end of the book, there are also suggestions for teachers and parents on how to get the best results from the reading. Eiza-guirre was serious about getting young readers to experiment with emotion when they read about the patria. His instructions for reading book 1 in-clude this recommendation: "Following the reading, students should think about personal experiences of holidays, focusing on that first sensation of joy and enthusiasm felt on great patriotic days when citizens parade with soldiers to the sound of regal music, waving the flag proudly. Questions should be directed to this end." Similar approaches were advocated to get students to realize the connection between the home and the patria.[20]

What comes out clearly in the book is the idea of a shared national history that enables and inspires the reader to participate in the national community. The patria functions as a big family of families connected by affection and love, and by the supposed desire of a better life. Life outside this family is impossible—a situation Eizaguirre compares to a child trying to survive when separated from his or her parents.[21] In short, patria is about feeling. It is something the reader was to make into a reality, thanks to the passages of the book, for they introduced the reader—child, parent, worker, or immigrant—to what the nation meant and to Argentines' shared past, and in the process sought to bridge the individual experience of reading with the collective experience of community.

This was exactly what the books of H.D. (Hermano Damsceno) accomplished. H.D. authored the best-selling and most widely read by far textbooks on national history in Uruguay. Ironically, his books never made it to the lists of official textbooks, in large part because he was a professor at the religious Colegio Sagrada Familia (School of the Holy Family). The battle waged by liberal statesmen and educational bureaucrats against church authorities led him to sign his books with his initials.[22] Nevertheless, his *Ensayo de historia patria* (Essay on patriotic history) and the two-volume *Curso de historia patria* (Course on patriotic history) were adopted in public and private schools across Uruguay for the half century following the appearance of the first editions, in 1900 for *Ensayo* and 1903 for *Curso*. Later editions of these books sold like hotcakes to the general public as well, for they combined concise, well-synthesized explanations of Uruguayan history with reader-friendly layouts and images—just the type of book on national history members of the growing middle class wanted to have in their personal libraries.

Even today, most Uruguayans born before the 1980s are familiar with H.D.'s books: many have an old copy at home, and older generations still talk about having encountered his books in school some fifty years ago. His popularity and the use of his "unofficial" history books in public schools earned him a bad name with educational administrators. His religious affiliation did not help in this respect, especially given that the DGIP had barred all teaching or mention of religion in public schools in 1909.[23] In the end, though, H.D.'s reputation has remained intact, thanks to the lessons in patriotism contained in his histories.

Good examples come from the first book of the *Curso*. In the book's dedication to young readers, the author explains that kids have suffered from a lack of texts on national history written for beginners. They have the same right—and need—to learn to love the patria as older citizens, and they should study the book's lessons well, for, in his words to them, "You are the future hope of the patria: be good and virtuous, and one day you will be the source of her glory." The book for you, he writes, is this course on patriotic history: "What do you think? Look at the beautiful prints! See how short and easy the lessons are?" The author also announces to his readers that they will learn about a man who deeply loved his country—Artigas—and patriots who fought for the nation's independence—the Thirty-Three Orientales.[24]

The preface addresses teachers and older readers and echoes the dedication. In it, H.D. adds that teaching national history is the best way to help students understand moral and patriotic values. To achieve this, it was imperative for the readings to "connect to both the imagination and the hearts of young students."[25] Keeping the lessons brief was one of the author's strategies for keeping readers hooked. Bold text and the flagging of vocabulary words with asterisks were used to this end as well. Take lesson 1, for instance, on the "discovery" of Uruguay. Its first lines state, "**We are Uruguayans.** Our patria* is the República Oriental del Uruguay, the country that we love the most."[26] "Patria" and other terms marked with asterisks—the key words to remember—reappear at the back of the book as part of a list of definitions. These techniques are used throughout the book: In the lesson on the May Revolution, **25 May 1810**—the date to remember—appears in bold, and in the chapter on the Thirty-Three, **19 April 1825**, the name **Juan Antonio Lavalleja**, and **Thirty-Three** are likewise all in bold print. Words such as *estridentes* (strident, in reference to Uruguayan patriots fighting against Brazilian soldiers) and *destituir* (overthrow, in reference to what the people of Buenos Aires did to the old viceroy of the Plata) are flagged.[27] In addition, each lesson is followed by short exercises that sum up the main points of the reading.

The important thing, then, about teaching about the patria is to make the lessons interesting. In addition to the narrative strategies mentioned, this meant including images (even in color) alongside text, for H.D. thought they often do more to help kids learn than extensive descriptions. Like other books on national history and civics, the *Curso de historia patria* includes the national anthem at the end for the multiple reading publics, aiming to provide a total package of lessons in patriotism.

Other authors offered textbooks animated with dialogues, skits, and short theatrical scenes. Some called for students to be creative and act out

Figure 4.1. A heroic gaucho rides across the grasslands of Uruguay bearing a flag with the slogan "Libertad o Muerte" (Liberty or Death). This flag is known as the flag of the Thirty-Three Orientales. This image appears on the cover of H.D.'s *Curso de historia patria, libro primero*, 3rd ed.

ARTIGAS EN 1810
Ayud.te Mayor del Cuerpo de Cabal.ría de BLANDENGUES de la FRONTERA
(Copia del celebrado cuadro del pintor nacional D. Juan M. Blanes)

Figure 4.2. Juan Manuel Blanes's representation of what José Artigas looked like on the eve of independence. This copy comes from H.D.'s *Curso de historia patria, libro primero,* where it appears between pages 76 and 77.

the lessons they were learning. This was the case with the Spanish immigrant Ricardo Monner Sans's *Teatro infantil* (Children's theater), a collection of plays for schoolchildren to act out in order to learn what it means to be "good Argentines." The prologue highlights the importance of creativity and suggests some general rules for reading aloud the plays that constitute the book's lessons: "Recitation consists of conducting oneself with careful art, according to the situation that is at hand, in *feeling* what one pronounces and in making others *feel* it too, thus giving fiction the appearance of reality."[28] The importance of feeling is definitely part of the short play titled "La patria," a dialogue between mother and son.

The play begins with the two listening to the sounds of the national anthem. The son asks his mother what all the noise is. She corrects him

124   GUERRAS DE LA INDEPENDENCIA

Sobre las Lecturas del CAPÍTULO VI

IV.—**31.** ¿Adónde fué Artigas a principios de 1814? ¿Qué hizo cuando supo que había capitulado la plaza? ¿Quién ganó la batalla de Guayabos? ¿Cuándo entró *Otorgués* en Montevideo? ¿Cómo era la bandera de Artigas? ¿Qué palabras se leían en el escudo?—**32.** ¿Dónde pasó Artigas en marzo de 1815? ¿Qué hizo el Director *Alvear?* ¿Qué hizo el sucesor de éste para amigarse con Artigas?
V.—**33.** ¿Cuándo nació el P. *Larrañaga?* ¿Dónde recibió las sagradas órdenes? ¿Por qué lo desterró Elío

de Montevideo? ¿A qué cargo fué elevado en 1825? ¿Cuándo murió?—**34.** ¿Qué día se dió la batalla del *Catalán?* ¿Qué hicieron los invasores poco después de esta derrota?
VI.—**35.** ¿Quién ganó la batalla de *las Guachas?* ¿Donde huyó el jefe vencido? ¿Quién fué vencedor después? ¿Qué hizo Artigas al ver su causa perdida?—**36.** ¿Cuál era el gobernador del Paraguay en 1820? ¿A qué pueblo envió al general Artigas? ¿Cuál fué el sucesor de Francia? ¿Dónde y cuándo murió Artigas?

En la Agraciada «juraron **libertar la patria o morir.**» (pág. 125)
(cuadro de Blanes)

Figure 4.3. A lesson illustrated with a print of Blanes's *Juramento de los Treinta y Tres Orientales*, depicting the pledge of the group to liberate the Banda Oriental. The state had commissioned Blanes to complete a set of historical paintings, including this one. In H.D., *Curso de historia patria, libro primero*, 124.

Figure 4.4. The Argentine coat of arms and flag appearing with the date 25 May 1810 on the patriotic cover of Igón's *El mosaico argentino*. The cover art hints at the nature of the content students would find within.

by explaining that it is the soul of the nation that he hears. Naturally, he follows up, inquiring what "patria" means. Like Eizaguirre, the mother launches into an elaborate description of the qualities of the patria and concludes by admonishing her son to love the nation with all his heart. The boy agrees to do so, but only if she teaches him how. She tells him that "there is no word in the world as beautiful as *PATRIA*. But to love her means to serve her loyally, to work day and night with hopes of augmenting her glory." These words ignite the national spirit in the son: "Today I'm going to dedicate my time to my studies so I can be a good citizen tomorrow." As the play draws to a close, the mother shows her pride in her son, tells him to think of the independence hero Manuel Belgrano when the going gets tough, and then ends the dialogue in a way that sums up the lesson and links the home to the school and the nation: "Don't ever forget, my son, these words that my father once uttered: 'He who learns to be a good son and a good student will not fail when he becomes a man, and he will always deserve the embrace of the patria.'"[29]

A similar performative spirit infuses a book of lessons in patriotism published for the centenary celebration in Buenos Aires, *El niño y la patria: Poesías, monólogos, diálogos y escenas patriótico-infantiles ofrecidas por su autor a los niños argentinos en el primer centenario de la patria* (Youth and the patria: Poetry, monologues, dialogues, and patriotic, youth-friendly scenes offered by the author to Argentine children for the first centenary of the patria). Publishing this collection of lessons in the year of the centenary was not just a rhetorical act. Students were actively encouraged to recite passages from the book during the activities commemorating the May Revolution and independence. Again, the affective dimension of reading is where the texts were to be most effective. As the author states in his note at the beginning of the book, "I will be content if I am able to instill true love for the patria in your tender hearts."[30] The titles of some of the poems and songs reveal the nature of the book's content and how the author sought to touch his readers' hearts: "My land," "To my flag," "Patria!," "Long live the patria!," and "To those who died for the patria."[31] For good measure, the national anthem was included, too.

Where the narrative strategy really came to life was in the various scenes and dialogues, ideally to be performed by students. One of these was titled "Los soldados" (The soldiers), featuring a mother and her five-year-old son, Ricardito. The scene begins with Ricardito on the balcony shouting to his mother that a group of soldiers is marching in the street. She leaves her sewing project ("proper work for her condition") and heads to the balcony, where her son poses a series of questions: What do soldiers do? Who are our enemies? Is the cloth of the flag so expensive that it has to be defended with arms? The mother has all the right answers for Ricardito, of course: Soldiers defend the patria against the bad people who want to rob our houses and resources, and the flag is the portrait of the patria, even though it is just a piece of cloth. She then asks Ricardito what he would do if somebody tried to steal the portrait of Grandpa hanging in the living room. Ricardito cries and says he would go after the thief. Well, responds his mother, that is what soldiers do—protect the flag and the patria, just like Ricardito would do with the family member's portrait. The scene ends with the mother defining "patria" and Ricardito proclaiming that when he is a bit older he wants to become a soldier.[32]

These examples of textbooks with lessons in patriotism offer us just a glimpse of what was an immense publishing effort during the 1890s and 1900s to produce books that would shape future citizens, driven primarily by the state. Books were not the only types of print media that were employed for this purpose, either. Student notebooks were more numerous, as we saw in the last chapter, and many of them carried powerful patriotic messages. As the reader may remember, the Vázquez Cores series of notebooks had writing exercises where students traced over printed words and sentences on the pages. The sentences the students traced told of turning moments in Uruguayan history. In Argentina, the titles of popular notebooks included *Zorrilla, Belgrano, San Martín, Rivadavia,* and *Alvear*—all appropriately patriotic in their reference to heroes of increasingly national stature. And then there was the Uruguayan series of Cuadernos Nacionales, whose covers boasted of *over a million* copies sold. Divided into a historical set, a biographical set, a descriptive set, and a set of notebooks on monuments, the front covers of the Cuadernos Nacionales presented images of historical scenes, portraits, and important places in Montevideo and the interior. The back covers consisted of narratives for children about the images on the front.

The editors of these notebooks, which were sold in bulk quantities of one hundred and one thousand, were certain of their success and proudly declared one of their goals to be that of augmenting civic pride in readers. They commissioned images with this goal in mind, to pique the curiosity

Figure 4.5. The front cover of a Cuadernos Nacionales notebook in the historical series, circa 1900. The scene portrays the "exodo del pueblo oriental" (exodus of the Orientales)—in this case, the departure of Artigas and his followers leaving the Banda Oriental in 1811. The junta in Buenos Aires had reached a deal with royalists in the Spanish holdout of Montevideo and rescinded support of Artigas and his troops in their siege of the city. (Courtesy of the Museo Pedagógico José Pedro Varela, Montevideo.)

Figure 4.6. The back cover of the same notebook, with a lesson in patriotism: "The history of independence explained to children." (Courtesy of the Museo Pedagógico José Pedro Varela, Montevideo.)

of the student in matters of the patria. For some of the illustrations of the wars of independence, the painter Diógenes Héquet and the editors made trips to the scenes of battle to study the land and look for vestiges of what took place. This was true of the painting *La Batalla de Las Piedras* (The Battle of Las Piedras), which depicted the first important victory for Artigas's revolutionary forces.[33]

The paintings that embellished the Cuadernos Nacionales were another state-funded effort to create a national imaginary. Some fifteen years earlier, Juan Manuel Blanes had been commissioned to carry out a series of historical paintings that had similar goals.[34] His paintings are the ones that have lived longer, so to say, for they are still a vibrant part of the Uruguayan national imaginary, and reproductions can be found at just about any street fair or souvenir store. Around 1900, though, his paintings were just beginning to see massive distribution on par with the scenes on the Cuadernos Nacionales, thanks to their appearance in textbooks and on postcards (more on these in the Epilogue).

In discussing the strategy of their covers, the editors of the Cuadernos Nacionales wrote that, for example, a student might see "a group of gauchos with lances raised, or a battle scene. The caption indicates what the image depicts, but it is not enough. The student wants more explanations." They remind the reader that the student will find those explanations on the back cover of the notebook, which "the student reads; and by reading, the student learns, without realizing it. Then conversations follow on the theme the child has read about. 'Look,' the student will say to a friend, 'those gauchos were raring to fight,' or 'Look what Artigas did,' or 'During the moment of independence, people traveled in wagons pulled by oxen through the countryside.'"[35] While these claims may sound exaggerated, they were right in line with the reading of notebooks and textbooks in actual practice, and in harmony with what students were saying about the lessons they learned.

Words of Young Patriots

As documented in written assignments on patriotic themes and in student notebooks, kids took such lessons in patriotism to heart. Writing about the Argentine flag in 1890, the sixth grader María Balech finished her short composition with the following words of praise: "You remind us of our heroes, and when torments arise you give valor to your children. . . . My beloved flag! Preserve your purity forever, and grant protection to your daughters, who gratefully salute you and send words impregnated with love and admiration."[36] Mariano Olaciregui, a fifth grader, took this reverence to another level: "Today, 9 July 1890, marks the seventy-fourth anniversary

of the independence of my patria. As one of her true sons, I consecrate my-
self to defend her, willing to take up arms and die on the battlefield for her.
I have a special place in my heart for the heroes of independence."[37] Similar
words of devotion can be found in pamphlets of exam-day speeches and
compositions.[38] In one of these compositions, titled "Far from my patria,"
a young girl who had made the voyage from Montevideo to Buenos Aires
wrote about her memory of the moment when sailors motioned to her that
it was time to set sail from Montevideo. She vowed she would never forget
her patria.

More authentic student perspectives—or at least ones that teachers
did not polish or correct for publication of some type—come from student
notebooks. In August 1908, Carmen Biasotti, a second grader in a rural
school outside Montevideo, offered a summary of the codes of behavior
befitting citizens. Titled simply "Advice," the summary reads:

> Love your parents, brothers, and sisters.
> Be good, obedient, and kind.
> Do not get angry.
> Do not scream or respond in an unbecoming way.
> Always keep your face and hands clean, and your hair brushed.
> Do not put your fingers in your nose.
> Do not play with needles, knives, or scissors.

These codes are complemented by other exercises throughout the notebooks where, for example, in a writing exercise Biasotti equates those who
do not work with thieves.

To refrain from nose-picking and to keep a good temper may seem far
removed from hoisting the national flag and singing the national anthem,
but they were in fact intimately related, for all these activities had to do
with the making of good future citizens and preventing the formation of
unwanted ones (i.e., those who would be lazy, unproductive, and lacking in
patriotism). Biasotti also crafted compositions on the meaning of independence day and who she regarded as national heroes.

The affective dimension of the lessons in patriotism was evident in
simpler exercises, too. On 25 August 1908, for example, in a writing exercise
allowing students to elaborate creatively on the word "patria," Biasotti tells
us:

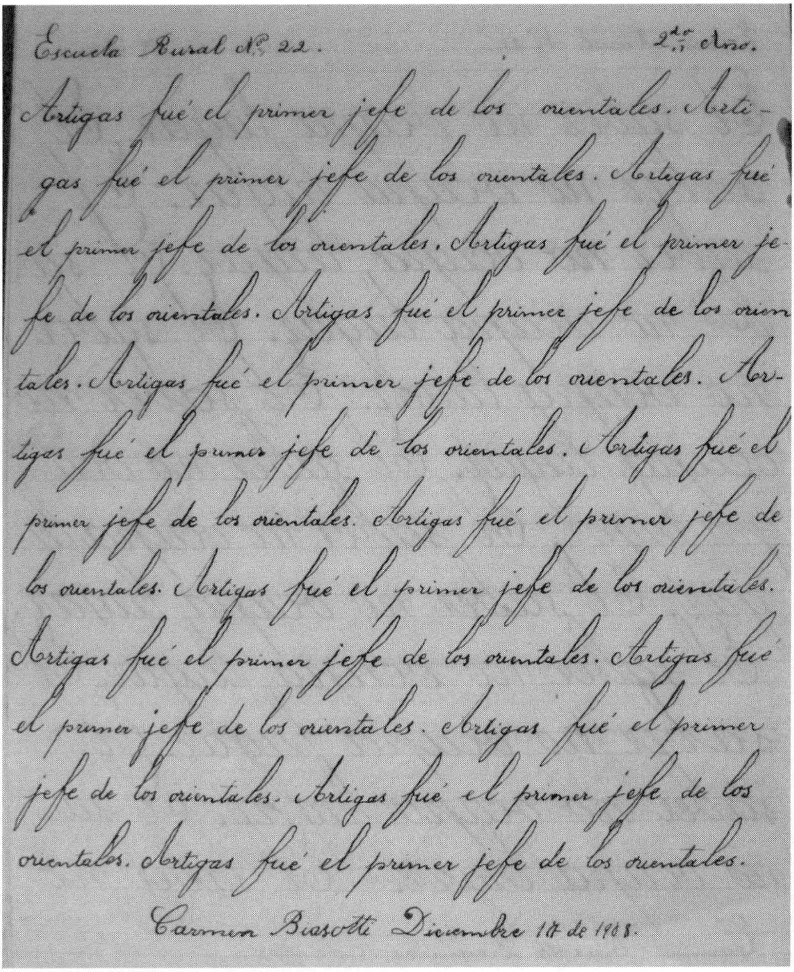
Escuela Rural Nº 22. 2do Año.
Artigas fué el primer jefe de los orientales. Artigas fué el primer jefe de los orientales. Artigas fué
el primer jefe de los orientales. Artigas fué el primer jefe de los orientales. Artigas fué el primer jefe de los orien
tales. Artigas fué el primer jefe de los orientales. Artigas fué el primer jefe de los orientales. Artigas fué el
primer jefe de los orientales. Artigas fué el primer jefe de
los orientales. Artigas fué el primer jefe de los orientales.
Artigas fué el primer jefe de los orientales. Artigas fué
el primer jefe de los orientales. Artigas fué el primer
jefe de los orientales. Artigas fué el primer jefe de los
orientales. Artigas fué el primer jefe de los orientales.
Carmen Biasotti Diciembre 10 de 1908.

Figure 4.7. An exercise in one of Carmen Biasotti's notebooks, dated 10 December 1908, where she repeats "Artigas was the first leader of the Uruguayans" down the entire page. (Courtesy of the Museo Pedagógico José Pedro Varela, Montevideo.)

Patria
We should respect the flag, because it reminds us of the patria.
Patria
The patria is the country where we were born.
Patria

August 25 is a patriotic holiday because it commemorates the day when
the famous Thirty-Three Orientales gathered in the department of
Florida to declare our patria independent.
Patria
We should love our patria and do all that is in our power for her
exaltation.
Patria

In another writing assignment, she had to repeat phrases such as "Artigas was the first leader of Uruguayans" and "My country's coat of arms is
beautiful."[39]

A Uruguayan student from the rural town of San Fructuoso (today
Tacuarembó), Raudelinda Pereda wrote homages to national symbols in
one of her notebooks, too. Her tributes were similar to Biasotti's, albeit
more elaborate: "Lavalleja was a brave *Oriental*. . . . The Thirty-Three in-
flamed the spirit of patriotism among Uruguayans and the veteran warriors
who defended the patria with Artigas and shed generously their blood in
tremendous battles." In another exercise that she titled "Our Flag and Coat
of Arms," Pereda wrote that "when one goes off to war, the flag always always accompanies the brave. When it has been raised on a field of battle
the Uruguayan flag signals victory, although its fabric has been pierced by
the bullets that have touched our glorious insignia." She continues to paint
a scene of glory—of soldiers returning from war holding the flag high—
and describes how both the flag and coat of arms dot public buildings such
as police headquarters. "Whenever we see the flag at places like this we
should salute it. We should always defend the flag, because speaking of it is
like speaking of the patria."[40] It was these types of expressions that led one
national inspector of the school system in Uruguay to proclaim that whenever students are asked something about national history, "they respond
with vibrant and deeply felt patriotism."[41]

Lessons in patriotism were reinforced by *fiestas de fin de año* (end-of-
the-year parties). These events accompanied final exams and were true
community celebrations oriented around the students' work and their expressions of patriotism. Such gatherings gave students the chance to perform the lessons they had learned for teachers, parents, and neighbors,
leading to feelings of collective pride in the school and its contribution
to the patria. This was the explicit rationale behind the participation of

schoolchildren in fiestas cívicas, be these on 25 May or 9 July in Argentina, or on 18 July or 25 August in Uruguay, showing off how children were indeed learning to become citizens.[42]

A secondary motive was present, too: if learning lessons in patriotism in books proved difficult or ineffective for some students, then taking part in these sorts of events would help fill in the gaps, so to say. Schoolchildren always enjoy days when they do not have to engage in normal class work, and field trips—even ones to the town square a couple blocks away—are always welcomed. When organized around national holidays and patriotic content, these activities were sure to inspire the boy or girl who had not followed the lesson in the textbook. Singing the national anthem and engaging in practices such as raising the flag every morning were group activities that by their very nature (and by the mirror system in the brain) bound children together and to lessons in patriotism. Singing the national anthem, especially during holidays, was not something a student could or would want to opt out of. There was something to be said for repetitive physical action and singing in a group.[43]

In sum, then, what are the lessons in patriotism? One of them teaches students about a group of historical figures who are presented as national heroes. Another relates the meaning of patria and of national symbols. Like national heroes, these meanings are meant to be cultural referents for readers. Other lessons touch on morals and on codes of behavior befitting patriotic citizens. As we learned in Chapter 3, there were many reasons to make reading part of these codes. Reading also led to economic gain and progress. A farmer's son who goes to school and is able to read about crop protection and market prices of grains can make all the difference in the world to the success of the family farm.[44] Moreover, lessons in patriotism were about respecting parents and elders and not playing hooky. They were about being studious and generous and becoming good citizens and parents who could, in turn, help shape a future generation of patriots. Another lesson highlights the role of the family and its connection to the school.

Ultimately, the lessons in patriotism were about looking toward the future and transforming the experience of reading into the reality of daily life as a good citizen. All together, these lessons communicated highly charged symbolic messages that allowed readers to claim "I am Uruguayan" or "I am Argentine" at the end of the day, every day. On a daily basis, the lessons reached a wide reading public composed of young students, parents, and

Figure 4.8. A postcard of male students marching through downtown Montevideo, circa 1900. That postcards were made of the event suggests the activity was popular and worth remembering. (Courtesy of the Museo Pedagógico José Pedro Varela, Montevideo, Photography Collection.)

Figure 4.9. A postcard of female students marching through downtown Montevideo, circa 1900. (Courtesy of the Museo Pedagógico José Pedro Varela, Montevideo, Photography Collection.)

Figure 4.10. "Visión de la patria" (View of the Patria), 1923. Students participating in the *fiesta de promoción* at the Escuela de 2ndo Grado, Rivera, Uruguay. The end-of-the-year party celebrated the promotion of students to the next grade level. In addition to the patriotic costumes the students are wearing, the stage is full of symbols, including portraits of José Enrique Rodó (left), José Artigas (center), and José Pedro Varela (right). (Courtesy of the Museo Pedagógico José Pedro Varela, Montevideo, Photography Collection.)

working adults, thus promoting and permitting the popular appropriation of an official brand of nationalism.

The production of books on national history and civic and moral education did not slow down after the 1910 centenary celebration, nor did lessons in patriotism stop appearing in textbooks. If anything, they grew more ardently nationalist, such as in Felisa Latallada's *Hogar y patria* (Home and patria).[45] By 1910, though, the lessons in patriotism had already made their mark, instilling a sense of national identity and pride in the patria across several generations. Of course, their success depended on a constant linking of the home to the patria and the national community, as well as on the young women who were growing up to be future mothers.

Lessons in Motherhood

The second group of textbooks with lessons for a nation consisted of manuals written expressly for female students, with the intent being the formation of morally upright, patriotic mothers who would understand their education as a civic duty and carry the well-being of the nation in their hearts as parents and spouses. They provided young girls with lessons in motherhood designed to shape them into ladies exuding national pride and eager to do their share to raise good citizens, especially ones who would identify more with the nation than with a political party.

Books with lessons in patriotism were more numerous, but during the 1890s and early 1900s, male and female authors on both sides of the Río de la Plata wrote dozens of texts for girls in grades three to seven, whose ages ranged from ten to sixteen. The titles were popular sellers and appeared in multiple editions. Primarily the work of women, this group of texts breaks down into a few distinct categories: home economics and hygiene, libros de lectura using creative narrative to advise young women along their path to motherhood, and books explicitly linking school—and the reading of such texts—to home and the patria. The differences in content between the books of these three groups, however, are nuanced, and often more identifiable in their titles than anywhere else. The main dissimilarities appear in narrative strategy and the reader-friendliness of the lessons.

Studied together, these textbooks for young girls yield a handful of common messages relating to the social role of the mother, to codes of behavior that are gender specific and that lead to the formation of a specific gender identity, to social practices and appropriate work for women, and to education as a family affair and, ultimately, a national priority dependent on women being good mothers. The point about education being a family affair was reinforced by mothers reading the lessons with their daughters, and, as in the case of lessons in patriotism, by parents visiting schools on exam days and for awards ceremonies. These messages reveal what constituted lessons in motherhood, as well as ways in which print media contributed to the formation of female and motherly identity. The best-crafted of these messages managed to tie what the girls were learning in school to the motherly love they experienced at home and to an idealized vision of their future lives as loving mothers. Put differently, good readings—on topics such as how to hold a needle properly, the importance of cleaning the house frequently, and the correct number of months to breast-feed the children one *will* have—went a long way toward defining motherhood and raising the female gender role to a position of national importance.

A look at some examples will make these points clear, though a note of clarification regarding the meaning of "home economics" is in order. While these books on *economía doméstica* (home economics) deal with activities that fit under the rubric of home economics as we understand it today (cooking, sewing, cleaning, and proper etiquette for hosting guests in the home), the teaching of home economics at the turn of the century was more expansive: it encompassed a whole philosophy toward life within its most private space. Home economics was the domain of women; it was a holistic approach to maintaining order, raising a family, and caring for a spouse. That said, even though the philosophy of home economics concerned itself chiefly with the private realm of the home, there was an ever-present link between the practice of home economics and the public sphere, which was understood to be an extension of the home or as the conglomerate community of homes. Hence the need to teach home economics in public schools.

In Uruguay, textbooks for girls had been a concern since the early 1880s. One author and pedagogue even argued that public education's success, and that of all civilization, depended on mothers and on educating girls to become good mothers.[46] By the turn of the century, a flood of these texts had appeared in the Plata, including Emma Catalá de Princivalle's three-volume series. Simply titled *Lecciones de economía doméstica* (Lessons on home economics), it received the official stamp of approval for use in Uruguayan public schools. The books were dedicated to the memory of Catalá's aunt, Martina Gadea de Moreira (unfortunately—for the sake of our story—not related to Juan Moreira), who had belonged to a generation of patriotic heroes "whose only goal was independence." Martina was one of the women who had "turned every home into a temple of virtue and sacrifice."[47]

So from the outset, the books praise the wife and mother who can make a house a home and who contributes to building a better nation. This idea is expressed explicitly in the note to teachers that precedes the lessons in book 1. "Home economics," writes Catalá, "is for young women what civic education is for young men. One can go so far as to argue that forming good mothers and spouses should be a greater concern for edu-

Figure 4.11. "Lección de higiene: El corsé" (Lesson on Hygiene: The Corset). Escuela de Aplicación para Señoritas, Montevideo, August 1912. The sketches on the chalkboard illustrate the natural position of the organs (right), and their position when a corset is worn too tightly (left). Note the portrait of Varela on the back wall. Escuelas de aplicación (roughly, practice schools) were primary schools that fed into normal schools and were often located in the same vicinity or building as normal schools. (Courtesy of the Museo Pedagógico José Pedro Varela, Montevideo, Photography Collection.)

cators than the formation of good citizens, for mothers exercise a funda-mental influence over the development of their children's character, as well as their feelings and habits." The idea was that "frivolous" women would raise improper citizens, and while the school could go a long way toward putting children on the right path, it would be difficult to compete against bad lessons learned at home. "If civic education is indispensable for shap-ing citizens conscious of their rights and duties," the note continues, "then home economics is indispensable for shaping the mothers who will exercise direct influence over what those citizens learn in the home."[48]

A sample of the lesson titles illustrates the nature of the book's con-tent: "Substances for removing stains and how to properly use them," "Ironing light-colored clothes," "Ironing sheets," "Advice and hygienic concepts regarding the importance of frequent changes of underwear," and "The corset." Female students were encouraged to practice in their homes the lessons they learned in school. Thus, their assignments included making breakfast, cooking steak, and serving coffee to their fathers. Teachers, for their part, were to discuss with the students how their practice exercises went and, more importantly, they were to be in direct contact with the students' mothers.

There is little evidence to shed light on teacher-mother relations around 1900, aside from accounts of mothers visiting schools during exams and other special events. Today, in the United States, there is a paper trail for teacher-parent conferences, but casual phone calls and conversations between teachers and parents when they run into each other at the grocery store are not recorded with such formality. In the small towns and rural interiors of Uruguay and Argentina, teachers and parents lived in close proximity to each other, so it is easy to imagine a street corner discussion of a student's performance between a teacher and a mother. Anonymity was greater in the capital cities, but such communication would still have been easy, given that schools were neighborhood institutions and that social interaction was usually neighborhood-based. This sort of contact was yet another means of facilitating the popular appropriation of lessons for a nation.

There are plenty of practical exercises in Catalá's book 1. One of these exercises detailed how girls should open all the windows, shake their mattresses, and dust their rooms when they wake up in the morning. Another focused on how to remove stains from clothing. That lesson ends with the following suggestions for teachers: "When a girl stains her clothing at school, most likely with ink, make her clean the stain herself. Accustom them to removing any stain that appears because of their carelessness or lack of attention. The oldest students should clean the hats and sweaters of their siblings." Additional pointers for teachers dealt with the cleanliness of mourning gowns and supervision of student practice: "Girls who are in mourning should clean the stains from their black dresses and iron them if they are wrinkled. The girls whose mothers or sisters use gloves should try to wash these and take them to school so the teacher can see and comment on the work."[49]

The theme of all three volumes in Catalá's series is clear. The main drawback of the books was that they were not all that engaging, lacking a young narrator to invite readers to follow along. That said, they were replete with advice, which helped keep them on the official list of books year after year. Book 2, for example, focuses on running a household, with particular emphasis on cleanliness. In addition to the usual pointers for keeping the kitchen, bathrooms, and bedrooms clean, several lessons included some out-of-the-way advice. Take this one: students could read that in houses with rats, roaches, ants, and other pests, the way to protect the family food supply was by moving the furniture and cupboards away from the wall and placing the legs of the furniture in cans full of kerosene. This was called an "indispensable precaution, not only for preserving food from the invasion of ants and the like, but also for its effectiveness in ridding the house of such pests by starving them and pursuing them tenaciously."[50]

Designed as a review of the material in books 1 and 2, the third book in Catalá's series on home economics spells out even more clearly the main features of the state-supported gender identity for women. Many are summed up in the boldface section headings listed at the beginning of the first lesson, which appear later in bold type at the head of or within the lesson's paragraphs:

Women are in charge of the inside of the home
A home without cleanliness, order, and economy is not one where happiness can exist[51]
Young girls should learn to consider domestic chores as pleasant and honorable work
All young girls should take part in household chores in order to help their mothers as much as possible

In addition to the constant mentions of cleanliness throughout the text, students read in the first lesson that from the youngest age possible, women must grow to understand their role in the home as a noble one.[52] This may sound like a strange statement coming from a female author, especially if we read it from a modern perspective on women in the home, but Catalá was not by any means alone in thinking of the social role of women in this light.

Cipriano Torrejón's *Lectura de economía doméstica* (Study of home economics) and Aurora Stella del Castaño's *El vademécum del hogar* (The household guidebook), a reference book of sorts that included four hundred illustrations and some sixty pages of recipes, were similar to Catalá's text in narrative style and structure. The mentions of gender roles in these and Catalá's textbooks overwhelmingly dealt with the work of women. Occasionally the role of men was brought into the discussion for comparative purposes: the man was supposed to make money outside the house. When men ended up staying in the house, it was a sort of aberration. Torrejón went as far as to claim that such men "should be considered intruders or queers, never as men."[53] This is an exaggerated take on gender divisions, but it goes to show that stereotypes of gender cut both ways. Males, by nature, went the thought, were destined to work outside the home and fight for the patria.

Educators were successful in instilling official visions of these gender roles, though that did not mean that men and women did not challenge them from within. But even with modifications made to gender-specific codes of behavior over time, the lessons for a nation that gender roles fed into remained strong. Imagining the future was a key part of lessons in motherhood, and it was also crucial to their success. What was most important was getting students to look forward to their lives as mothers, which in turn made them enthusiastic about learning lessons in motherhood.

Of course, a good read could go a long way toward turning readers' attention toward the future in the first place. This is exactly what a large group of books with lessons in motherhood did. The tone and narrative style of these, similar to some of the textbooks with lessons in patriotism that we covered, were more friendly and animated than those of Catalá de Princivalle's series of books. One example comes from an anonymously written textbook titled *Economía doméstica al alcance de las niñas* (Home economics within the reach of young girls). The author of this little book directly addressed its young female readers as intimate friends, though always referencing the young readers' future: "Today's girl, my little friends, is the woman of tomorrow who will share with her spouse and children the pleasures and pains of life—the one who will educate her children so that they will benefit society and honor the nation." The narrative strategy incorporated short stories with morals on motherhood and engaging exercises such as creating a "museum for teaching home economics," in which students were to make small exhibits with dolls, cloth, and drawings, to demonstrate key practices in the home. There is also an interesting lesson on reading: reading together as a family following a meal is praised as an activity that will yield countless fruits. Such sessions "open the minds of children; they teach them to think critically and prepare them for lively discussions . . . and rouse in young hearts the most noble sentiments, which in turn leads parents to exude pride."[54]

This type of reading was at the heart of *Consejos a mi hija: Lecturas de propaganda moral* (Advice to my daughter: Readings in moral rectitude), written by the prolific Argentine Amelia Palma.[55] The first of a four-volume series titled *La vida práctica* (Practical life), this textbook received the CNE's stamp of approval, as well as that of the educational boards of the provinces of Buenos Aires and Córdoba. Its status as an official textbook was a definite boost for sales. As noted on the cover, the first edition had already sold seven thousand copies. As the title suggests, the book is all about advice to a young girl on her path toward becoming a wife and a mother (in that order). One of the letters of praise to the author that open the book qualifies it as a literary work fit for "the hands of the young woman who is starting out in life, as well as in those of the teacher or the mother who should be accompanying her in this venture." Another letter came from the Argentine poet Carlos Guido y Spano, who concluded his encomium by declaring Palma's hands "blessed" for keeping the lamp of home economics shining bright. The director of public schools in Mendoza offered equal words of support, stating that he was going to ask the CNE to send copies of the book to all the schools in the province.[56]

Testimonials aside, what was innovative about the first book in *La vida práctica* was its conversational depiction (albeit one-sided) of a mother relating her life experiences *through writing* to her fourteen-year-old daughter, Laura. Since Laura's mother was "on the downhill slope of life's mountain," she wanted to leave her words of wisdom for when her daughter learns about marriage and what to look for in a husband. And of course Laura is told all about the basics of home economics. The second book of the series, *El hogar modelo* (The model home), continues the conversation between the characters of Laura and her mother.[57] Like the first one, it was geared for

Figure 4.12. A daughter reading to her mother on the cover of Amelia Palma's *Consejos a mi hija*. (Courtesy of the Biblioteca Nacional de Maestros, Buenos Aires.)

use in the classroom and envisioned as a textbook whose contents daughters could discuss, if not read, with their mothers. The mother-daughter link of these conversations and all lessons in motherhood not only led to their reinforcement, but also gave them unmatched credibility as proponents of a gender-specific identity. Calling Palma's textbooks works of quotidian literature is not a misnomer.

The same can be argued for several other books that presented lessons in motherhood in even more creative ways, employing narrative techniques meant to engage the reader. Take, for example, *El primer libro de las niñas: Lecturas morales e instructivas* (The first book for young girls: Instructive and moral readings) by José M. B. Mareca, one of the earliest books of this type in Argentina. This book consists of fifty lessons on topics ranging from love of God to love of the national flag. What was new about this book, and what made it so attractive, was that young girls are the protagonists of the lessons, which address their readers in a friendly tone. The goal was to enable the reader to see herself in the stories, following the advice presented in them. The idea is clearly stated in an introductory note: "Girls: this book is for you. Read it and reflect on the little stories you find herein.

. . . Caring and hardworking girls, respectful and obedient ones, they are angels from heaven who were born and live on the earth."[58]

In order for readers to achieve this angel-like status, each reading is followed by a series of questions designed to summarize the selection and drive home the proper interpretation—a sort of modified catechism. In lesson 3, for instance, "A Happy Father," a young girl arrives home from school and conveys to her father that the teacher told her that good daughters should help their parents rest and make them happy. This means helping their mothers with chores around the house so they can take care of other maternal duties. When the father hears his daughter's new resolution to behave in this way, he weeps with joy. The follow-up questions include lines such as: "What are the responsibilities of 'good girls'? How will Amalia behave from now on? What happiness will this kind girl find in her change of behavior?"[59]

Subsequent readings reiterated their points in even more forceful questions. One lesson on personal hygiene was followed by these provocative questions: "When is a young girl repugnant and unattractive? What effect do filthy girls produce? What does their appearance inspire? What is personal hygiene? What sensation does the body feel when it is accustomed to cleanliness?" A later lesson stages its demonstration of love for the patria with the figure of a mother expressing sadness over her son's departure to become a soldier. Her husband grows angry seeing her in this state, and claims that it's a young man's duty to serve his country and fellow citizens. Of course the mother quickly acknowledges that her husband is right, and when the son's first letter arrives home, she cries, but this time out of pride in her patriotic offspring rather than out of sadness.[60] The examples abound. Suffice it to say that after lessons and questions such as these, what young girl would not aspire to become the angel spoken of at the beginning of the book? With all the "wisdom" presented in the vignettes, capped with the last two lessons on the flag and the nation, young readers complete *El primer libro de las niñas* prepared to become good Argentine matrons and are sent off contemplating their duties.

The three volumes of *La niña argentina* (The young Argentine girl) were similar to *El primer libro de las niñas* in their format. In the prologue to book 1, the author bluntly states his goal to be that of writing books that will prepare and instruct the future matrons of Argentine society [*damas argentinas*].[61] The first couple of readings are enough to let readers know what they are in for. Lesson 1 presents young Ernestina, the narrator throughout the book, who is awed by the quality of her citizenship: "I'm Argentine. I'm Argentine because I was born in the Republic of Argentina. What a beautiful name! Argentina!" In lesson 2, Ernestina offers thanks to her mother for teaching her to love God, to sew, to have good manners, and to know that the patria was "born" in 1810. And in lesson 4, the narrator speaks with her grandmother about family members who fought for the patria, including a brother who had died shouting "¡Viva la patria!"[62] There are other lessons that deal with home economics, but lessons in patriotism are never far off.

Across the river, another book on home economics was growing in popularity and earning its authors handsome profits: *Lecturas sobre moral, higiene y economía doméstica* (Readings on morals, hygiene, and home economics), by Alejandro and Elvira Lamas. Alejandro had written an earlier book of lessons in motherhood: tellingly titled *Maternología* (Mother-

Figure 4.13. The lady of the house arranges the table on the cover of *Lecturas sobre moral, higiene y economía doméstica*, by Alejandro Lamas and Elvira Lamas. The caption reads, "To create habits of thinking, feeling, and behaving, for these are the essence of education."

ology), it was used in Uruguay's normal schools and promoted as a book for all current and future mothers. *Lecturas* was for a different audience—namely girls in primary schools—and it was written in a different style, beginning with the type of intimate connection the authors aimed to establish with readers. This was manifest in a note admonishing girls to "love this book and consult it frequently. When you leave school, take it with you, and take good care of it. This textbook is a loyal friend." As quoted on the cover, the authors' intent was "to create habits of thinking, feeling, and behaving, for these are the essence of education," a goal that informed the narrative strategy. In the note to teachers, the authors wrote: "We have tried to reach the emotions of our readers and stir profoundly their interest in the book, which explains why we have broken with the old mold for writing textbooks."[63] As in *La niña argentina* and *El primer libro de las niñas*, young girls narrated the lessons, specifically in the form of letters sent by Blanca to her younger sister Sofía, in which she explains all the basics of womanhood and how Sofía should prepare for her future.

Lecturas sobre moral, higiene y economía doméstica touches on all the themes we have seen mentioned in the other books discussed up to this point. Like the most successful texts with lessons in motherhood, it was written in a way to allow readers to see themselves in the narrative—the voices of Blanca and Sofía impart nuggets of gender identity easy for readers to swallow. Its simplicity and its format of the epistolary conversations and informative lessons are complemented by pages featuring short moral statements and proverbs, beginning with the note about taking care of the book. The last such page deals with nothing less than life itself: "Life is a continuous battle," the authors explain to readers, "and it is imperative to prepare for it at school and at home, first by being good students and daughters, and then later affectionate spouses and loving mothers."[64] Once again, then, we meet here the emphasis placed on the future of everyday life that is at the core of this and other books with lessons in motherhood.

The World of the Young Female Reader

To understand the dynamics of this moment in the development of Rioplatense print culture, it is essential to recognize the production of textbooks and messages for young girls aimed at crafting a female identity. An

Figure 4.14. Young students learning to weave at the Internato Normal de Señoritas, Montevideo, circa 1893. (Courtesy of the Museo Pedagógico José Pedro Varela, Montevideo, Photography Collection.)

equally important step is to look at how readers received and were affected by such print media, but it is a much more complicated task to perform because of the nature of limited sources and the difficulty of approaching how people in the past felt about and absorbed what they read.

A few examples, like those we saw regarding the reception of lessons in patriotism, take us from the books and their messages to the world of the young female reader. Photographs from the period show female students diligently reading in school, engaging in activities such as weaving and sewing, and participating in classes on subjects ranging from music to hygiene.

The words of students also illustrate well how readers literally put into practice the words they read and studied. Raudelinda Pereda (quoted earlier in this chapter and the one preceding) drafted a sentimental letter to her mother in one of her notebooks, praising her for the example she sets. Reflecting on her advancements along the path toward motherhood, she goes on to tell her mother, "My conduct and my tenderness will give you new reasons to rejoice at having been born."[65] Thirteen-year-old María Za-

Figure 4.15. Students in a music class at the Escuela de Aplicación, Montevideo, 1893. They are singing the national anthem, written on the board. (Courtesy of the Museo Pedagógico José Pedro Varela, Montevideo, Photography Collection.)

Figure 4.16. A sewing class at the Escuela de Aplicación, Montevideo, circa 1912. (Courtesy of the Museo Pedagógico José Pedro Varela, Montevideo, Photography Collection.)

pater wrote a similar composition about the home and her mother's care for her children: "There is nothing so sweet or beautiful . . . as the love of parents for their children. . . . When we think about the love of a mother, there are no words that duly express her affection or our adoration of her. With that tender heart, she spends all her days devoted to us, taking care to protect us from sickness and life's perils."[66] The class notebooks of Carmen Biasotti help us here, too. They are filled with pages that hint at how she interacted with lessons in motherhood. In one instance, she practices form-ing past tenses using the verb "to iron"—definitely not an innocent verb: "I ironed, I have ironed, I had ironed, you ironed, you have ironed, you had ironed, we ironed, we have ironed, we had ironed." On another occasion, she recalls the routine of her father quizzing her after dinner about what she learned at school, reading over her notebooks with her, and then telling her stories about "good girls" who live happily and "disobedient" ones who are not well liked. And in exercises where sentences are repeated twenty or thirty times per page, she writes, "Your mother is your best friend," "Be

Figure 4.17. A reading lesson at the Escuela José P. Varela 3er Grado No. 2 in Montevideo, August 1912. While this was a posed photo, it is worth pointing out that every student in the room has her own copy of the day's book. (Courtesy of the Museo Pedagógico José Pedro Varela, Montevideo, Photography Collection.)

good, friendly, and obedient," "Good girls work hard," and "What is the best ornament of a young girl? Education."[67]

By now it should be abundantly clear that cultivating modes of behavior and social graces befitting proper ladies was part and parcel of lessons in motherhood. These lessons did not stop appearing after 1910.[68] In all the textbooks mentioned in this section, instructions for how to behave in different social situations constitute key lessons, regardless of which social class the reader was from. This is true of other textbooks that we have not analyzed in detail, such as the prolific Isidoro de María's *El libro de las niñas* (The young girls' book) and the more explicitly titled *Urbanidad y cortesía* (Manners and courtesies).[69] Again, the mother was the model to follow, and the codes of behavior fit into the larger picture of women being linchpins in the formation of upright citizens and by extension a healthy national community.

The engineering of motherhood in the ways we have seen in these lessons most likely seems unsettling to us today. Some of the lessons are downright startling in their direct statements that women should be subordinate to their husbands and occupy themselves with chores in the home. Others may come across as exaggerations, or as sarcastic and humorous bits of advice. But to condemn these lessons in motherhood as mere efforts to prolong traditional gender roles would be both anachronistic and shortsighted. These lessons were serious, and they were for a rapidly growing school population. By 1910, females accounted for nearly half the total number of students in both Uruguay and Argentina. Many of these would go on to become teachers; as we learned in Chapter 3, women made up 85 percent of the teaching force in Argentina by 1910.[70] My point here is that education—including lessons in motherhood—was an empowering, *new* experience for women, illustrated best by those who joined the workforce as teachers, but also more subtly by new mothers, who were now educated ones.

My claim is that educated women enjoyed better social status precisely because of their education, regardless of whether they stayed at home or joined the workforce.[71] Education certainly led some to improve their social standing and others to subvert assigned gender roles, despite being homemakers and despite being advised not to go against established social norms. What is certain is that the lessons in motherhood were intimately connected to lessons in patriotism. Through education, and the role of mothers in the education of their children, women were becoming key players (in some instances, they were considered the most important players) in the formation not only of new citizens but also national communities. This point is made in Wagner Sosa's *Patria, hogar y fraternidad*. In a lesson titled "Sara's unhappiness," the protagonist Sara puts down the book on national history she is reading and exclaims, "How sad it is to be a woman!" Her friend Teresa asks why Sara thinks this way and states that women have a beautiful mission to undertake. Sara does not comprehend this, which leads Teresa to explain that it is up to women to form future citizens. When Sara does not buy the argument, her friend then tells her about the moral influence women have on the world, thanks to their roles in the home and as mothers. By the end of the lesson, Teresa has convinced Sara of the importance of women in the making of a successful nation.[72]

In short, the lessons for female students institutionalized motherhood and made it a matter of national importance, which in turn led to greater numbers of girls attending schools.

■

From the first large-scale creation of public schools in the region around 1880 to the one-hundredth anniversary of the May Revolution in 1910, inhabitants of the Río de la Plata experienced a second printing revolution that consisted of dramatic increases in literary production, a flood of newspaper and magazine publications, and much greater interaction between the popular classes and print media. Textbooks constituted a major force behind this cultural revolution, and they were by far the most influential texts in the formation of national and gender identities at the turn of the century. The ramifications of these changes did not stop with mere statistical jumps in literacy or lucrative contracts for textbook authors.

Lessons in patriotism are at the heart of hundreds of titles on national history and geography, and they appear prevalently in books that are not solely devoted to these subjects. These lessons instilled a sense of family and a passion for the notion of a unified nation in young readers' hearts. Such lessons dealt in sentiment, attempting to link a common or shared history to the pride of feeling part of a national community. Female students were targeted with a special set of books that provided lessons in motherhood, which prepared young readers to become model mothers and influenced the formation of a type of collective identity related to gender. These lessons in patriotism and motherhood offered a sense of collective identity that children *and* parents of different political stripes could share. They promised a path toward a more cohesive national unity on both sides of the river.

Some readers remained untouched by what they read, and some surely rejected the concisely packaged role of "mother" presented to them or the attempts to establish a national history that any citizen could tap into. But the overwhelming majority of children took these daily lessons in patriotism and motherhood to heart. The formation of national identities was a process that took shape through many practices and in many venues. But when it comes down to the connections between print culture and collective identity, no other publication or institution could rival the school and the home and their everyday lessons for a nation.

Epilogue

Spreading the Word and Image
(1880–1910)

■ On a spring morning in October 2005, I was faced with a daunting task. I had traveled to Salto, Uruguay, along the country's western edge, to meet with children at an elementary school on the outskirts of town. Precariously constructed houses lined the dirt roads, and nestled among them was La Amarilla (The Yellow School), as it was called. It brimmed with life as I arrived that morning. After sitting down to breakfast with a group of first graders—children who attend the school are guaranteed at least two meals per day—I went to a third-grade classroom where the students eagerly introduced themselves. Then it was my turn. I told them a little about me—where I grew up, what I was doing in Uruguay. My task for that class period was to explain to them the meaning of literature—nothing more, nothing less. While I had thought about how to accomplish this prior to going to La Amarilla, it was nevertheless a challenge. I talked, they listened, and then with great enthusiasm they all wrote: short stories, poems, tales of monsters, short autobiographical narratives.

Did they understand my explanation? Did it mean anything to them? At the morning recess, I got answers to my questions. A group of boys asked me to join them in a game they were playing, a sort of slapjack with trade cards whose images carried different point values. When the game ended, each student gave me one of his cards—invariably the most valuable one. The girls from the class asked me to dance with them and the boys as they rehearsed the *pericón*—a traditional folk dance—for the upcoming talent show. They too offered me gifts: the compositions they'd written earlier; thank-you notes; one even tried to give me a two-peso coin. And those were the answers to my questions—they wanted to express their gratitude, be it because they'd had such fun with this strange guy visiting their school, or because they had indeed gotten something meaningful out of that class devoted to the meaning of "literature."

Only later did I begin to think about the powerful implications of that experience. I had been in the interior of Uruguay, on the edge of a small city cropped just like the lettered city of Angel Rama's description.[1] The Uruguayan coat of arms hung above the school's front door—that same coat of arms we learned about in Chapter 1. There was a framed portrait of José Pedro Varela inside. The young children of lower-class families were literate. And some of them had given me their prized printed possessions, which I still hold dear—those bent and scratched collector's cards with their curious images. In short, it had been a firsthand experience of the reach and the lasting impact of print culture, and one far from the capital city of Montevideo.

For those children in Salto, their collectible cards were normal, everyday objects, and they were strikingly similar to the collectible cards that began circulating in the region in the 1880s. In fact, almost parallel with the growth of the public primary education system in the Plata, a new printing industry had emerged that produced media for mass distribution. These media included cigarette cards inscribed with episodes of national history, decorative tickets to be used on new tramway lines, new national currencies in the form of paper bills, postage stamps, postcards, matchboxes, and cigarette boxes, not to mention colorfully illustrated magazines and loose-leaf publications. All these new forms of everyday reading spread words and symbolically charged images to all sectors of Rioplatense society. All were novel at first, but they would soon become the stuff of daily life. And all owed much to the way print culture had developed in the region—a process that, as we have learned, had effectively linked print to politics and the public sphere by the early 1900s. We will sample some of these sources here and see how they helped spread the word and image.

Postal Imagery, Postal Stories

On 19 July 1906, envisioning a good meal after the voyage across the river, Luis Reyes asked María Sicardi in Buenos Aires to "make spaghetti, and take care," scrawling the words across a view of what is today the Plaza

Figure 5.1. A postcard with poetic lines sent to a woman in Melo, Uruguay, dated 16 July 1905. Note the embossed illustrations of coins. (Courtesy of the Estudio Filatélico de Carlos Hernández Rocha, Montevideo.)

Matriz in Montevideo.[2] "Enrique, I hope to see you today at three at the university," wrote a new friend sometime in 1899.[3] And on 16 July 1905, an admirer wrote the following poetic lines to Máxima Rodrígues in Melo, Uruguay: "I would like to be the night shadow in order to see you peacefully asleep, and then be the light of dawn to wake you with a kiss on your eyelids."[4] All these messages were transmitted on postcards. They depended on rapid delivery, which did indeed happen, although this form of communication—the postcard—was radically new around 1880. On both sides of the Plata River, initiatives had been proposed earlier in the century for some form of an organized postal system in the capital cities. But administering the makeshift system that emerged prior to the 1870s had been difficult. There were few established delivery routes, and these did not reach much beyond urban centers. Moreover, the transport of mail was slow and infrequent in Uruguay and even slower in Argentina, where its carriers traveled on horseback or in carriages [*diligencias*].

During the second half of the nineteenth century, private and public capital funded the construction of national roads and the creation of rail lines for transporting agricultural products from the interior to port capitals and manufactured imports to the countryside. The development of railroad lines started just after the midcentury in Argentina, and slightly later in Uruguay. In both places, the lines expanded exponentially thanks to British investment.[5] What concerns us here is that these transportation networks also facilitated the rise in postal communications and a faster and more far-reaching distribution of print media. One of the results was that by the end of the 1880s, truly national postal services became a reality in the Río de la Plata.

These services brought post offices to neighborhoods throughout the cities and on their outskirts, and scattered them throughout the countryside. They stipulated that drop boxes would be established at certain points, with stamp dispensers next to them, and new laws provided for mail delivery to homes and required official postage to be used on all mail. The new postal service also stimulated a flood of diverse stamps, postcards (some with embossed postage), and prepaid letter-envelopes, which allowed citizens to send, consciously and unconsciously, ornate symbolic images in stupefying quantities.

Postal imagery ranged from busts of national heroes and renderings of symbols—most commonly coats of arms and flags—to cityscapes, attractive vistas of geographical landmarks, celebrated battle scenes, and allegorical representations of progress. Beginning in the 1880s, the region saw the advent of more advanced photographic printing machines and a greater availability of specialty paper. Photographic scenes covering aspects of life as diverse as countryside traditions (seen best in the *Reminiscencias Camperas* postcard series in Uruguay), new paper money in circulation, buildings and monuments erected in city squares, and the bustling docks of Buenos Aires and Montevideo began appearing on postcards and in miniature on stamps.[6]

Both the Uruguayan and Argentine postal services, later administered with telegraph and telephone services, were state agencies. As such, they enjoyed exclusive control over the political messages and goals behind the images on stamps and on the official postcards, postal letter paper, and letter-envelopes. Thus, stamps featured figures such as liberal leaders Bernardino Rivadavia, Domingo Sarmiento, and Bartolomé Mitre in Argentina, and the caudillo José Artigas and President Joaquín Suarez in Uruguay. Neither Juan Manuel de Rosas nor Manuel Oribe was considered among the options, though Justo José de Urquiza was.[7] Examples of

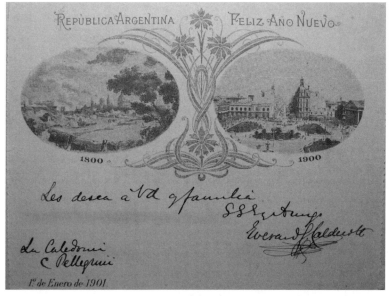

Figure 5.2. A Happy New Year postcard dated 1 January 1901, depicting the Plaza de Mayo in Buenos Aires in 1800 (left) and 1900 (right). (Courtesy of the Estudio Filatélico de Carlos Hernández Rocha, Montevideo.)

Figure 5.3. A postcard dated 1 January 1901, celebrating the expansion of rail lines in Uruguay. Note the driver of the carriage looking back at the train roaring by while his horses casually graze. (Courtesy of the Estudio Filatélico de Carlos Hernández Rocha, Montevideo.)

Figure 5.4. A colorful postcard of a colorful "country memory," with a woman "handing her man a gourd of bitter mate" as a rooster looks on. Sent from Salto, Uruguay, to Montevideo, September 1907. (Courtesy of the Estudio Filatélico de Carlos Hernández Rocha, Montevideo.)

Figure 5.5. A postcard from the *Reminiscencias Camperas* series, circa 1905, representing "a rest along the trail." Note the man drinking mate under the wagon. (Courtesy of the Estudio Filatélico de Carlos Hernández Rocha, Montevideo.)

Figure 5.6. A postcard showing the Palacio Legislativo in Montevideo, sent 25 April 1908. Writing in English to a Mrs. Florence Leslie in Rio de Janeiro, the author noted that "all S. American countries seem to have good government buildings." (Courtesy of the Estudio Filatélico de Carlos Hernández Rocha, Montevideo.)

Figure 5.7. A postcard dated 11 January 1905, with the Uruguayan coat of arms (top left) and a spread of Uruguayan stamps. (Courtesy of the Estudio Filatélico de Carlos Hernández Rocha, Montevideo.)

scenes portrayed on official postcards include an elegant Plaza de Mayo, Montevideo's Central Post Office, and a pastoral glimpse of the country-side. Tenement houses, growing shantytowns, and scenes of poverty in the interior were obviously not featured. Private printers also began selling postcards in the late 1880s, offering alternative designs, albeit ones as con-genial as the scenes on the official versions.

Suffice it to say that there were certain types of images these print media were carrying, and in the broader context of visual culture, as Bea-triz González-Stephan and Jens Andermann have argued, they engaged collective memory and modes of seeing.[8] Most postcards suggested some forward-leaning vision or appreciation for modernization, though this was not always the case. On a postcard with a photograph of a carriage crossing the St. Lucía River in Uruguay, the writer noted that "locomotives are great, but, damn it, what's even better is traveling across our countryside the old way [al estilo viejo]."[9] Granted, the author of that note was the poet of popular verse Alcides de María: his work celebrated rural traditions and a slower way of life, and he was editor in chief of the illustrated criollo maga-zine El Fogón (Campfire). Some scholars have argued that postal images helped shape a civic identity and that there was a "foundational quality" to them, and there is truth in both these claims.[10] Though it is more difficult to prove how postal imagery disciplined vision, what is sure beyond doubt is that these everyday reading materials were making their way into the hands of tens of thousands of new readers and writers.

Some of the numbers on stamp and postcard production bear out this point. In 1883, the first Uruguayan stamp to feature an image of Artigas was produced, depicting the hero as an octogenarian. A portrait of a slightly younger Artigas was circulated in 1884, along with stamps displaying the coat of arms and decorative numbers corresponding to postage. All these stamps were printed in New York by the American Bank Note Company in sheets of one hundred. The emissions of both the 1884 Artigas and the coat of arms stamps were in quantities of one hundred thousand each, which were small print runs compared to that year's batch of two million five-cent stamps.[11] Toward the end of the decade, the printing of Uru-guayan stamps shifted to London, and in the late 1890s stamps began to be produced in Montevideo. In 1895 and 1897, the so-called first and second Catedral stamp series was launched; it included images of a gaucho, a steer's

Figure 5.8. Stamps from the 1895 *Catedral* series in Uruguay:
a gaucho, the Teatro Solís, and a locomotive. (Courtesy of the
Estudio Filatélico de Carlos Hernández Rocha, Montevideo.)

head, the Teatro Solís, the first locomotive, and an allegory of electricity, all
representing different strengths of Uruguay's past, present, and future. In
addition to this series, which remained valid throughout the first decade
of the 1900s, five hundred thousand copies of a special stamp reading "Paz
1897" (Peace 1897) were released and sold in Montevideo between 26 and
28 September of that year to mark the end of civil war.[12]

Symbolic capital continued as a staple of stamps at the beginning of
the twentieth century. The 1900 series showcased several animals in reference to the country's agricultural wealth. In 1904, just as in 1897, another
commemorative stamp celebrating the end of civil war—this time Uruguay's last—was released. 1908 saw special stamps on 25 August, the anniversary of the declaration of independence, and the two days surrounding
it. In 1909, stamps celebrating the opening of Montevideo's new port were
circulated. And in 1910 and 1911, there were special stamps marking the
centenary of the May Revolution (ironically, these were printed in Buenos
Aires) and the Battle of Las Piedras, honored in Uruguayan military history and still a national holiday. During the second part of the decade, the
publication quantities shot up. In 1906, five million stamps bearing the coat
of arms were issued. In 1910, a multicolored set of stamps with a new image
of Artigas (based on the 1884 painting by Juan Manuel Blanes) broke all
records: eight million purple, four million green, four million red, twelve
million blue, two million gray, and several hundred thousand in other hues
swarmed around the country.[13] That added up to more than thirty million thumbnail-sized representations of Blanes's young, dashing, and bold-
featured Artigas. Fifteen years earlier, he had been a pointy-nosed elder

Figure 5.9. Stamps from 1883 (left), 1884 (center), and 1910 (right) showing the evolution of José Artigas's image toward a bold, youthful look. (Courtesy of the Estudio Filatélico de Carlos Hernández Rocha, Montevideo.)

statesman who was losing his hair. At any rate, by 1910, Artigas's place in the pantheon of patriotic symbols was guaranteed. In subsequent years, postal stamps were printed in increasing numbers, with dates, people, allegories, and places in Uruguayan history continuing to drive the imagery. The total volume of mail, which increased from forty-four to ninety-five million pieces from 1900 to 1910, indicates that these images were definitely moving from one correspondent to another, with plenty of people coming into contact with them along the way.[14] There is also evidence of the use of postcards as simple notes passed between friends without sending them through the mail.[15]

Stamps in Argentina underwent a similar process. They were first printed in New York by the same American Bank Note Company, later in London, and then Buenos Aires. Their imagery gradually became more complex, too. Like the Correo Uruguayo, the Correo Argentino also sold pre-stamped envelopes and *fajas* (bands stamped or embossed with postage for the mailing of newspapers or other print media). The postage on these fajas often replicated stamp designs. In 1892 and 1896, fifteen million bands carried between them the Argentine coat of arms and a bust of Bernardino Rivadavia. If this figure seems high, consider that more than fifty-two million fajas with an embossed profile of Lady Liberty's head—drawing on the female imagery of republicanism—were sold to send "impresos" (print media such as newspapers and pamphlets) in 1902. Four years later, the independence military hero José de San Martín's bust was on another faja that had a print run of almost eighty-nine million.[16] Standard print runs for both bands and envelopes were commonly in the tens or hundreds of thousands, and they continued to increase as years went by. While not all of them were indeed used, they nevertheless point to the surge in available print media and their growing circulation networks.

There were also sheets of paper designed to double as their own envelopes, displaying one blank side and the other filled with advertisements when folded. Some of these letter-envelopes, as they were called, had simple, preprinted messages such as "Happy New Year" that correspondents could sign or add to. The same was true of postcards, some of which had ready-made notes. Another type of postcard had an image on one side and only lines on the reverse for the addressee. A series of this type from 1897, with a print run of thirty thousand, presented vistas of Argentine cities, buildings, landscapes, and markets. There were also cards from 1899 to 1902 that carried the lone silhouette of Lady Liberty. The publication quantities of these postcards ranged from the tens or hundreds of thousands to close to three million.[17]

On 20 January 1905, a young man named Alberto wrote to his family in Buenos Aires. He reacted to news of a family friend passing away, recounted the movement of cattle on the estancia where he worked in the province of Buenos Aires, and told his family he had gained weight and grown taller. Another writer with an illegible signature folded a prepaid sheet of paper dated 10 August 1907 and sent it to a Señor Flandrach, requesting that he "please come fix the doorbell that for days has not been working." Someone with the initials B. E. H. wrote a postcard to his or her grandmother in Buenos Aires to tell her that "the indigestion has passed." The candid note was next to a photograph of a statue of Belgrano.[18] From the town of Minas, east of Montevideo, a woman named Rosa wrote to her cousin on 23 April 1901 to tell her about her experience as a pilgrim to the new shrine of the Virgin of Verdún.[19] A father selected a postcard with an image of Montevideo's new Palacio Legislativo to send to his son on 18 July 1906, the anniversary of the signing of the constitution. He wrote, "At the age of 62 your father sends you warm greetings on this glorious day, and you'll receive them in your town of Florida, historic too."[20] And in December 1907, a woman living in Montevideo wrote to her sibling in Buenos Aires: "My dearest sister: I have received the postcard where you say that Ernesto Sans desires to come to Montevideo. If you see him again, you can tell him that it would give me great pleasure for his desired plan to become a reality."[21] These are just a handful of the stories abundantly recorded on postcards that relate the everyday experiences of residents in the Plata region.

Symbolic Power of New National Currencies

While citizens could choose whether or not to use the forms of communication the postal service offered and thus had some control over the symbolic images they encountered, the same could not be said of their interaction with new national currencies, specifically paper money. Paper money became a new form of exchange during the independence period in the region, and over the next several decades, private banks opened (and closed) their doors, emitting bank notes that were occasionally used. Paper slips called *vales* were also fairly common forms of payment (or at least a promise of payment) throughout the 1800s. But it was not until the last two decades of the nineteenth century that the national governments in either Uruguay or Argentina established a uniform monetary system. Through the privileging of a single state-backed currency in both countries in the mid-1880s and the creation of national banks—the Banco de la Nación in Argentina (1891) and the Banco de la República in Uruguay (1896)— money and the physical space it offered for visual communication became nationalized. The symbolic imagery of new national currencies, specifically on bank notes, spread rapidly through both republics with the required use of official tender.

The process by which this form of everyday print grew to become part of everyday life played out almost identically on both sides of the river. In Argentina, the Banco Nacional joined the fray of the private banks on its creation in 1872, and it would soon acquire a much more public role. In 1881, a national mint was formed, and a few years later legislation stipulated that bills of a certain value were to be circulated nationally by the Banco Nacional, effectively leading to an end to provincial currencies and to tender issued by other banks. Throughout this decade, the American Bank Note Company in New York—the friendly printer of postcards— published the bank notes emitted by the Banco Nacional as well as those of many provincial banks.[22] A financial meltdown forced the Banco Nacional to close, and the Argentine government created the Banco de la Nación in

1891.[23] The new bank was located in the first Colón Theater next to the cathedral, right in the heart of Buenos Aires, where thousands passed by its doors daily. It was the new financial headquarters of the nation, set in an imposing building.

There was a Banco Nacional in Uruguay, too. Established in 1887, it was one among many private banks and exchange outfits that produced loosely regulated bills, bonds, certificates of deposit, and *pagarés* (IOUs), all loaded with patriotic representations.[24] It had the semi-official charge of circulating currency nationwide, though the institution lasted only a few years after the economic storm hit Uruguay. In 1896, the state created the national Banco de la República, granting to it exclusive rights to issue coins and bills; all the paper money was printed in Buenos Aires, London, and Germany.

As with stamps and official postcards, paper money in the Plata from the 1890s on features visual content with explicit meanings, and the quantity of bills in circulation points to the contact people had with this new symbolic power. Sarmiento, Mitre, Urquiza, Nicolás Avellaneda, and an allegory of progress appeared on the faces of the first Argentine bills circulated nationally in the 1880s.[25] On the back of these notes, the images

Figure 5.10. The Banco Nacional's 1887 hundred-peso bill. On the left is a portrait of Fructuoso Rivera. In the center, angels surround the coat of arms. And in the lower right, two peasants watch a train steam through the countryside. In Banco Central del Uruguay, 260. (Courtesy of the Banco Central del Uruguay.)

included a Lady Liberty figure, a circle of young girls discussing a book, a steer's head, and (ironically opposite Sarmiento) a gaucho running wild through the countryside. These same images were printed on the Banco de la Nación's first series of notes in the 1890s, which were reissued into the 1930s. They were joined by portraits of other liberal statesmen and the ever-present coat of arms.[26]

The images on early Uruguayan bills ranged from the bland to the distinctly rural—assorted species of trees, animals such as ñandú and deer, and a man on horseback herding cattle—as well as the calmly patriotic, such as the indistinct bust representing the general idea of Lady Liberty.[27] In the 1870s and 1880s, the symbolism grew slightly stronger: a female soldier holding both a sword and the coat of arms decorates a bill from 1872.[28] The Banco Nacional's bills routinely featured coats of arms in tandem with engravings of the Palacio Estévez in Montevideo's Plaza Independencia and of figureheads of state, as well as the portrait of an old Artigas (the same rendition that appeared on the 1884 stamp), which in 1887 was cast against a dark background to show his visage all but radiating from the bill.[29]

A handful of these Banco Nacional notes provided motifs for the Banco de la República's new bills, which began to be printed in large quantities in 1896. A meager two hundred thousand copies of the first of these was produced in Buenos Aires that year, it being a temporary bill to be circulated only until the main order of ten million notes from Germany arrived.[30] On the front of the temporary bill, a young boy holds up the coat of arms; on the reverse, there is a country scene. The second through eighth bills emitted between 1896 and 1898 represent values from fifty cents to five hundred pesos. The imagery grew more complex and scaled a symbolic ladder corresponding to the face value of the notes. On the fifty-cent bill, for example, of which three million were issued, rural motifs appear on the front, and the coat of arms on the reverse. A female figure representing the republic is really the only distinct marker on the five million one-peso bills. One million ten-peso bills began circulating in 1898: the printer had received instructions to include the image of a gaucho, but lacking sufficient information, it ended up substituting a sailor, with another female allegorical representation of the patria on the reverse.[31] Fructuoso Rivera starred on the fifty-peso bill, and on the highest value bill, the elder Artigas presides over all. Another ten-peso bill was issued in 1899, with a youn-

Figure 5.11. The Banco de la República's 1896 ten-peso bill, with a sailor and Lady Liberty on the front, and Montevideo's port and the ubiquitous railroad on the reverse. In Rubens Bonino, Martín Valdez, and Villaamil, 11. (Courtesy of the Banco Central del Uruguay.)

ger woman representing the republic, and it was printed in London by the same company that had printed several Argentine stamps. These new national bills and their imagery defined the paper money landscape until 1914. Then another printer in London—the same company in charge of the early postage stamps in Uruguay—produced a series of bills in massive quantities, all bearing Blanes's interpretation of Artigas (the young, handsome one).[32]

There was simply no escape from the symbolic power of national currencies. The use of the same printers to generate both stamps and paper money helps explain some of the similarities—and, at times, the presence of identical images—that can be found among these media. While the de-

Figure 5.12. A luminescent Artigas decorates the Banco de la República's 1896 500-peso bill. In Rubens Bonino, Martín Valdez, and Villaamil, 17. (Courtesy of the Banco Central del Uruguay.)

cisions behind the explicit undercurrent of patriotism they communicated are hard to trace, they were easy enough to view, which was what mattered most, especially to those fingering the new bills or pasting stamps onto their correspondence. The growing popularity of such imagery and stories was likewise observable on the unofficial media that was also enjoying massive distribution at the turn of the century, such as cigarette boxes, matchboxes and the cards [*figuritas*] they contained.

The Excitement of the Ordinary

The connection of politics to print is easily visible in the world of tobacco products that became so lucrative at the turn of the century. What is surprising about this connection is the extent to which companies exploited patriotic symbols to market their products. Images were of course crucial in this regard, but so too were product names, as well as taglines, verses, and even the short prose printed on cigarette boxes and matchboxes or on material included inside them. This is what made such ordinary objects extraordinary.

Cigarette brand names were suggestive of the images used to promote them, some more creative than others. They included *El Gaucho Oriental* (a gaucho on horseback charging across the box like the one on the mast-

Figure 5.13. The not-so-subtle imagery appearing on Uruguayan cigarette boxes. (Collection of Marcos Silvera Antúnez, Montevideo, Uruguay. Used by permission.)

head of Hilario Ascasubi's 1843 newspaper), *La Democracia* (whose boxes portrayed republican women, flags, and coats of arms), *La Universal, La Rueda de la Fortuna* (The Wheel of Fortune), *La Industrial* (Industry, represented by a republican woman revealing one breast), *El Tiro Nacional* (The National Shot), *La Nacional, El Progreso* (Progress, symbolized by a train proudly rolling into a station somewhere in the Río de la Plata), *La Independencia*, and *La Honradez* (Honor; the box shows men drinking "honorably"). In Argentina, *El Paisano* featured a peasant on the top of the box; the back of the box listed the names of other brands manufactured by José León and Company, including *Unión, Ejército Argentino* (The Argentine Army), and *Guardias Nacionales* (National Guard). The logo for *Dos Americanos* (Two Americans), a brand with stores located in both Buenos Aires and Montevideo, depicted an indigenous figure holding a bow and arrow, peering out over the horizon; in the valley below, he sees a train roaring through.

A closer look at several brands reveals some of their powerful appeal to consumers and the sales tactics employed. One of these was the inclusion of certain prizes to help boost sales, such as maps, portraits of famous figures, and illustrations. *Tango* cigarettes offered chances to win musical instruments. Others followed the serial novel approach, releasing simple yet meaningful cards in installments. Such was the "Country Life" series of scenes, which included drawings of "a first kiss," "barbecuing," "an amorous encounter," and "a farewell." The verses on the back of these cards told "a country story." Consumers had to purchase another box of cigarettes to see what happened next.

A similar figurita series, albeit much larger in scale, was called "Dramas Criollos" and produced by the Argentine tobacco maker La Popular in the late 1880s. The name of this series should sound familiar, for it was a direct reference to the crowd-pleasing circus acts also labeled "dramas criollos." Like several of the most successful plays, the content of this series was based on Eduardo Gutiérrez's novels and José Hernández's *Martín Fierro*. Tapping into (as well as feeding) the nativist spirit at the turn of the century, the criollo dramas series consisted of colorful lithographs depicting certain scenes from these works. The cards were included in cigarette boxes and later sold or given separately as sets. Take, for example, the twenty-two cards representing *Juan Moreira*. Created with the assumption that consumers would know enough of the novel to fill in the blanks, the drawings covered highlights of the story, such as its fight scenes, moments of danger and sorrow, Moreira's acts of revenge, and of course the finale, in which Moreira is stabbed in the back while scaling a wall to escape police. All the images portray Moreira as a hero—which was only natural—and that added to the excitement of opening up a new pack to find the latest installment. Thirty-six figuritas related Gutiérrez's *Juan Cuello* and shared many of the same qualities. The *Fierro* cards combined excerpts from the poem with images to outline the plot and its moments of drama. One of the largest sets of figuritas was the story of Juan Manuel de Rosas according to Gutiérrez. It was told in two volumes, so to speak, the first of which had sixty cards, and the second one hundred and one. They featured the same characteristics as other criollo drama cards, though this time the portrayal of violence aimed to paint Rosas and his supporters in a negative light.

Figure 5.14. Scenes from *Juan Moreira* as told in the criollo dramas series of cards included in cigarette boxes. (Collection of Marcos Silvera Antúnez, Montevideo, Uruguay. Used by permission.)

Founded in 1874, La Popular also distributed cards based on Bartolomé Mitre's historical studies, as well as announcing that it was preparing to feature stories of independence and the colonial period that would go "all the way back to the discovery." Mitre's portrait was the most widely disseminated among the "famous figures" collection, so much that La Popular later could not calculate how many boxes had carried the historian and president's visage throughout the republic over the course of eighteen years. But the simple fact that around one hundred thousand boxes of cigarettes were produced on a daily basis for twenty-four days each month hints at the number of consumers who saw Mitre, Moreira, Martín Fierro, and others when they purchased La Popular cigarettes, and the regularity of this contact.[33]

Across the river, the French immigrant Julio Mailhos was making similar waves with his newly established tobacco factory La Republicana. It was no surprise that Mailhos selected the Phrygian cap as his iconic logo; what was so impressive about the enterprise was the variety and the long life spans of his tobacco brands, as well as the imagery used to market them. Among the dozens of these that were sold over multiple decades, a couple staple lines are worth mentioning here. First, several products employed countryside motifs: *El Pingo* (Trusty Horse) cigarettes were represented by a gaucho on his trusty horse, and the boxes containing *Los Gauchitos* displayed a gaucho closing a deal with a well-dressed urban type, among other images. These two brands went on sale beginning in 1898. *Criollos* cigarettes, whose boxes evolved and contained many scenes, were sold from 1896 through the 1930s. *La Paz* first appeared in 1897, the brand a harbinger of a spirit of brotherhood after civil war; it was on the market throughout the twentieth century. The countryside could be consumed as well in the form of tobacco brands named after animals such as *El Venado* (The Deer) and *El Ñandú* (The Rhea). Mailhos appealed to collective moral codes, too, with brand names such as *El Progreso*, *La Constancia* (Determination), and *El Porvenir* (Horizon).[34] Just like La Popular, La Republicana was a veritable printing center, with presses at the factory that produced its box labels.

Given the widespread consumption of tobacco in the Río de la Plata, as well as in every other part of Latin America, Mailhos and his fellow makers clearly saw the imagery and the names of their products as more than successful marketing ploys: they helped create customer bases speaking about peace, progress, and the national traditions illustrated on the boxes, and in this way were also effective means to instill such beliefs.[35] The changing political culture at the dawn of the twentieth century (with tensions building between recently arrived immigrants and more established communities of citizens) and the increasingly prevalent myth of the gaucho also played a role in the popularity of criollo brands. After all, the criollo spirit was all about celebrating what was considered authentically "from the land," as opposed to what came from "outside"—hence the presence of gauchos and references to rural tradition. But Mailhos was not one to miss out on a business opportunity, in this case of appealing to the newcomers: he manufactured cigarettes with Italian brand names and references to Spain, too.

A range of other strategies helped make these objects of daily consumption special. The increasingly popular magazine *Caras y Caretas* marketed its own *Caras y Caretas* cigarettes. Playing off the success of the brand, advertisements often adopted the voice of the magazine editors to note that "we have never tasted cigarettes this good, and don't think we're saying this just because the product carries our name."[36]

Many vendors deployed explicit patriotic imagery (as if gaucho themes and portraits of national heroes were not enough) to tug at customer senti-

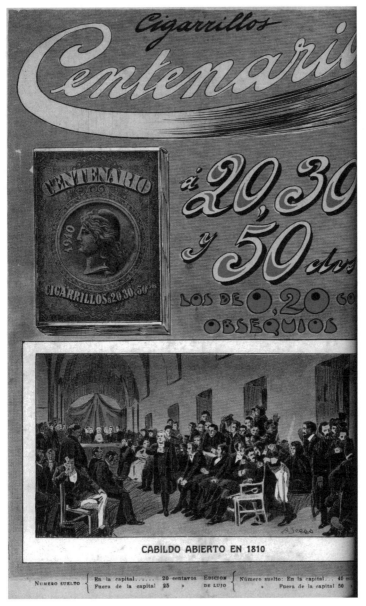

Figure 5.15. One of the many creative ads for *Cigarrillos Centenario*. In this instance, participants in the 1810 *cabildo abierto* (town hall gathering) discuss the idea of forming a junta to take the place of the Spanish viceroy. Those who smoke *Centenario* cigarettes can experience this collective patriotic sentiment. *Caras y Caretas*, 2 April 1910.

ments of loyalty. On a poster advertising *La Argentina* smokes, two lions pull Lady Liberty through a crowd of well-dressed men in suits, women, and gauchos. Curiously, one of Lady Liberty's breasts is bared, which apparently was necessary for her task of throwing sample cigarettes out to the joyful onlookers. The Compañía General de Fósforos was one of the region's largest producers of matches, responsible for brands such as *La Paz*, *Victoria*, and one that simply paired the company name with humorous scenes on the tops of its boxes. *La Paz* matches capitalized on the relief felt at the end of Uruguay's civil wars, as was the case with *La Paz* cigarettes. Some of this brand's boxes show two hands clasping in the spirit of brotherhood. Both La Republicana and another maker sold *Patria* cigarettes in Uruguay, while smokers of *Por la Patria* saw a particularly touching tableau of a soldier bidding farewell to two tearful women while a compatriot awaits him. Argentine smokers of *Ideales* and *Patria* cigarettes found in the boxes slips they could exchange for a two-peso coin or a book from a list that included Mitre's history of San Martín and Samuel Smiles's self-help books.[37] In the advertisement for this deal, the maker claimed that "amenable, relaxing, and instructive literature is what we offer our smokers to cultivate good literary tastes."[38] And around 1910, in Argentina, *Cigarrillos Centenario* appeared in honor of the centennial celebration of independence with creative advertisements illustrating historical scenes related to May 1810 and the lead-up to the wars.

Of course, cigarettes, matches, and other tobacco-related paraphernalia are just a sample of the everyday objects in which the proliferation of print at the turn of the century is evident. Advertising in print exploded during the last decade of the 1800s for all sorts of products, from shirt collars to healing creams to a portlike wine called El Abuelo (Grandfather) promoted in 1910—drink it and you, too, will live to be a hundred, just like the patria.

Such ads were part of the larger expansion of the region's printing industry, which turned out reading material like never before during these years, as should be evident by now. Along with increases in the number of active printing presses and newspapers, the number of bookstores and libraries (and their clients and patrons) rose, as did the number of places where print media could easily be found, which by now included train stations, corner stalls, and the neighborhood barbershop.[39] Multiple book series were created to provide affordable titles to people who did not usu-

Figure 5.16. An ad for a portlike wine: "Celebrate the Argentine centenary with this delicious wine, and always drink El Abuelo if you want to celebrate your own centenary." *Caras y Caretas*, 25 May 1910.

ally read books. Many of these, such as the *Biblioteca Popular de Buenos Aires* in the early 1880s, were ended soon after they started because of poor sales. Yet others turned out to be commercially viable, such as *Biblioteca La Nación*, which lasted close to twenty years.

One of the best indicators of the growing reach of the publishing industry was popular literature, especially after 1900. There was, of course, criollista writing in Argentina and Uruguay, which Adolfo Prieto and Hugo Achugar have so effectively studied.[40] This literature made characters such as Juan Moreira and Juan Cuello mythic figures all across the region. When their stories became material for dramas at circus performances or shows in theaters, essentially jumping from one medium to another, there was no stopping their spread. This explains why we found them in cigarette boxes as marketing tools. Not everyone liked such texts, however. Miguel Navarro Viola, the man of letters who founded the not-so-popular *Biblioteca Popular de Buenos Aires*, regularly disparaged Gutiérrez's novels. And in 1905, Emilio Becher wrote to a friend regarding the publication of a recent novel that "in Argentina only a work of mediocrity can please five thousand people."[41] Their stance, however, was clearly becoming one shared by a minority of readers.

And then there was the new genre of the inexpensive illustrated magazine, which became a commercial and cultural phenomenon. Though an in-depth study of this medium (along with the exploding market for newspapers) would require another, separate book, a few points can be made here to illustrate its impact. Beginning in the 1890s, magazines emerged that featured colorful and often humorous covers dealing with current events, captivating readers on a weekly, biweekly, or monthly basis. They offered entertainment, tidbits of information, and often biting social critique. In Montevideo, *El Amigo del Obrero* (The worker's friend) was one of these, and its press (like those publishing other magazines) also issued an annual almanac. In 1900, four thousand copies of the almanac were sold; by 1910, the number had grown to fifteen thousand, each of which sold for less than a pack of cigarettes.[42] *Rojo y Blanco* (Red and white) and *El Fogón* were two other popular magazines in Uruguay, and their readerships were much larger than that of *El Amigo del Obrero*.[43]

The most successful of these publications was *Caras y Caretas*, which got its start in Montevideo in 1890 and moved to Buenos Aires in 1898. An icon of Rioplatense popular culture, it served theater reviews, jokes, stories, poems, histories, and advertisements to its readers every week. On holidays such as 25 May or 25 August, its covers, like those of other illustrated magazines, featured patriotic imagery. Such issues were chock full of advertisements that either riffed on the spirit of patriotism to sell the products in question or functioned as public service announcements of sorts, such as a full-page color spread devoted to Argentine stamps.[44] And they sold extremely well, the price of each copy about equal to the cost of a pack of cigarettes. The average print run jumped from close to 81,000 copies per issue in 1904 to almost 110,000 in 1910.[45] For the 1910 centenary celebration, more than two hundred thousand copies of the special 25 May edition of *Caras y Caretas* were published and distributed in Buenos Aires and the interior, as well as across the river in Uruguay.[46] Such a print run was by that point nothing short of a mark of pride.

■

I have outlined here some of the most significant forms of everyday print media that were distributed in massive quantities and circulated on a large scale from 1880 to 1910. There were many others that I have not named that likewise grew to become a part of daily life during these years (such as the era's newspapers) and that would help shape Rioplatense print culture in the following decades. That said, by 1910, the uniqueness of the region's print culture and the ways in which people interacted with it were set. Print had become ordinary. But just like the slapjack cards given to me by the young readers in Salto, the printed materials of the early 1900s were no less powerful, meaningful, or valuable for being everyday reading.

We can trace the story of this power, meaning, and value back to the three moments in the development of print culture in the Río de la Plata from 1780 to 1910: the revolutionary moment, the high point of cattle culture, and the establishment and expansion of national public primary schools. During the revolutionary moment, the region's first printing presses drove the first printing revolution, which went hand in hand with the wars of independence. Following the May Revolution of 1810, revolutionary newspapers, public ceremonies, and symbolic repertoires fashioned the first attempts at patriotic poetry and the elaboration of national symbols for new republics. The first public libraries in the region created new public meeting spaces that not only brought the worlds of orality and print together, but also allowed citizens—both literate and not—much greater access to print.

The second scene in our story encompasses the period from the moment Juan Manuel de Rosas became governor of Buenos Aires, in 1829, up to the 1870s, when fragile state institutions began to consolidate themselves. These were years of civil war that saw a war of words between supporters of a colonial-style social order and its liberal opponents. The phenomenon of gauchesque writing in newspapers, pamphlets, and loose leaves—a form of literature not seen on a similar scale elsewhere in Latin America—drove the popularization of print. Gauchesque writing served to instill political identity and politicize the non-elite classes, and toward the end of the period it became a vehicle for expressing growing social concern about the transformations modernization was bringing.

The last defining moment in the development of Rioplatense print culture is that of the establishment of public primary schools across Uruguay and Argentina. In the last quarter of the century, sowers of alphabets not only built the foundation for Latin America's most successful public education systems but also participated in the region's second printing revolution, in the form of textbooks that taught lessons for a nation. Public primary education changed the relationship between the state, its citizens, and print media. It did this by increasing dramatically the contact between print and students (and their families), and by giving the state the authority to determine the content of textbooks and distribute these throughout both Uruguay and Argentina to captive audiences. The results were abundantly clear: literacy rates in Uruguay and Argentina became the highest in Latin America, a new reading public was formed, and children as well as adults appropriated official discourses of national and gender identities. The success of public education in the region was nothing short of a cultural revolution.

By 1910, then, print culture had reshaped forms of communication in Uruguay and Argentina. With national currencies entering circulation in the 1880s, patriotic symbols and scenes decorating cigarette boxes and matchboxes, criollo dramas retold in sets of figuritas, and the newfangled way of contacting friends and family through postcards, print media had become a part of daily life for all Uruguayans and Argentines—even illiterate ones.

As we have seen in each chapter, the story of everyday reading often deals with forms of print media that at first are extremely novel or extraordinary (the revolutionary newspaper, the loose-leaf gauchesque diatribe, the textbook on home economics, the paper money with new visual images of the nation) but soon become the stuff of daily life. The most powerful forms of reading materials, at least when it comes to influencing collective identities and instilling affection for a political party or the national community, are those that can be integrated with established patterns of sociability or those that usher in new ways to communicate. Over the course of the nineteenth century, the quantity of reading materials that opened new spaces for widespread association increased exponentially. Though it is not possible to establish firm cutoff periods for the jumps in production of everyday reading, the periods I have established for understanding the development of Rioplatense print culture (1780–1830; 1830–1870; 1870–1910) serve well to demarcate the different moments when the amount and types of everyday reading materials increased substantially.

Just as everyday reading materials changed throughout the century, so too did reading practices and the composition of reading communities and readerships. What I hope this book has made obvious is that the biggest transformation in reading and reading practices from the early 1800s to the early 1900s was the gradual progression from collective, group reading to individual silent reading on a large scale. Group reading was hands down the most frequently exercised reading practice up through the 1870s. Whether it was performed at churches or in town squares during the revolutionary moment, at bars and pulperías at midcentury, or around the family dining table, group reading was essential to imparting information, entertaining, communicating party values, and sharing lessons learned at school with the wider family. By 1900, a much higher percentage of the Uruguayan and Argentine populations was literate, with many more participants in silent, individual reading. As readerships grew and transformed toward the end of the century, new image-based reading practices and forms of communication gained a foothold through materials such as postcards, stamps, and national currencies. However, the collective experience of enjoying reading in groups did not come to an end at the turn of the twentieth century. Educators continued urging children to read with their siblings and parents to read with their children, and cafés remained popular as places to read with other people.

In many ways, the evolution of readerships and reading practices paralleled developments in modes of association. Chapter 3 detailed the rise in literacy rates as one index for measuring the growth in readership. The "sites of everyday reading" multiplied as the years passed, a fact that also sheds light on the increase in numbers of readers (those who listened and those who could in fact read on their own). The category of places such as churches and pulperías now included classrooms and the home, as well as the venues that hosted events such as awards ceremonies and *fiestas de promoción* (parties celebrating the promotion of students to the next grade level). All these sites orchestrated meetings of orality and print, and all were places where group identities were formed or grew stronger thanks to reading. Moreover, reading at these places became a central activity that *brought people together.*

Our study of everyday reading in the Río de la Plata has also examined the changes to the role of reading and writing in society. During the wars of independence, writing was a limited social practice that was quickly transformed into a new weapon. Reading was open to much larger groups by virtue of collective reading. During the years of cattle culture's apogee, writing remained a political weapon, wielded in the slogans and popular poetry that damned one's enemy. Yet its power to persuade became much more fully developed. At the end of this period, we witnessed writers shifting their attention to aesthetic goals and social situations that no longer hinged on partisan politics. This shift in focus led to calls for good citizens to become literate ones, and for hardworking citizens to become educated ones. During the last third of the century, educators, bureaucrats, and politicians intertwined the social role of writing and reading with the making of a patriotic citizenry. In doing so through the public primary school system, they were so effective that reading and writing as common social activities became essential to what it meant to be Uruguayan or Argentine, and the public concern with print culture likewise became key to Rioplatense identity.

How people interacted with print culture throughout the era this book covers depended on the increasing power of everyday reading to be just that—material they came into contact with on a regular basis. Bernardo Monteagudo understood this principle long before it was a reality when he encouraged fellow patriots to read aloud newspapers promoting republicanism. Joaquín Fretes helped bear out its beginnings when he read excerpts from the *Gaceta de Buenos Aires* to slaves and freedmen in

Mendoza in 1812. Luis Pérez's popular papers exemplify daily reading in the 1830s. They created a new reading public and became the most widely read materials of the decade largely by dealing with daily affairs. A frustrated Florencio Varela wanted his liberal friends to appeal to people from the countryside by creating texts that those people could relate with more easily—that is, ones they could laugh *with* while cooking dinner or sitting around a campfire. At the end of the century, generations of students—both children and adults—studied their lessons in the new world of textbooks. Raudelinda Pereda wrote in her notebooks regularly, at times about patriotic heroes and at times about her own behavior as a young woman, in doing so documenting how public schools were achieving the goals their architects had set. And the quantity of bills circulating as the sole form of exchange once national banks were founded signal that no citizen could have escaped the symbols passing from hand to hand in daily transactions.

Such sources are but glimpses of the vast spectrum of connected print media during the nineteenth century. They show the need for the study of print culture both to encompass texts that often go beyond the written or printed word, and to focus on more inclusive meanings of reading. The development of print culture in the Río de la Plata throughout the long nineteenth century was a regional process that resulted in the formation of a unique relationship between print, politics, and the public sphere in the larger context of Latin America. That reading was such a pervasive, common, and even mundane activity by 1910 among Uruguayans and Argentines bears out this point. The stories we have followed—from that of poetry filling main squares to those of children commenting on their patriotic sentiments, up to the figuritas of the third graders at La Amarilla—demonstrate clearly the extraordinary impact of ordinary reading on the lives of citizens young and old, and male and female, from the countryside to the port capitals.

Abbreviations

AAL	Academia Argentina de Letras, Buenos Aires
AGN Ar	Archivo General de la Nación, Buenos Aires
AGN Ur	Archivo General de la Nación, Montevideo
BN Ar	Biblioteca Nacional de la República Argentina, Buenos Aires
BNM	Biblioteca Nacional de Maestros, Buenos Aires
BN Ur	Biblioteca Nacional, Montevideo
BPC	Biblioteca Pedagógica Central, Montevideo
EFCH	Estudio Filatélico de Carlos Hernández Rocha, Montevideo
HA	Colección Horacio Arredondo, Biblioteca de la Facultad de Humanidades y Ciencias de la Educación, Universidad de la República, Montevideo
MHN	Museo Histórico Nacional, Montevideo
MPJPV	Museo Pedagógico José Pedro Varela, Montevideo
UNC	University of North Carolina at Chapel Hill

Notes

Introduction

All translations in this book are my own unless noted otherwise.

1. Eizaguirre, 17; emphasis in the original.

2. Ibid., 14.

3. In addition to being the name of one of the largest estuaries in the world, the term *Río de la Plata* has several significant meanings. During the late colonial era, it served as part of the title of the last royal administrative unit in Spanish America—the Viceroyalty of the Río de la Plata, created in 1776. With its center in Buenos Aires, the viceroyalty encompassed a stretch of territory that included what are today Argentina, Bolivia, Paraguay, and Uruguay. Following the wars of independence, Bolivia, Paraguay, and Uruguay split off from the land that would become Argentina, though Uruguay would maintain close political and cultural connections to its neighbor across the river. When not speaking about the river, scholars today use *Río de la Plata* to refer to the region that includes Argentina and Uruguay in general, and more specifically to refer to the coastal areas and cities on both sides of the Plata River. I will be using *Rioplatense*, *Río de la Plata*, and *Plata* (the abbreviated form of the term) in this way, in part to stress how print culture developed along the same lines in both Uruguay and Argentina, and in part to draw attention to the regional unity of concerns, questions, cultural meanings that are often deemed merely "national."

4. In the 2007 United Nations Human Development Reports on literacy rates for ages fifteen and older, Uruguay was ranked slightly ahead of Argentina. Cuba, which had been ranked third in literacy among Latin American countries in 2003, moved up to first. See *hdrstats.undp.org/en/indicators/89.html*. For measures of literacy in the Río de la Plata during the late nineteenth and early twentieth centuries, see Chapter 3.

5. De la Fuente, *Children of Facundo*; Scobie, *Argentina*, 88–111; Halperín Donghi, *Politics, Economics, and Society*. For a recent account of the development of the state in Argentina, see Halperín Donghi, "Argentine Counterpoint." On state formation in Uruguay, see Barrán, *Apogeo y crisis*; Frega, "La virtud y el poder"; and Chasteen, *Heroes on Horseback*, 43–59.

6. Anyone familiar with the demographics of Buenos Aires and Montevideo is aware of the fact that they are notably different from the rest of Latin America due to the mas-

sive waves of immigration to the Río de la Plata from the 1850s up to the First World War. By the outset of the war in 1914, the portion of immigrants in Argentina's total population had risen to 30 percent, more than the proportion of the population im-migrants accounted for in the United States during the same years. Around the cen-tenary celebration of independence in 1910, more than half the population in Buenos Aires Province consisted of immigrants or children born to immigrant parents. The numbers from Uruguay indicate a similar history. Half the residents of Montevideo during the Guerra Grande (1839–1851) were foreigners. In contrast to Argentina, im-migration to Uruguay occurred on a smaller scale, and with the important difference being that immigration to the country declined after 1900, dropping to slightly over 17 percent of the population in the 1908 census. See Arteaga and Puiggrós, 268–69, 371. Explanations for this shift include the fact that Argentina's phenomenal agricultural success promised more attractive work opportunities to immigrants after the turn of the century, making Argentina a more popular destination than Uruguay, as well as the idea that Uruguay was "saturated" and could no longer absorb newcomers. See ibid., 269.

7. Scott, xv–xvii; Scott and Kerkvliet; Joseph and Nugent.

8. On sociability in nineteenth-century Argentina, see González Bernaldo de Quirós.

9. For a more in-depth definition of popular literature in the region, see Acree, "Luis Pérez."

10. Johnson and Socolow; Arredondo.

11. The May Revolution refers to 25 May 1810, when a local junta declared self-rule in the name of the deposed Spanish king, Fernando VII. It was a rhetorical and political move carried out first in print and later on the battlefield. Since that day in 1810, 25 May has been celebrated in both Uruguay and Argentina as a milestone in the fight for independence and as a key feature of regional political identity.

12. See, for example, Blossom; Renan Silva; Nariño; Palacio Montiel; Conway; and Kaempfer. On the subject of journalism in Spanish America, see chapters 1–4 in González.

13. Cattle culture (or "cattle civilization," as James Scobie terms it) refers to the power structures and social relations that developed around an economy based on the sale and export of cattle products—hides, fats, and dried meat—that grew during the late eighteenth century and the first half of the nineteenth century. This economy domi-nated the Río de la Plata up to the 1850s and struck fear into lettered liberal elites for its preservation of practices and characteristics of the colonial era. See Scobie, *Argentina*, 64–87.

14. See Andrews, *Afro-Argentines*; Andrews, *Blackness*; Lewis; Solomianski; and Coll.

15. Wilson, 295–318.

16. Vaughan.

17. Loreto Egaña, Núñez Prieto, and Salinas Alvarez, 15–17, 61–68; Núñez.

18. Newland, "La educación elemental."

19. For recent assessments of Anderson's arguments regarding Latin America, see Chas-teen, Introduction; and Lomnitz.

20. Sommer; Shumway; Alonso; Jaksić; Unzueta, 144–55; Achugar, *La fundación*; Achugar, *Derechos*; Caetano; Eujanián; Rivera; Sagastizábal, *Diseñar una nación*; Diego; Prieto, *El discurso criollista*.

Chapter 1

1. A previous version of this chapter was published in Acree and González Espitia, 32–58.
2. Mitre, 200; Torre Revello, 214; Canter, *La imprenta*, 38–39.
3. Archivo Histórico de la Provincia de Buenos Aires, 1–4.
4. Ibid., 5–6; Mitre, 201, 208.
5. Canter, *La imprenta*, 43.
6. Furlong, 14; Newland, "La educación elemental," 341. See also examples in Heras, xxi–xxiii; and Juan María Gutiérrez, 388–93.
7. Solá, 42–45; Canter, *La imprenta*, 67–68. In *La edición*, Sagastizábal suggests that the melted lead formed the bullets used to pursue the *montoneras* (mounted peasants who formed impromptu armies) headed by the mythic Facundo Quiroga (29), but with Quiroga acting in the early 1830s, this claim does not fit well with the press's fifty years of production in Salta.
8. Solá, 44.
9. Two of the best examples from the late 1700s and early 1800s are Jacinto Ventura de Molina and the Cuban Juan Francisco Manzano. See Acree and Borucki; Acree, "Jacinto Ventura de Molina"; and Manzano.
10. For examples of scholarship focusing on other areas, see Guerra, "Forms of Communication." A look at writing in the public sphere in early 1800s Mexico, it is one of the most successful views into how print began reshaping forms of communication. See also Guerra, *Modernidad e independencias*. In "The Role of Print," Rebecca Earle examines newspaper production in Mexico, New Granada, Chile, and Peru, though like Guerra she is most concerned with political culture. Other recent considerations can be found in Alonso.
11. De María, *Montevideo antiguo*, 2:61; emphasis in the original.
12. Ibid., 61–62. *The Southern Star / La Estrella del Sur*, facsimile ed.
13. Canter, Introduction to *Gazeta de Montevideo*, xxxix, xlix.
14. *Gazeta de Montevideo*, l. See also Acree, "La otra batalla."
15. BN Ar, Tesoro: *Bando de la Real Audiencia de Buenos-Ayres*, 12 June 1807.
16. Ibid.
17. Canter, Introduction to *Gazeta de Montevideo*, lvi. The name *Banda Oriental* refers to the "eastern shore"—that is, the territory located east of the Uruguay River. Inhabitants of the Banda Oriental identified themselves as "Orientales." After the declaration of Uruguayan independence in 1825, citizens and officials gradually began employing the terms "Uruguay" and "Uruguayan." While today "Orientales" and "Uruguayans" are used synonymously to speak of citizenship and identity, for over a century they expressed competing views of Uruguayan history, specifically the role of the territory during the revolutionary moment and independence leader José Artigas's place in official history. For more on the debates surrounding these terms, see Frega, "Uruguayos y orientales," and Prado, 194–245.
18. See Zinny, *Efemeridografía argirometropolitana*.
19. Examples can be found in Furlong, 141–43, 216–17, 228–30.
20. Ibid., 240–44, 321–25.
21. Binayán, 137.
22. *Gaceta de Buenos Aires*, 71.

23. On the changing meaning of the term *Americanos* and its inclusiveness during independence, see Chasteen, *Americanos*.

24. Bragoni, 121.

25. Ibid., 118. Dated 9 April 1812, the junta's decree prohibiting slave ships from docking in the region also granted freedom to slaves introduced to the area after the law was passed.

26. Ibid., 120–21. The conspiracy to rebel was ultimately discovered and its conspirators imprisoned. A local tribunal studied the case and granted the leaders and their followers their freedom so that they could enroll in patriot troops.

27. *Gazeta de Montevideo*, 3 (8 October 1810).

28. Ibid., 7–8.

29. Ibid., 3.

30. Ibid., 4.

31. Ibid., 42.

32. Ibid., 42–45.

33. González Demuro, "*El Sol*"; González Demuro, "Un gallego"; Praderio, 3–40.

34. *El Grito del Sud*, 45.

35. Ibid., 47. The 27 October 1812 issue (173–80) directly addresses what was printed in "esos insulsos papelorios"—that is, in the *Gazeta de Montevideo* (173).

36. Ibid., 48–50.

37. Taken from the first book of Tacitus's *Histories*, the epigraph reads, "It is at rare moments of good fortune when one can think how one wants and say what one thinks," an appropriate choice of words for the moment of independence.

38. De Gandía, preliminary study to *El Grito del Sud*, 16.

39. *El Grito del Sud*, 63–68.

40. Ibid., 255.

41. *El Independiente*, 33.

42. Ibid., 33–36.

43. Ibid., 41.

44. De Gandía, preliminary study to *Los Amigos de la Patria*, 19.

45. Rómulo Fernández, 219–26.

46. Joyce, 100.

47. Ibid., 129–30.

48. See Seco; and Levene, *El fundador*.

49. Levene, *El fundador*, 34.

50. Ibid., 34, 64.

51. Ibid., 115–16.

52. Ibid., 61, 114; Beruti, 210.

53. *Gaceta de Buenos Aires*, 3:146.

54. *El Censor*, 92.

55. Blanchard.

56. *El Redactor*, 30, 35–36. See also Wilde, 196–97.

57. *Descripción de las fiestas*.

58. Ibid., 6–7.

59. Ibid., 7.

60. Ibid., 9–11, 13–14.

61. Ibid., 29–30.

62. See Acree and Borucki; Gortázar; Andrews, *Blackness*; Lewis; and Abella, 49–103.
63. See Pérez Rojo de Aldana.
64. *Descripción de las fiestas*, 66–69 (letters from Artigas to Dámaso Antonio Larrañaga and from Artigas to the Cabildo de Montevideo).
65. Paladino, 126, 135.
66. Hidalgo, *Obra completa* (Praderio), 144.
67. Wilde, 212.
68. Ibid., 179.
69. Burucúa and Campagne.
70. Achugar, "Parnasos fundacionales," 43.
71. Ibid., 50.
72. Ibid., 54.
73. Quoted in Barcia, xii–xiii.
74. Ibid., xiii.
75. *La lira*, 7–8.
76. Barcia, xxi.
77. Poch, "Himnos nacionales"; Wilde (195–96) described the debut of the "Marcha" at the 1813 fiestas mayas.
78. BN Ar, Tesoro.
79. Poch, "Himnos nacionales," 99.
80. Zeballos, 10. See also Binayán, 228; Cánepa, 129–54.
81. On symbols from the French Revolution and their influence in the region, see Burucúa, Jáuregui, Malosetti, and Munilla.
82. Burucúa and Campagne, 438.
83. Zeballos, 13; emphasis in the original.
84. Beruti, 231.
85. Ibid., 232.
86. Ibid., 234–35.
87. See the *Gaceta de Buenos Aires*, 4:409 and after.
88. De María, *Montevideo antiguo*, 1:121–22.
89. *Descripción de las fiestas*, 17.
90. See Andrés Lamas, 56–58; Goldaracena, 69–94; and AGN Ur, Archivos Particulares, caja 333, carpeta 1: "Escudo de armas de la República Oriental del Uruguay, ley de su creación."
91. Malagón, xv.
92. Poch, "Aura de inicio," 77.
93. Malagón, viii.
94. Ibid., 131.
95. De María, *Montevideo antiguo*, 2:342–44.
96. Ibid., 344–45.
97. Ibid., 345.
98. AGN Ur, Ex Archivo General Administrativo, Ministerio de Gobierno, caja 890. According to an 1836 inventory for the Hospital de la Caridad, home to one of the city's main presses, there were 530 "left over" copies of the constitution and sixty of the declaration of independence. My thanks to Alex Borucki for sharing this source.
99. De María, *Montevideo antiguo*, 2:347–51.

Chapter 2

1. See Chapter 1, note 13 for a definition of cattle culture. For an overview of the rise of cattle culture in the Plata and its structures, see Scobie, *Argentina*, 64–87; Slatta, *Gauchos*; Duncan Barretta and Markoff, 590–93; Lynch, *Argentine Caudillo*, 7–8, 136–38; Chasteen, "Violence for Show," 47–64; and Chasteen, *Heroes on Horseback*.

2. Vestiges of these party divisions are still present today in the region. In Uruguay, the Colorado and Blanco Parties are two of the three principal political forces and they adhere to the same image of tradition versus liberal progress.

3. De Ugarteche, 320.

4. Rosas, 38–40.

5. AGN Ur, Archivos Particulares, caja 320.

6. Wilde, 231–35. See also Garavaglia; and Gelman.

7. AGN Ur, Ex Archivo y Museo Histórico Nacional, libro 376. See also Ex Archivo General Administrativo, caja 351, carpeta 6: "Imprenta de Montevideo."

8. Lynch, *Argentine Caudillo*, 50.

9. BN Ar, Sala del Tesoro: *El Gaucho*, 31 July 1830 (no. 1: 1–2). See also Rodríguez Molas, *Luis Pérez*.

10. Lynch, *Argentine Caudillo*, 42.

11. See Weinberg, *Juan Gualberto Godoy*, for a facsimile reproduction of Godoy's *El Corazero*; Schvartzman, *Microcrítica*, 117–33; and Lucero.

12. For a close biographical portrait of Pérez and a broad study of his papers, see Acree, "Luis Pérez."

13. Rodríguez Molas, *Luis Pérez*, 6.

14. Soler Cañas, 10.

15. Ayestarán, 25–28; Acree, "Luis Pérez."

16. Soler Cañas, 54–57.

17. Schvartzman, "A quién cornea *El Torito*," 14–15. On the connections between cielito, pericón, and media caña (similar song and dance forms), dance, and their political force, see Chasteen, *National Rhythms*, 149–54. The widespread readership of popular (Federalist) verse was reinforced, if not guaranteed, by their ties to popular dance forms. As Chasteen puts it, "Because everyone knew cielito melodies, topical cielito lyrics could easily be transmitted, remembered, and launched at their targets like musical missiles" (150).

18. Rama, *Los gauchipolíticos rioplatenses*, 1:61–63.

19. BN Ar, Tesoro: *El Gaucho*, July 1830 (Prospejo: 2).

20. BN Ar, Tesoro: *El Gaucho*, 7 August 1830 (no. 3: 3).

21. See, for example, *La Negrita*, 21 July 1833 (no. 1: 1–2); *El Negrito*, July 1833 (nos. 1–4 and 6); *La Gaucha*, broadsheet circa May 1830; *La Gaucha*, December 1830 (nos. 15–22); and a series of broadsheet letters Pérez created with the characters Ticucha and Cunino. All these are archived at BN Ar, Tesoro.

22. BN Ar, Tesoro: *El Gaucho*, 25 August 1830 (no. 8: 4). The original Spanish reads: "El es ... negro felelá / Y agradecido a la Patria / Que le dió la libetá. / Esi negro cara noche / Sueña con don JUA MANUE; / y luego de mañanita / Otra vesi hablando del." See Becco.

23. Celesia (1954), 413–14.

24. Celesia (1969), 1:264–66; 2:481.

25. BN Ar, Tesoro: *El Gaucho* (no. 20: 3).

26. Pérez's plight is recorded in the pages of *El Clasificador ó El Nuevo Tribuno*, 11 January–3 March 1831 (nos. 78, 79, 80, 82, 83, 84, and 99). Archived at AAL.

27. See de Ugarteche, 322–24, for the articles of the decree (published in the *Registro Oficial*) and for details on the consequences of transgressing the points Rosas laid out.

28. Quoted in ibid., 328.

29. These were *Boletín del Comercio, Diario de Anuncios y Publicaciones Oficiales de Buenos Aires, Museo Americano*, and *El Recopilador*.

30. Leguizamón, *Papeles de Rosas*, 26–27; Chávez, 14–18; Trostiné, *Bacle*.

31. The original Spanish reads, "¡Viva la Confederación Argentina! ¡Viva Nuestro Ilustre Restaurador de las Leyes! ¡Mueran los Salvajes, Asquerosos Unitarios!"

32. The original Spanish reads, "¡Oribe, Leyes o Muerte! ¡Mueran los salvajes Unitarios!"

33. Lynch, *Argentine Caudillo*, 83.

34. Ibid., 84.

35. Leguizamón, *Papeles de Rosas*, 33.

36. Wilde, 205–9.

37. Ingenieros, 136.

38. AGN Ur, Archivos Particulares, caja 320, carpetas 2 and 3.

39. On dress and the use of divisas during the Rosas years, see West, 14–38.

40. Quoted in Wilde, 210–11.

41. Myers, *Orden y virtud*, 82. In addition to personal adornments, other materials such as paintings, flags and banners from black "naciones" and other Federalist supporters, and knife cases conveyed political messages. For more on these, see Pradere; and the items for sale in the *Catálogo descriptivo*.

42. Librería Linardi y Risso (Montevideo), private collection.

43. Librería Linardi y Risso, private collection: Oribe to subordinates, 5 December 1846; AGN Ur, Archivos Particulares, caja 320, carpetas 2 and 3.

44. Fructuoso Rivera was a Colorado leader who had been president of Uruguay for a short time (1830–1834). AGN Ur, Archivos Particulares, caja 328, carpeta 4; caja 6, carpeta 5: 20 August 1848.

45. AGN Ur, Ex Archivo y Museo Histórico Nacional, caja 206, carpetas 10 and 11.

46. Blomberg, 45.

47. Ibid., 71.

48. Ibid., 78, 87–88.

49. Ayestarán, 223–25. For other examples of anonymously authored pieces in Uruguay, see 219–40.

50. Blomberg, 89.

51. For a particularly forceful example, see *El Oriental en Campaña*, 11 May 1839: 1.

52. For examples of such use of these terms, see Blomberg, 90, 93, 96, 98, 100.

53. Andrews, *Afro-Argentines*.

54. Trostiné, *Cancionero*, 35–38.

55. These included *El Guerrillero de la Línea, El Telégrafo de la Línea*, and *El Artillero de la Línea*.

56. *El Tambor de la Línea*, 1843 (no. 2: 3). The original reads, "Le encargo que no pierda los calzones, el dia que se lo dirija, pues tengo un niño de dos años que . . . dice. . . Puf . . . tata . . . ese tene caca."

57. *Rasgos*, 211–14.

58. Ibid., 221–22.

59. There are no page numbers in the book. Perhaps the idea was for readers to read Rosas's story in one fell swoop, without becoming distracted by page numbers.

60. A handful of older works study the newspaper press in the Plata. For a narrative account, see Fernández, *Historia*, 57–95. A more detailed look at different papers can be found in Beltrán, 161–255. Weinberg's *Florencio Varela y "El Comercio del Plata"* is a more detailed study of a paper from Montevideo and the intellectual climate of the late 1840s. Lastly, indispensable are Zinny's bibliographical studies; Praderio; and Estrada. The newspaper press during the Rosas years is carefully studied in Weinberg, "El periodismo."

61. See Fernández, *Historia*, 226–29.

62. Boullosa, del Carmen Bruno, and Cantarelli, 268–69.

63. Amante.

64. Myers, *Orden y virtud*, 29–44.

65. Fernández, *Historia*, 229–31.

66. Praderio, 59–114.

67. Blomberg, 28–29.

68. Ibid., 32–33.

69. Myers, *Orden y virtud*, 100.

70. Sastre was one of the great Rioplatense pedagogues of the nineteenth century, and he authored several textbooks that were best sellers across all Latin America: the *Anagnosia* series for learning to read and write—used prevalently in the Rio de la Plata through the 1920s—and *El tempe argentino* (The Argentine paradise).

71. For an overview of Sastre's bookstores and the literary salon, see Weinberg, *El Salón Literario*.

72. Ibid., 95–98.

73. See Myers, "Aquí nadie vive," 310.

74. Boullosa, del Carmen Bruno, and Cantarelli, 265, 267.

75. Quoted in ibid., 274.

76. Valentín Alsina was another Argentine in Montevideo who edited papers, including *El Comercio del Plata* following the assassination of Florencio Varela in 1848.

77. See Eujanián, 600; AGN Ar, Museo Histórico Nacional, legajo 31, doc. 3703: 10 July 1834.

78. Benjamín Poucel relates Ascasubi's popularity and cites more praise from Florencio Varela in *Los rehenes de Durazno*, 39–40.

79. See Ansolabehere.

80. BN Ur, Materiales Especiales: *El Gaucho en Campaña*, 26 October 1839 (no. 4: 2).

81. Ascasubi, *Paulino Lucero*, 63–80.

82. Ibid., 49–62.

83. See Myers, *Orden y virtud*, 52–72, for a thorough analysis of nativism during the Rosas years and the "sistema americano."

84. López-Alves, 12.

85. From 1852 to 1872, the year Antonio Lussich published *Los tres gauchos orientales* and José Hernández's *Martín Fierro* was first printed, 380 newspapers alone—a formidable number—appeared across Argentina. In 1852, the year of the defeat of Rosas, thirty papers were started or restarted. See Fernández, *Historia*, 231–43. Montevideo was a ripe center for an expanding printing industry, too. According to Estrada, 444 catechisms for children, letters, newspapers, novels, works of theater, textbooks, and,

among others, administrative documents were printed between 1852 and 1865 (the last year that factors into Estrada's study). See Estrada, *Historia y bibliografía*, 183–311. The point here is that the printing industry in the Plata picked up steam following the Rosas years, and the partisan thread was not the only one that made it into print media.

86. Rama, *Los gauchipolíticos*, 1:59.

87. Quintana, xii. See also Román, "La vida color rosao." The War of the Triple Alliance, or Paraguayan War, lasted from 1865 to 1870 and pitted Paraguay against Brazil, Argentina, and Uruguay.

88. Battistessa, 27. The book contained a prologue by José Mármol.

89. Quoted in Quintana, viii.

90. Rama, *Los gauchipolíticos*, 1:95.

91. Myers, "Aquí nadie vive," 321–23.

92. Rama, *Los gauchipolíticos*, 2:165–66. Rama suggests that fostering the development of this reading public was closely connected to the emergence of writing as a professional practice.

93. Lussich, 3.

94. Ibid.

95. Ibid., 14–17.

96. Ibid., 99–100.

97. Hernández, *Martín Fierro* (Leumann), 268.

98. Ibid., 269.

99. Prieto studies such publications in the context of Argentina in *El discurso criollista*.

100. Gallareta; Fuentes; *Carta del gaucho Cipriano*; Eduardo Gutiérrez, *Juan Moreira*. This is just a representative handful of the hundreds of similar titles published from 1870 to 1900.

101. Gutiérrez's novels enjoyed print runs that far surpassed the initial printings of *Martín Fierro* and Lussich's poem. See Quesada, "El 'criollismo,'" 137; and Prieto, *El discurso criollista*.

102. The Scotsman Robert Cunninghame Graham recorded that he had come across countless people in the countryside who were illiterate but had memorized *Martín Fierro* from the many times they heard it recited (Cunninghame Graham, 40).

Chapter 3

1. Children age five to fifteen attended primary schools. While some public secondary schools opened their doors in the 1880s and 1890s, they were institutions meant to prepare elite children to enter the university. Students older than fifteen who had not been to primary school could attend night schools for adults, where immigrants and rural workers constituted the majority of the student body. Normal schools were an exception to this scheme, serving as both primary and secondary schools where students trained to become teachers.

2. The period of the foundation of public education in the Río de la Plata varies slightly according to different scholars. Some highlight the passage of the 1875 law of public education in Buenos Aires Province as a logical "starting" point; others suggest that the early 1880s would be more appropriate, given the 1882 international pedagogical conference held in Buenos Aires and the 1884 Argentine law of public education. Common end points include 1910, the year of the centenary celebration of indepen-

dence, and 1914, by which time public education was solidly established in the region. See, for example, Puiggrós, *Sujetos, disciplina y curriculum*; and Puiggrós, *Sociedad civil y estado*. The period in focus in this chapter—1870–1910—should be regarded more as a framework for understanding a significant block of time when the major initiatives establishing public education were carried out, rather than years marking a specific beginning and a specific end.

3. Varela's death resulted from a pulmonary condition, though it is not clear if the root cause was tuberculosis or a form of cancer. His family ties ran the political spectrum of Colorados and Blancos, but there was no doubt that he came from a long line of lettered elites. His father had fought against the English invasion of Buenos Aires at the beginning of the century, and moved the family to Montevideo after Rosas took office. His uncles were the editor Florencio Varela and the poet Juan Cruz Varela. José Pedro was also a relative twice removed of Dámaso A. Larrañaga, head of the first public library in Montevideo. His mother's side of the family connected Varela to the Blanco president of Uruguay in the early 1860s, Bernardo Berro.

4. Víctor Lima (1921–1969) was a poet and musician who collaborated with the schoolteacher Rubén Lena. "Sembrador de abecedario" was made popular by the folk duo Los Olimareños and thousands of children who sang the tune in Uruguayan schools. The verse in the original Spanish reads: "Don José Pedro Varela / Pastor de mi escuela jamás morirá." I found inspiration for the title of this chapter partly in the lyrics of Lima's song, though primarily in the sources I study here, from documents on the bureaucracy of education to reading and writing materials for students.

5. Araújo, *Historia de la escuela uruguaya*, 462. Though dated, Araújo's history of education in Uruguay remains the most complete interpretation.

6. Ibid., 470, 463.

7. Ibid., 463.

8. Quoted in Monestier, 3. Monestier's study is one of the most recent accounts of the birth of public education in Uruguay. It is full of excerpts from the periodical press of the time.

9. Quoted in Araújo, *Historia de la escuela uruguaya*, 464.

10. Quoted in Monestier, 23–24.

11. Ibid., 37–39. See Araújo, *Historia de la escuela uruguaya*, 465.

12. Quoted in Monestier, 40.

13. MPJPV: Carmen Biasotti, planas, 1908.

14. For a concise overview of this debate in Argentina, see Tedesco, 25–35.

15. Tedesco's main argument regarding public education in Argentina from 1880 to 1910 is that it fulfilled a political function more than an economic one. It was political insofar as it aimed to contribute to political stability and form citizens capable of taking on political obligations, one of which was being productive (64–65). There is a fine line, however, between the political and economic functions of the school, given that producing industrious and loyal workers and citizens was both a political and an economic aim.

16. Quoted in Monestier, 55.

17. Quoted in Araújo, *Historia de la escuela uruguaya*, 324; emphases in the original.

18. Quoted in Puiggrós, *Sujetos, disciplina y curriculum*, 157; emphasis in the original.

19. De Miguel.

20. Rodríguez.

21. Nunn, 45, 47, and 123–27. The law mandating compulsory military service for all males beginning in December 1901 (126) was also part of the modernizing endeavor.
22. Ibid. 2–3.
23. Ibid., 22–23.
24. Rodríguez, 206–9.
25. Nunn, 47.
26. Puiggrós, *Sujetos, disciplina y curriculum*, 77.
27. The Elbio Fernández School created by the society is still operating today. One of the public libraries was the library of the society. Its doors were open for anyone who wanted to consult its more than five thousand volumes, but only members (that is, those who paid dues) were allowed to borrow books. The collection consisted of novels, poetic and dramatic works, miscellaneous books, philosophy texts, legislative documents, travel books, and works on politics and agriculture. There were also a substantial number of books in French. For a list of titles, see *Biblioteca de la Sociedad*.
28. José Pedro Varela, *Obras pedagógicas: La legislación escolar.*
29. José Pedro Varela, *Obras pedagógicas: La educación del pueblo.*
30. Araújo, *Historia de la escuela uruguaya*, 522.
31. See "Ley de Educación Común," in Pimienta, 141–54.
32. Monestier, 515. On the idea of the "model country," see Vanger, *Model Country*.
33. Bottarini, 77–79.
34. See Biagini, 94–101.
35. See Tedesco, 98–139.
36. Tedesco makes the claim that schools fed *distinction*, to be understood along the lines of Bourdieu's notion of distinction being a class structure whereby elites create a system of cultural codes and meanings that preserves their status as elites. At the outset of the twentieth century, this may very well have been the case at the elite Colegios Nacionales (national colleges) and secondary schools where students went to prepare for the university. The public primary school, however, was not a conducive place to the development of Bourdieu's distinction.
37. For more on the departmental commission in Uruguay, see articles 29–36 of the "Ley de Educación Común" in Pimienta, 150–52.
38. In Argentina and in studies on the history of Argentine education, this law is commonly referred to as Ley 1420.
39. See de Luca.
40. Marengo, 79 and 87.
41. These included the Junta Económica Administrativa de Montevideo (Montevideo Council of Economic Administration) and the Comisión Nacional de Educación in Argentina (National Commission of Education).
42. See the *Memorias* of José Pedro Varela and Jacobo A. Varela as Inspectores Nacionales de Instrucción Primaria corresponding to the years 1877–1880.
43. Spregelburd, 154.
44. Ibid., 154–55.
45. Ibid., 162. Spregelburd's point about this new genre is limited to the libro de lectura. However, the competition normalized many types of books that became "regulars" in the curriculum and constituted the new form of print that was the textbook.
46. Ibid., 164–66. See also Rostan on aspects of the new industry for reading in Uruguay.
47. Marengo, 103.

48. See Linares.
49. Ibid., 188–90.
50. See Pérez, *Memoria correspondiente a los años 1902–1903*, 645.
51. In 1874, for example, Bishop Jacinto Vera came out swinging against "seditious texts" that Varela and the Society had promoted. In a *pastoral* dated 18 February of that year, he wrote: "It is every Christian's duty to abstain from any reading [of those seditious writings] that can inspire thoughts or maxims opposed to our saintly religion, good behavior, and public order; it is also his duty to impede the spread of these writings by any and every means possible." Quoted in Monestier, 260–61.
52. Marengo, 123–27.
53. Dirección General de Instrucción Pública, *Legislación escolar vigente*, 5:88–90.
54. Anonymous, "El libro en la Argentina: Lo que se compra y lo que se desdeña," *La Nación*, 4 January 1898; quoted in Prieto, *El discurso criollista*, 49.
55. Quoted in Spregelburd, 163. See also Linares, 180–87.
56. Araújo, *Historia de la escuela uruguaya*, 493.
57. For a detailed look at women in education and their "natural" teaching abilities, see Morgade, *Mujeres*, in particular Morgade's chapter, "La docencia para las mujeres."
58. The normalist tradition has often been associated with the project of disciplining young citizens. On schools as a place for disciplining the minds and bodies of children, and on the science and politics of discipline behind curricular decisions, see Puiggrós, *Sujetos, disciplina y currículum*, 115–65; de Miguel; and Tedesco, 149–57. For a look at writing as a form of disciplining children, see Ossanna.
59. Sarlo, *La máquina cultural*, 9–92.
60. Ibid., 25–26, 28.
61. Dirección General de Instrucción Primaria, *Lista de los libros . . . 1902*, 9; archived at BN Ur, Sala Uruguay. Also available in the Sala Uruguay are lists published in pamphlet form in 1901, 1904, 1907, 1908, and 1910. These lists were distributed to all public primary school teachers. See also, for example, Circular 17 in Dirección General de Instrucción Pública, *Legislación escolar vigente*, 5:178.
62. This practice led the inspector Abel Pérez to issue a circular in June 1901 reiterating that only official texts should be used in the classroom. See Dirección General de Instrucción Pública, *Legislación escolar vigente*, 5:133–34.
63. Article 34 of the Uruguayan "Ley de Educación Común," in Pimienta, 151–52. Departmental school inspectors also had to review the hygienic condition of schoolhouses, monitor the availability of materials, and keep a record or archive of all documents (including textbooks) related to educational administration in their jurisdiction. See also de Luca.
64. See, for example, Chucarro, *Memoria correspondiente á los años 1890 y 1891*, anexo 27; Chucarro, *Memoria correspondiente al año 1895*, anexo 19; Chucarro, *Memoria correspondiente al año 1896*, anexo 19; Pérez, *Memoria correspondiente al año 1900*, cuadro 19; Pérez, *Memoria correspondiente a los años 1902–1903*, cuadro 19.
65. Monestier, 517.
66. Compte y Riqué introduced students to the alphabet, as well as other subjects. On the organization of her kindergarten classes, see Palomeque, 57–71.
67. An example of the division of class time in Uruguayan schools following the reform can be found in Jacobo A. Varela, *Memoria correspondiente*, 605–16.
68. Vázquez Cores, various *Cuadernos*.

69. Vázquez Cores, *Cuadernos Vázquez Cores . . . Letra inglesa*, 7:10, and 8:1 and 7. The original Spanish reads:"El 25 de agosto de 1825 la Banda Oriental proclamó en la Florida su independencia del Brasil,""Montevideo es una hermosa ciudad," and "¡Vuelvo a verte, patria mía!"

70. MPJPV has a substantial number of these notebooks. Almost all of them are without writing; they probably ended up in the museum's library as leftovers from shipments to schools around the country.

71. Barreiro y Ramos, 6:4, 7; and 8:10. The original Spanish reads:"En boca cerrada no entran moscas,""No es oro todo lo que brilla," and "Artigas fue el fundador de la República Oriental."

72. Jacobo A. Varela, *Memoria correspondiente*,18, 100; Jacobo A. Varela, *Informe correspondiente*, cuadros 13 and 16; and Chucarro, *Memoria correspondiente al año 1895*, cuadros 11 and 14.

73. Up to now, there has been no systematic study of textbooks. With titles numbering in the hundreds, it is a daunting task. Most scholarship on these texts has focused on history books. See Chapter 4 for a closer look at this debate.

74. Some of the other important books for learning to read, published in a smaller number of editions, but still with significant content messages, include Nuñez; Osuna, used in both Uruguay and Argentina; Igón; Imbert de Moles; Berra, *Ejercicios de lectura (curso progresivo), primera parte*; Berra, *Ejercicios de lectura (curso progresivo), segunda parte*; Miranda, *El lector infantil*; and Ledesma, *Mi primer libro*.

75. Chucarro, *Memoria correspondiente á los años 1890 y 1891*, cuadro 16; Chucarro, *Memoria correspondiente al año 1896*, cuadro 14; and Pérez, *Memoria correspondiente a los años 1902–1903*, 644.

76. Dirección General de Instrucción Pública, *Legislación escolar vigente*, 6:130.

77. Dirección General de Instrucción Pública, *Legislación escolar vigente*, 5:88–89.

78. Pizzurno, iv–vi.

79. Palma, *El hogar modelo*, viii.

80. Araújo, *Episodios históricos*, v.

81. See Comisión Departamental de Instrucción Pública.

82. Comisión Departamental de Instrucción Primaria, 43.

83. In class notebooks from 1908 and 1909 (archived at MPJPV), Carmen Biasotti writes about parents at the school during exam days.

84. On prizes in Uruguay, see Araújo, *Historia de la escuela uruguaya*, 307–9, 379. See also Jacobo A. Varela, *Informe correspondiente*, relación de cuadro 16. The MPJPV has a good collection of prizes.

85. The covers of textbooks from the Río de la Plata as well as from other parts of Latin America vary widely in their symbolic imagery and offer a rich source for understanding book content and summations of messages that publishers and the boards of education aimed to communicate.

86. Pérez, *Memoria correspondiente al año 1901*, 48.

87. Pérez, *Memoria correspondiente al año 1900*, cuadro 14bis, and Pérez, *Memoria correspondiente al año 1901*, 270.

88. See, for example, Figueira, *¿Quieres leer?* (1908 edition), 4.

89. Dirección General de Instrucción Primaria, *Lista de los libros . . . 1904*, 5.

90. Ibid., 5–6, 11–16.

91. The numbers of schools noted in this section only refer to public schools. Private

schools functioned during the same period in both countries, but they were by far fewer in number than public ones and their enrollment steadily decreased. Enrollment in public schools indicates the number of students officially registered for the year. The *asistencia media*, or average attendance (based on the records of students who did not miss class more than three times per month), was usually around a third lower than the total enrollment for the year.

92. Jacobo A. Varela, *Memoria correspondiente*, 18, 31; Chucarro, *Memoria correspondiente a los años 1890 y 1891*, cuadros I, II, and 15; Pérez, *Memoria correspondiente al año 1900*, 65, 77, 78; Pérez, *Memoria correspondiente a los años 1909 y 1910*, 117, 120, 125, cuadro 3. Statistics on asistencia media are available in these same sources.

93. José Pedro Varela, *Memoria correspondiente*, lxxxvi.

94. Gandulfo, 314, 316, 323–25.

95. See Consejo Nacional de Educación, 9. For a look at how these statistics were compiled, see Nelson, 5–43.

96. *Anuario estadístico . . . años 1902 y 1903*, 1:110–12, cuadro 15. The majority of departments reported a slightly greater number of literate men than literate women for the population older than fourteen. Interestingly, for ages six to fourteen, the opposite was the case, with most departments reporting higher literacy rates among females. See *Anuario estadístico . . . años 1904 a 1906*, 1:55.

97. See Rial, 147.

98. MPJPV, caja 19: Delia Beramendi to A. Gómez Ruano, 23 November 1901; Oscar Laporiti to A. Gómez Ruano, 23 November 1901.

99. MPJPV: Raudelinda Pereda, cuaderno de escritura, 1898.

Chapter 4

1. Hudson, 125–31.
2. Díaz, 34–35.
3. Ibid., 55–56.
4. See, for example, circular 19, titled "Manifestaciones partidistas: Su prohibición a los funcionarios escolares y a los educandos," and circular 18, which prohibited students from wearing any emblems symbolizing party affiliation. In Dirección General de Instrucción Pública, *Legislación Escolar Vigente*, 5:13–16.
5. Navarro Viola, *Anuario bibliográfico de la República Argentina*, año 2, 286–87. See also Navarro Viola, *Anuario bibliográfico de la República Argentina*, año 3, 399–400.
6. On the phenomenon of *criollismo* in Argentina and the creation of criollista societies (groups that formed around the criollo spirit through the Plata) at the turn of the century, see Prieto, *El discurso criollista*. See also Chasteen, *National Rhythms*, 51–70; Castagnino, *El circo criollo*; and Bosch.
7. See Riekenberg for an introduction to history textbooks in Latin America.
8. Prieto, *El discurso criollista*, 13.
9. Amid the limited scholarship on textbooks from these years, good overviews include Fontana, "Los primeros textos . . . Primera parte"; Fontana, "Los primeros textos . . . Segunda parte"; and Leone.
10. Cecilia Braslavsky makes the argument that textbooks carried diverse messages on patriotism (41–45). While variations are no doubt present in the texts, and although some authors have, for example, conflicting ideas about the immigrant population in Argentina, the hundreds of titles with patriotic lessons do indeed rally around

the formation of a national community based on a shared past and a common set of heroes.

11. Bolívar fulfilled these in Venezuelan books. See Werz.

12. Wagner Sosa, 16–19.

13. See, for example, *Liga Patriótica de Enseñanza*. See also Islas, *Liga*.

14. MPJPV: Carmen Biasotti, planas, 1909.

15. See Quiroga; de María, *Catecismo constitucional*; Ortega, *Compendio de instrucción cívica*; and Miranda, *Educación cívica*.

16. Miranda, *Educación cívica*, 33–35.

17. Examples of rather dry histories include Peacan; Benigno T. Martínez, *Curso elemental*; and Antuña. Antuña's books sold well, however, both in bookstores in Montevideo and in post offices in the interior.

18. Bernárdez.

19. Eizaguirre, 7, 8–10, 14–15; emphasis in the original.

20. Ibid., 117–18.

21. Ibid., 20–21.

22. Achigar, Varela Brown, and Eguren, 155–56.

23. Ibid., 170–83. Beginning around 1915, debates about H.D.'s books became heated, and attempts were made to discredit them based on his historical methodology.

24. H.D., *Curso*, 6.

25. Ibid., 7–8.

26. Ibid., 13.

27. Ibid., 75–76, 125–26.

28. Monner Sans, *Teatro infantil*, 14–15; emphasis mine.

29. Ibid., 53–55; emphasis in the original.

30. Alexis, 1.

31. "Mi tierra," "A mi bandera," "¡Patria!," "¡Viva la patria!," and "A los muertos por la patria."

32. Alexis, 19–23.

33. *Cuadernos históricos*, 4–7.

34. See Achugar, "Blanes y el cuerpo."

35. *Cuadernos históricos*, 47–49.

36. *El Monitor de la Educación Común*, 1890 (no. 185: 346).

37. Ibid., 377. Other illustrative examples may be found in this volume. See in particular 343, 373, 374, and 376.

38. See *Discursos del profesor Don Cayetano Centorami*; and *Composiciones presentadas*, 16–17.

39. MPJPV: Carmen Biasotti, planas, 1906, 1908, 1909.

40. MPJPV: Raudelinda Pereda, cuaderno de escritura, 1898.

41. Pérez, *Memoria correspondiente al año 1901*, 51–52.

42. For more on patriotic celebrations and the school, see Cecilia Braslavsky; and Pérez, *Memoria correspondiente a los años 1902–1903*. On the "mission of the teacher on patriotic holidays," see Dirección General de Instrucción Pública, *Legislación escolar vigente*, 6:137–38.

43. Recent research on mirror neuron theory and social interaction suggests new ways for understanding the power of collective sentiment and the formation of identities. The claim is that neurons in the brain fire in the same way when one experiences

stimuli or sees or hears someone else experience stimuli, the neurons in the brain fire in the same way—hence the name of "mirror system" for these neurons. So when one is in the middle of a patriotic crowd that sings praises to the nation, the person who is not initially drawn into the fray can count on his or her mirror system to respond, perhaps leading him or her to join the crowd. See Glenberg; Gazzola et al.; and Elfenbein.

44. Vásquez Acevedo, 222–26.
45. See, for example, Latallada, 38–41.
46. Roldós y Pons, 14, 20–21, 129.
47. Catalá de Princivalle, *Lecciones de economía doméstica, primer libro.* 3.
48. Ibid., 5.
49. Ibid., 34–41.
50. Catalá de Princivalle, *Lecciones de economía doméstica, segundo libro,* 24.
51. Here, the term *economy* corresponds to "proper management of the domestic environment."
52. Catalá de Princivalle, *Lecciones de economía doméstica, tercer libro,* 7–10.
53. Torrejón, 24.
54. *Economía doméstica al alcance de las niñas,* 3, 23, 57–58. Anyone could do the reading, although ideally at least one parent would be literate and could oversee the selection of books or newspapers to read as a family.
55. Palma, *Consejos a mi hija: Lecturas de propaganda moral.* The subtitle is a little misleading, for in English today propaganda has negative overtones. In Spanish, *propaganda* has its negative political meaning, but it also refers to common publicity, which is generally understood in a positive light. It is this second, positive *propaganda* that is referred to in the subtitle.
56. Ibid., iv–v.
57. Palma, *El hogar modelo.* Palma also wrote *Veladas del hogar* (Evenings at home) for male and female readers.
58. Mareca, 8.
59. Ibid., 12–14; emphasis mine.
60. Ibid., 31–32, 74–77.
61. Fragueiro, 7–8.
62. Ibid., 9–15.
63. Lamas and Lamas, 9.
64. Ibid., 193.
65. MPJPV: Raudelinda Pereda to her mother, in her cuaderno de escritura, 16 November 1898.
66. *Composiciones presentada,* 25–26.
67. MPJPV: Carmen Biasotti, planas, 1906–1908.
68. In *Hogar y patria,* Latallada issues a call for young women to serve the patria, specifically those who have learned well their lessons in motherhood (281–83). According to the call, which ends the textbook, the nation will continually search for such women in all Argentine schools and homes.
69. We met de María in Chapter 1, where his writings about the *Southern Star* and the swearing of the Uruguayan constitution were discussed.
70. Morgade, "La docencia para las mujeres," 68.

71. This idea was expressed by some teachers and educational bureaucrats. See Palumbo. For critical perspectives on this question and on gender roles in schools, see the essays in Morgade, *Mujeres*.
72. Wagner Sosa, 25–29.

Epilogue

1. Rama explains how those who exercised power through writing (a group that made up the "lettered city") were able to implement the standard-grid layout now so characteristic of big cities and small towns throughout Latin America. See especially chapter 1, "The Ordered City," in Rama, *Lettered City*.
2. EFCH.
3. Loeb, 224.
4. EFCH.
5. See Baracchini, 90–93, 95–103, 135–45; Silvera Antúnez, *Historia del transporte*, 16–25; and Scobie, *Buenos Aires*, 91–99.
6. For a complete survey of these scenes and others skillfully printed by C. Galli Franco and Co., see Loeb.
7. See Kloetzel, 1:316–19, 6:571–73.
8. González-Stephan, "Forms of Historic Imagination." For a recent comparative study of visual culture within state formation in Argentina and Brazil, see Andermann. See also González-Stephan and Andermann.
9. EFCH: 23 July 1904.
10. Preston and Rosenthal; Achugar, "Foundational." A recent general overview of stamps is Child's "Politics and Semiotics." In *Miniature Messages*, Child argues that Argentine politics did not become intertwined with stamps until after 1910 (100–105). On postcards as source material and in comparative perspective, see Vanderwood.
11. *Catálogo especializado*, 19–21.
12. Ibid., 24–26.
13. Ibid., 28–32. Many artists participated in the competition to depict Artigas, including Alfredo Demersay, Eduardo Carbajal, and Juan Manuel Blanes. See Comisión Nacional de Homenaje a Artigas; and Ribeiro, 107–66.
14. Silvera Antúnez, *El correo*, 97.
15. Hundreds of postcards without postage archived in the collections of EFCH, Loeb, and Silvera Antúnez contain such notes. While thousands of others were sent between people living in the same town or city, it would have been easy for a note writer to take his or her message a few blocks to the recipient's house or place of work, or to exchange postal messages and images upon running into a friend.
16. Vasen and Riese, 25–26.
17. Ibid., 16, 20, 53–54.
18. Estudio Filatélico Marcelo Loeb.
19. Loeb, 225.
20. EFCH.
21. Ibid.
22. Shafer and Cuhaj, 6–83.
23. For an overview of the evolution of monetary policy in Argentina and the nationalization of the banking system, see Hansen, 390–415, 418–59.

24. Shafer and Cuhaj, 1169–84.
25. Avellaneda served as minister of education under Sarmiento, and then as president of Argentina.
26. Shafer and Bruce, 61–64.
27. Banco Central del Uruguay, 81–145.
28. Ibid., 153.
29. Ibid., 256–62.
30. Williman, 263–325.
31. Rubens Bonino, Martín Valdez, and Villaamil, 10–11.
32. Ibid., 20–28.
33. *La Nación*, 7 June 1892. The newspaper published a loose-leaf as well with information on La Popular. Each box contained fourteen cigarettes.
34. The brands mentioned here are but a fraction of La Republicana's total production.
35. Borucki.
36. See, for example, *Caras y Caretas*, 2 August 1891.
37. While lettered elites in Argentina and elsewhere in Latin America read books by Smiles in English, the Argentine general Edelmiro Mayer was one of the first to translate several of the books into Spanish, thus helping to boost their circulation among new readers toward the end of the 1800s. See Smiles, 398–401.
38. *Caras y Caretas*, 2 April 1910.
39. Eujanián; Pastormerlo; Merbilháa.
40. Prieto, *El discurso criollista*; Achugar, *Poesía y sociedad*.
41. Quoted in Merbilháa, 52.
42. *El Almanaque del Amigo del Obrero*, 1910:50.
43. See Barité; Romano.
44. *Caras y Caretas*, 25 May 1910.
45. Fraser; Pignatelli, 319.
46. See *Caras y Caretas*, 11 June 1910.

Bibliography

Magazines and Newspapers

El Almanaque del Amigo del Obrero, Montevideo
El Amigo del Obrero, Montevideo
Archivo Americano y Espíritu de la Prensa del Mundo, Buenos Aires
El Artillero de la Línea, Montevideo
El Avisador, Buenos Aires
Caras y Caretas, Montevideo and Buenos Aires
El Clasificador, Buenos Aires
De Cada Cosa Un Poquito, Buenos Aires
El Defensor de las Leyes, Montevideo
El Diario de la Tarde, Buenos Aires
El Fogón, Montevideo
La Gaceta Mercantil, Buenos Aires
La Gaucha, Buenos Aires
El Gaucho, Buenos Aires
El Gaucho en Campaña, Montevideo

El Gaucho Jacinto Cielo, Montevideo
El Gaucho Oriental, Montevideo
El Gaucho Restaurador, Buenos Aires
El Grito Arjentino, Montevideo
El Guerrillero de la Línea, Montevideo
Leyes o Muerte, Montevideo
El Monitor, Buenos Aires
El Monitor de la Educación Común, Buenos Aires
¡Muera Rosas!, Montevideo
La Nación, Buenos Aires
La Negrita, Buenos Aires
El Negrito, Buenos Aires
El Oriental en Campaña, Paysandú
Rojo y Blanco, Montevideo
El Tambor de la Línea, Montevideo
El Telégrafo de la Línea, Montevideo
El Toro de Once, Buenos Aires
La Tribuna, Buenos Aires

Published Primary Sources

Alberdi, Juan Bautista. *Bases y puntos de partida para la organización política de la República Argentina.* Buenos Aires: Ediciones Estrada, 1943.

Alexis. *El niño y la patria: Poesías, monólogos, diálogos y escenas patriótico-infantiles ofrecidas por su autor a los niños argentinos en el primer centenario de la patria, 1810–1910.* La Plata: Talleres Gráficos de J. Sesé, 1910. Archived at BNM.

Los Amigos de la Patria y de la Juventud, facsimile ed. With an introduction by Guillermo Furlong and a preliminary study by Enrique de Gandía. Periódicos de la Epoca de la Revolución de Mayo, 5. Buenos Aires: Academia Nacional de la Historia, 1961.

Antuña, Enrique M. *Lecciones de historia nacional: Artigas y la insurrección, segundo curso.* 3rd ed. Montevideo: El Ateneo, 1901. Archived at MPJPV.

Anuario estadístico de la República Oriental del Uruguay, años 1902 y 1903, vol. 1. Montevideo: Dornaleche y Reyes, 1905.

Anuario estadístico de la República Oriental del Uruguay, años 1904 a 1906, vol. 1. Montevideo: Dornaleche y Reyes, 1907.

Araújo, Orestes. *Episodios históricos.* 5th ed. Montevideo: Dornaleche Hermanos, n.d. Archived at MPJPV.

———. *Lecturas ejemplares.* 6th ed. Montevideo: A. Soury, 1908. Archived at MPJPV.

———. *Perfiles biográficos trazados para la niñez.* With a prologue by José H. Figueira. Montevideo: Dornaleche y Reyes, 1892. Archived at MPJPV.

Archivo Histórico de la Provincia de Buenos Aires. *Orígenes de la imprenta de Niños Expósitos.* With an introduction by Carlos Heras. La Plata, Argentina: Taller de Impresiones Oficiales, 1941.

El Arriero Argentino, facsimile ed. In Rodríguez Molas, "Contribución a la bibliografía," between pages 80 and 81.

Ascasubi, Hilario. *Ancieto el Gallo: Gacetero prosista y gauchi-poeta argentino.* Paris: Imprimerie de Paul Dupont, 1872.

———. *Paulino Lucero, ó Los gauchos del Río de la Plata: Cantando y combatiendo contra los tiranos de las repúblicas Argentina y Oriental de Uruguay (1839 a 1851).* With a prologue by Manuel Mujica Lainez. Buenos Aires: Ediciones Estrada, 1945.

———. *Santos Vega, ó Los mellizos de la Flor.* Paris: Imprimerie de Paul Dupont, 1872.

Aubin, José María. *Lecturas sobre historia nacional, para los niños de segundo grado.* Buenos Aires: Angel Estrada, 1897. Archived at BNM.

Bacle, César Hipólito. *Trages y costumbres de la Provincia de Buenos Aires.* Buenos Aires: Bacle, 1834. Archived at BN Ar, Tesoro.

Barreiro y Ramos, Antonio. *Método Barreiro y Ramos: Curso graduado de escritura inglesa compuesto de 8 cuadernos, cuaderno 6.* Montevideo: A. Barreiro y Ramos, 1893. Archived at MPJPV.

———. *Método Barreiro y Ramos: Curso graduado de escritura inglesa compuesto de 8 cuadernos, cuaderno 8.* Montevideo: A. Barreiro y Ramos, 1893. Archived at MPJPV.

Barreto, Félix G., ed. *Papeles de Rosas, 1821–1850.* Santa Fe, Argentina: Imprenta de la Provincia, 1928.

Becco, Horacio Jorge, ed. *Negros y morenos en el cancionero rioplatense.* With a preliminary study by Horacio Jorge Becco. Buenos Aires: Sociedad Argentina de Americanistas, 1953.

Bernárdez, Manuel. *La patria en la escuela, cuaderno 1: Los atributos.* Montevideo: Imprenta Artística y Librería de Dornaleche y Reyes, 1894. Archived at MPJPV.

Berra, Francisco A. *Apuntes para un curso de pedagogía.* Montevideo: Sociedad de Amigos de la Educación Popular de Montevideo, 1883. Archived at MPJPV.

———. *Ejercicios de lectura (curso progresivo), primera parte.* 2nd ed. Buenos Aires: Angel Estrada, 1894. Archived at MPJPV.

———. *Ejercicios de lectura (curso progresivo), segunda parte.* Buenos Aires: Angel Estrada, 1890. Archived at MPJPV.

Beruti, Juan Manuel. *Memorias curiosas.* Buenos Aires: Emecé, 2001.

Biblioteca de la Sociedad de Amigos de la Educación Popular, Catálogo. Montevideo: Tipografía Liberal, 1889. Archived at MPJPV.

Binayán, Narciso, ed. *Ideario de Mayo.* Buenos Aires: Editorial Kapelusz, 1960.

Blomberg, Héctor Pedro, ed. *Cancionero federal.* Buenos Aires: Ediciones Anaconda, 1934.

Bunge, Carlos Octavio. *Nuestra patria: Libro de lectura para la educación nacional.* 17th ed. Buenos Aires: Angel Estrada, 1910.

Cambaceres, Eugenio. *Sin rumbo (estudio).* Madrid: Cátedra, 1999.

Cané, Miguel (h). *Charlas literarias.* Sceaux, France: Imprimerie de Charaire, 1885.

———. *Juvenilia.* Buenos Aires: Editorial Universitaria de Buenos Aires, 1964.

Carta del gaucho Cipriano relatando sus amores con una coqueta. Montevideo: Tipografía Nacional, 1885. Archived at BN Ur, Sala Uruguay.

Castañeda, Francisco de Paula. *Doña María Retazos*, facsimile ed. With a preliminary study by Néstor T. Auza. Buenos Aires: Taurus, 2001.

Catalá de Princivalle, Emma. *Ejercicios progresivos de lectura, ortología y ortografía, primer libro*. 2nd ed. Montevideo: Imprenta El Siglo Ilustrado, 1915. Archived at MPJPV.

———. *Lecciones de economía doméstica, primer libro*. Montevideo: Imprenta El Siglo Ilustrado, 1905. Archived at MPJPV.

———. *Lecciones de economía doméstica, segundo libro*. Montevideo: Imprenta El Siglo Ilustrado, 1906. Archived at MPJPV.

———. *Lecciones de economía doméstica, tercer libro*. Montevideo: Imprenta El Siglo Ilustrado, 1906. Archived at MPJPV.

Catálogo descriptivo: Colección época de Rosas; En venta: Casa Pardo. Buenos Aires: Ferrari Hermanos, n.d. Archived at HA, Foll. 109.

El Censor, facsimile ed. With an introduction by Guillermo Furlong and a preliminary study by Enrique de Gandía. Buenos Aires: Academia Nacional de la Historia, 1961.

Chucarro, Urbano. *Memoria correspondiente á los años 1890 y 1891*. Montevideo: Imprenta La Nación, 1892. Archived at BPC.

———. *Memoria correspondiente al año 1895*. Montevideo: Imprenta La Nación, 1896. Archived at BPC.

———. *Memoria correspondiente al año 1896*. Montevideo: Imprenta La Nación, 1897. Archived at BPC.

Colección general de las marcas del ganado de la Provincia de Buenos Aires. Buenos Aires: Bacle, 1830. Archived at UNC Rare Book Collection.

Comisión Departamental de Instrucción Primaria. *Exámenes generales de las escuelas públicas del departamento de Cerro Largo correspondientes al año escolar de 1891*. Melo: Tipografía y Encuadernación de El Deber Cívico, 1891. Archived at BN Ur, Sala Uruguay.

Comisión Departamental de Instrucción Pública. *Exámenes generales de las escuelas públicas del departamento de Rocha correspondientes al año 1895*. Rocha: Imprenta La Democracia, 1895. Archived at BN Ur, Sala Uruguay.

Composiciones presentadas por las alumnas en los exámenes del año 1893, Colegio San José. Montevideo: Imprenta y Librería Vázquez Cores y Montes, 1893. Archived at BN Ur, Sala Uruguay.

Cuadernos históricos de episodios de la independencia pintados por Diógenes Héquet. Montevideo: Sierra y Antuña Editores, 1896. Archived at HA.

Cunninghame Graham, Robert Bontine. "A Vanishing Race." In *The South American Sketches of R. B. Cunninghame Graham*, ed. John Walker, 35–41. Norman: University of Oklahoma Press, 1978.

del Campo, Estanislao. *Fausto: Impresiones del gaucho Anastasio el Pollo en la representación de esta ópera*, facsimile ed. With a preliminary study by Ernesto Mario Barreda and a prologue by Raúl Quintana. Buenos Aires: Imprenta de la Biblioteca Nacional, 1940.

———. *Fausto: Impresiones del gaucho Anastasio el Pollo en la representación de esta ópera*. Buenos Aires: Editorial de Belgrano, 1981.

———. *Fausto: Su prefiguración periodística*. Edited with a preliminary study by Angel J. Battistessa. Buenos Aires: Academia Argentina de Letras, 1989.

del Castaño, Aurora Stella. *El vademécum del hogar: Tratado práctico de economía doméstica y labores, ilustrado con 400 grabados conteniendo además recetas útiles y variadas*. Buenos Aires: Imprenta de Juan E. Barra, 1903. Archived at BNM.

de María, Isidoro. *Catecismo constitucional de la República Oriental del Uruguay*. 10th ed. Montevideo: Imprenta El Siglo Ilustrado, 1894. Archived at MPJPV.

———. *El libro de las niñas, compuesto expresamente para lectura de las uruguayas*. Montevideo: Imprenta El Siglo Ilustrado, 1891. Archived at MPJPV.

———. *Montevideo antiguo: Tradiciones y recuerdos*. 2 vols. Colección Clásicos Uruguayos, vols. 23–24. Montevideo: Ministerio de Instrucción Pública y Previsión Social, 1957.

Descripción de las fiestas cívicas celebradas en Montevideo, Mayo de 1816; Oración inaugural pronunciada por Larrañaga en la apertura de la Biblioteca Pública de Montevideo, 1816, facsimile ed. With an introduction by Edmundo M. Narancio. Biblioteca de Impresos Raros Americanos, vol. 2. Montevideo: Facultad de Humanidades y Ciencias, Instituto de Investigaciones Históricas, Universidad de la República, 1951.

Díaz, José Virginio. *Viaje por la campaña oriental*. With an introduction by Oscar Padrón Favre. Montevideo: Ediciones El Galeón; Durazno, Uruguay: Tierra Adentro Ediciones, 2005.

Diez, Gabriel, arranger. *Cantos escolares*. Vol. 1. Buenos Aires: Angel Estrada, 1886. Archived at BNM.

Dirección General de Instrucción Primaria. *Lista de los libros de texto adoptados para uso de los alumnos de las escuelas primarias durante el año 1902*. Montevideo: Imprenta El Siglo Ilustrado, 1902. Archived at BN Ur, Sala Uruguay.

———. *Lista de los libros de texto adoptados para uso de los alumnos de las escuelas primarias durante el año 1904*. Montevideo: Talleres de A. Barreiro y Ramos, 1904. Archived at BN Ur, Sala Uruguay.

———. *Lista de los libros de texto adoptados para uso de los alumnos de las escuelas primarias durante el año 1907*. Montevideo: Talleres de A. Barreiro y Ramos, 1907. Archived at BN Ur, Sala Uruguay.

———. *Lista de los libros de texto adoptados para uso de los alumnos de las escuelas primarias durante el año 1908*. Montevideo: Talleres Gráficos de A. Barreiro y Ramos, 1908. Archived at BN Ur, Sala Uruguay.

———. *Lista de los libros de texto adoptados para uso de los alumnos de las escuelas primarias durante el año 1910*. Montevideo: Imprenta y Encuadernación El Siglo Ilustrado, 1910. Archived at BN Ur, Sala Uruguay.

Dirección General de Instrucción Pública. *Informe de la Comisión nombrada para formular la lista de los textos que deberán ser adoptados en las escuelas públicas y aprobado por la corporación*. Montevideo: Imprenta El Siglo Ilustrado, 1901. Archived at BN Ur, Sala Uruguay.

———. *Legislación escolar vigente*. Vol. 5, *1898–1903*. Montevideo: Talleres A. Barreiro y Ramos, 1904. Archived at BPC.

———. *Legislación escolar vigente*. Vol. 6, *1904–1905*. Montevideo: Talleres Tipográficos de La Prensa, 1906. Archived at BPC.

Discursos del profesor Don Cayetano Centorami recitados en el día de los exámenes finales por los alumnos del Colegio de 2o grado, no. 1. Montevideo: Imprenta y Litografía La Razón, 1897. Archived at BN Ur, Sala Uruguay.

Domínguez, Luis L. *Historia argentina*. 2nd ed. Buenos Aires: Imprenta del Orden, 1862.

Echeverría, Esteban. *Dogma socialista*. Buenos Aires: Librería La Facultad de Juan Roldán, 1915.

———. *Obras completas de D. Esteban Echeverría*. Edited by Juan María Gutiérrez. Buenos Aires: Imprenta y Librería de Mayo, 1870–1874.

Economía doméstica al alcance de las niñas. 4th ed. Buenos Aires: Cabaut, 1914. Archived at BNM.

Eizaguirre, José Manuel. *La patria: Elementos para estimular en el niño argentino el amor á la patria y el respeto á las tradiciones nacionales.* 3rd ed. Buenos Aires: Angel Estrada, 1895. Archived at BNM.

Espora, Juan Manuel. *Episodios nacionales.* 12th ed. rev. Buenos Aires: Cabaut, 1911. Archived at BNM.

Ferreyra, Andrés. *Aventuras de un niño. Libro 1.* Buenos Aires: Angel Estrada, 1907. Archived at BNM.

Figueira, José H. *Adelante, libro segundo.* 5th ed. Montevideo: Dornaleche y Reyes, 1904. Archived at MPJPV.

———. *Un buen amigo, libro tercero.* New ed. Montevideo, 1908. Archived at MPJPV.

———. *¿Quieres leer? libro primero.* 4th rev. ed. Montevideo: Dornaleche y Reyes, 1897. Archived at MPJPV.

———. *¿Quieres leer? libro primero.* Rev. ed. Montevideo, 1908. Archived at MPJPV.

———. *Trabajo, libro cuarto.* 2nd ed. Montevideo: Dornaleche y Reyes, 1902. Archived at MPJPV.

———. *Vida, libro quinto.* Montevideo: Dornaleche y Reyes, 1902. Archived at MPJPV.

Fontanella, Agustín. *Los amores de Giacumina: Sainete cómico en un acto y cinco cuadros.* Buenos Aires: Editor Salvador Matera, 1906.

Fragueiro, Rafael. *La niña argentina: Serie primera, cuarenta y tres lecturas instructivas.* Buenos Aires: Cabaut, 1902. Archived at BNM.

Fuentes, Calistro. *El gaucho oriental: Colección de poesías campestres.* Montevideo, 1872. Archived at BN Ur, Sala Uruguay.

Gaceta de Buenos Aires, facsimile ed. 6 vols. Buenos Aires: Compañía Sud-Americana de Billetes de Banco, 1910–1915.

Gallareta, Aniceto. *La fiesta de los rurales.* Montevideo: Tipografía de la Escuela de Artes y Oficios, 1883. Archived at BN Ur, Sala Uruguay.

Gambón, Vicente. *Lecciones de historia argentina según el programa oficial.* Buenos Aires: Angel Estrada, 1907. Archived at BNM.

Gazeta de Montevideo, facsimile ed. With an introduction by Juan Canter and a preliminary study by M. Blanca París and Q. Cabrera Piñón. Biblioteca de Impresos Raros Americanos, vol. 1. Montevideo: Facultad de Humanidades y Ciencias, Instituto de Investigaciones Históricas, Universidad de la República, 1948.

González, Joaquín Víctor, ed. *Manual de la constitución argentina, escrita para servir de texto de instrucción cívica en los establecimientos de instrucción secundaria.* Buenos Aires: Angel Estrada, 1897.

———. *Patria.* Buenos Aires: Cabaut, 1906.

Gorriti, Juan Ignacio de. *Reflexiones sobre las causas morales de las convulsiones internas en los nuevos estados americanos y examen de los medios eficaces para reprimirlas.* Buenos Aires: Librería La Facultad de Juan Roldán, 1916.

Gorriti, Juana Manuela. *Cocina ecléctica.* Edited by María Rosa Loja. Buenos Aires: Aguilar, 1999.

———. *La tierra natal.* With a prologue by Santiago Sylvester. Buenos Aires: Fondo Nacional de las Artes, 1999.

Granada, Nicolás. *Cartas gauchas: Descripción de las fiestas del centenario, hecha por el gaucho argentino Martín Oro, en seis cartas, en versos gauchos, dirigidas a su mujer Benita Chaparro.* 5th ed. Buenos Aires: Talleres Gráficos La Mundial, 1942.

———. *La gaviota.* Buenos Aires: Plus Ultra, 1973.

———. *La piedra de escándalo / Martín Coronado / ¡Al Campo!* With a prologue and notes by Luis Ordaz. Buenos Aires: Centro Editor de América Latina, 1980.

El Grito del Sud, facsimile ed. With a prologue by Guillermo Furlong and a preliminary study by Enrique de Gandía. Periódicos de la Epoca de la Revolución de Mayo, vol. 2. Buenos Aires: Academia Nacional de la Historia, 1961.

Gutiérrez, Eduardo. *El Chacho*. Buenos Aires: Librería Hachette, 1960.

———. *El drama de Caseros*. Buenos Aires: J. C. Rovira, 1932.

———. *Hormiga negra*. Buenos Aires: Perfil Libros, 1999.

———. *Juan Cuello: El enemigo de la mazorca*. Buenos Aires: J. C. Rovira, 1933.

———. *Juan Cuello y los amores de Rita*. Buenos Aires: J. C. Rovira, 1933.

———. *Juan Manuel de Rosas: Los dramas del terror*. Buenos Aires: Harpón, 1944.

———. *Juan Moreira*. Buenos Aires: Perfil Libros, 1999.

Gutiérrez, Juan María. *Origen y desarrollo de la enseñanza pública superior en Buenos Aires*, rev. ed. Buenos Aires: La Cultura Argentina, 1915.

H.D. [Hermano Damsceno]. *Curso de historia patria, libro primero*. 3rd ed. Montevideo: A. Barreiro y Ramos, 1914.

———. *Ensayo de historia patria*. 6th ed. Montevideo: A. Barreiro y Ramos, 1929.

Heras, Carlos. Introduction to Archivo Histórico de la Provincia de Buenos Aires, *Origenes*.

Hernández, José. *Martín Fierro*. Edited by Carlos Alberto Leumann. Buenos Aires: Angel Estrada, 1945.

———. *Martín Fierro*. Critical edition by Elida Lois and Angel Núñez. Madrid: ALLCA XX, 2001.

Hidalgo, Bartolomé. *Obra completa*. With a prologue by Antonio Praderio. Colección Clásicos Uruguayos, vol. 170. Montevideo: Ministerio de Educación y Cultura, 1986.

———. *Obra completa*. With a prologue and notes by Walter Rela. Montevideo: Editorial Ciencias, 1979.

Hudson, W. H. *The Purple Land*. With an introduction by William McFee. New York: Modern Library, 1926.

Igón, J. B. *El mosaico argentino: Lecciones útiles de diversos caracteres de letra manuscrita para ejercitar á los niños y niñas en esta clase de lectura*. 9th ed. Buenos Aires: Angel Estrada, 1905.

Imbert de Moles, Ana. *El lector del Plata, primer libro*. Montevideo: Imprenta a vapor de El Siglo, 1894. Archived at MPJPV.

El Independiente, facsimile ed. With an introduction by Guillermo Furlong and a preliminary study by Enrique de Gandía. Periódicos de la Epoca de la Revolución de Mayo, vol. 4. Buenos Aires: Academia Nacional de la Historia, 1961.

Lamas, Alejandro. *Maternología: Estudio de la crianza, higiene y educación de los niños*. Montevideo: Librería Nacional de A. Barreiro y Ramos, 1899. Archived at BN Ur, Sala Uruguay.

———, and Elvira Lamas. *Lecturas sobre moral, higiene y economía doméstica*. 2nd ed. Montevideo: A. Barreiro y Ramos, 1909.

Latallada, Felisa A. *Hogar y patria, libro de lectura para grados elementales y superiores*. 3rd ed. Buenos Aires: Alberto Vidueiro, 1917. Archived at BNM.

Ledesma, Serafín. *Lecturas manuscritas, libro primero*. Montevideo: Juan J. Dornaleche, 1898. Archived at MPJPV.

———. *Mi primer libro*. Montevideo: E. Lagomarsino e Hijo, n.d. Archived at MPJPV.

Leguizamón, Martiniano. *Alma nativa*. 2nd ed. Buenos Aires: Juan Roldán, 1912.

———. *Calandria, costumbres campestres / Del tiempo viejo, boceto campestre*. With a preliminary study by Juan Carlos Ghiano. Buenos Aires: Solar / Hachette, 1961.

———. *Junto al fogón y otros relatos*. Buenos Aires: Editorial Universitaria de Buenos Aires, 1966.

———. *Papeles de Rosas*. Buenos Aires: J. Peuser, 1935.

Levene, Ricardo. *Cómo se ama a la patria*. With a prologue by Osvaldo Magnasco. Buenos Aires: Aquilino Fernández, 1910.

Liga Patriótica de Enseñanza a los habitantes de la campaña. Montevideo: Imprenta a vapor de La Nacion, 1896. Archived at BN Ur, Sala Uruguay.

La lira argentina, o Colección de las piezas poéticas dadas a luz en Buenos Aires durante la guerra de su independencia. Edited and with a preliminary study by Pedro Luis Barcia. Buenos Aires: Academia Argentina de Letras, 1982.

Lussich, Antonio D. *Los tres gauchos orientales*. With a prologue by Eneida Sansone de Martínez. Colección Clásicos Uruguayos, vol. 56. Montevideo: Ministerio de Instrucción Pública y Previsión Social, 1964.

Malagón, Javier, ed. *Las actas de independencia de América*. With a preliminary study by Charles C. Griffin. Washington, DC: Unión Panamericana, 1955.

Mansilla, Lucio Victorio. *Una excursión a los indios ranqueles*. With notes by Guillermo Ara. Buenos Aires: Editorial Kapelusz, 1966.

Manzano, Juan Francisco. *Autobiografía del esclavo poeta y otros escritos*. Edited and with an introduction by William Luis. Madrid: Iberoamericana; Frankfurt am Main: Vervuert, 2007.

Marcó, Susana, Abel Posadas, Marta Speroni, and Griselda Vignolo, eds. *Antología del género chico criollo*. Buenos Aires: Editorial Universitaria de Buenos Aires, 1976.

Mareca, José M. B. *El primer libro de las niñas: Lecturas morales e instructivas*. Biblioteca Elemental. Buenos Aires: Pedro Igón, 1897. Archived at BNM.

Mármol, José. *Amalia*. Buenos Aires: Editorial Kapelusz, 1960.

Martel, Julián. *La bolsa*. Buenos Aires: Imprima Editores, 1979.

Martínez, Alberto. *Censo general de educación: Levantado el 23 de mayo de 1909 durante la presidencia del Dr. José Figueroa Alcorta siendo Ministro de Justicia é Instrucción Pública el Dr. Rómulo S. Naón*. Buenos Aires: Taller de Publicaciones de la Oficina Meterológica Argentina, 1910.

Martínez, Benigno T. *Curso elemental de historia argentina*. 7th ed. Buenos Aires: Pedro Igón, 1896. Archived at BNM.

———. *Nociones de historia argentina extractadas del resúmen general del curso de historia*. 6th ed. Buenos Aires: Igón Hermanos, 1888. Archived at BNM.

Miranda, Julián O. *Apuntes sobre historia de la República Oriental del Uruguay, primer curso*. 10th ed. Montevideo: Librería Nacional A. Barreiro and Ramos, 1915.

———. *Apuntes sobre historia de la República Oriental del Uruguay, segundo curso*. 9th ed., rev. and enl. Montevideo: Librería Nacional A. Barreiro y Ramos, 1912.

———. *Educación cívica: Obra destinada a la enseñanza de la constitución*. Montevideo: A. Barreiro y Ramos, 1906. Archived at MPJPV.

———. *El lector infantil, libro de lectura elemental*. Montevideo: Librería Nacional de A. Barreiro y Ramos, 1898. Archived at MPJPV.

Mitre, Bartolomé. *Ensayos históricos*. Buenos Aires: La Cultura Argentina, 1918.

Monner Sans, Ricardo. *Mis dos banderas, poema hispano-argentino*. Buenos Aires: Imprenta Nacional, 1912. Archived at BNM.

———. *Teatro infantil: Monólogos, diálogos y comedias*. 2nd ed. Buenos Aires: Cabaut, 1913. Archived at BNM.

Moreno, Mariano. *Escritos*. Edited and with a prologue by Ricardo Levene. Clásicos Argentinos. Buenos Aires: Ediciones Estrada, 1943.

Nariño, Antonio. *La Bagatela, 1811–1812*, facsimile ed. Bogotá: Vanegas, 1966.

Navarro Viola, Alberto, ed. *Anuario bibliográfico de la República Argentina, año 2—1880*. Nendeln, Liechtenstein: Kraus Reprint, 1970.

———. *Anuario bibliográfico de la República Argentina, año 3—1881.* Nendeln, Liechtenstein: Kraus Reprint, 1972.

Núñez, José Abelardo. *El lector americano, libro primero.* Buenos Aires, n.d. Archived at BNM.

Obligado, Rafael. *Poesías.* 6th ed. Buenos Aires: Espasa-Calpe, 1951.

Olivera, J. V. *Método de Caligrafía.* Buenos Aires: Angel Estrada, n.d.

Ortega, Enrique. *Compendio de instrucción cívica para uso de las escuelas.* Buenos Aires: Pedro Igón, 1897. Archived at BNM.

———. *Manual de instrucción primaria.* Biblioteca Elemental. Buenos Aires: Pedro Igón, 1892. Archived at BNM.

Osuna, Trinidad S. *El nuevo Mándevil: Libro primero, para uso en las escuelas del Río de la Plata.* New York: D. Appleton, 1880. Archived at BNM.

Palliere, León. *Diario de viaje por la América del Sud (1856–1866).* Buenos Aires: Ediciones Peuser, 1945.

Palma, Amelia. *Consejos a mi hija: Lecturas de propaganda moral.* La vida práctica. Buenos Aires: Casa Editora de Jacobo Peuser, 1903. Archived at BNM.

———. *El hogar modelo: Curso completo de economía doméstica.* With a preface by Cecilia Griérson. La vida práctica. Buenos Aires: Imprenta, Litografía y Encuadernación de Jacobo Peuser, 1902. Archived at BNM.

———. *Veladas del hogar: Lecturas auxiliares de moral e instrucción cívica.* Buenos Aires, 1907. Archived at BNM.

Palumbo, Laura. *Educación especial que debe recibir la mujer.* Montevideo: Imprenta Rural, 1901. Archived at BN Ur, Sala Uruguay.

Peacan, Oscar L. *La historia patria explicada a los niños.* Buenos Aires: Cabaut, 1903. Archived at BNM.

Pelliza, Mariano A. *El argentino, texto de lectura.* 2nd ed. Buenos Aires: Igón Hermanos Editores, 1885. Archived at BNM.

Pérez, Abel J. *Memoria correspondiente al año 1900.* Montevideo: Imprenta El Siglo Ilustrado, 1901. Archived at BPC.

———. *Memoria correspondiente al año 1901.* Montevideo: Talleres de A. Barreiro y Ramos, 1902. Archived at BPC.

———. *Memoria correspondiente a los años 1902–1903.* Montevideo: Talleres de A. Barreiro y Ramos, 1904. Archived at BPC.

———. *Memoria correspondiente a los años 1909 y 1910.* Montevideo: Talleres Gráficos A. Barreiro y Ramos, 1911. Archived at BPC.

———. *Motivos de una ley de educación común.* Montevideo: Imprenta El Siglo Ilustrado, 1915.

Pérez Rojo de Aldana, María Leoncia. "Crítica de las fiestas mayas montevideanas de 1816." *Boletín histórico* 69 (1956): 79–84.

Pizzurno, Pablo A. *El libro del escolar, primer libro.* 15th ed. Buenos Aires: Aquilino Fernández, n.d. Archived at BNM.

Podestá, José J. *Medio siglo de farándula: Memorias.* Edited by Osvaldo Pellettieri. Buenos Aires: Galerna, Instituto Nacional del Teatro, 2003.

Poucel, Benjamín. *Los rehenes de Durazno.* Translated by Alicia Mercedes Chiesa. Montevideo: Ediciones El Galeón, 2001.

Pulido, Justino. *Urbanidad y cortesía.* Buenos Aires: Cabaut, 1902. Archived at BNM.

Quesada, Ernesto. "El 'criollismo' en la literatura argentina." In *En torno al criollismo: Ernesto Quesada, "El criollismo en la literatura argentina" y otros textos,* ed. Alfredo V. E. Rubione, 103–230. Buenos Aires: Centro Editor de América Latina, 1983.

——. *Nuestra raza: Discurso pronunciado en el teatro Odeón el 12 de octubre de 1900.* Buenos Aires: Librería Bredahl, 1900.

Quiroga, Clodomiro. *Manual del ciudadano argentino, o sea instrucción cívica para uso de las escuelas seguido de la constitución nacional.* 6th ed. Buenos Aires: Librería La Anticuaria, 1899. Archived at BNM.

Rasgos de la vida pública de S. E. el Sr. Brigadier General D. Juan Manuel de Rosas, Ilustre Restaurador de las Leyes, Héroe del Desierto, Defensor Heroico de la Independencia Americana, Gobernador y Capitan General de la Provincia de Buenos Aires. Buenos Aires: Imprenta del Estado, 1842.

El Redactor de la Asamblea de 1813, facsimile ed. Buenos Aires: La Nación, 1913.

Regules, Elías. *Versos criollos.* With a prologue by Lauro Ayestarán. Colección Clásicos Uruguayos, vol. 57. Montevideo: Ministerio de Instrucción Pública y Previsión Social, 1965.

Rodó, José Enrique. *Ariel* and *Liberalismo y jacobinismo.* Colección Clásicos Uruguayos, vol. 44. Montevideo: Ministerio de Instrucción Pública y Previsión Social, 1964.

Roldós y Pons, Jaime. *La madre y la escuela en sus relaciiones con la educación popular.* Montevideo: Librería Argentina de H. Ibarra, 1880. Archived at MPJPV.

La rosa de marzo, facsimile ed. With a prologue by Juan Canter. Buenos Aires: Ediciones Augusta, 1941.

Rosas, Juan Manuel de. *Instrucciones a los mayordomos de estancias.* With a biography by Pedro de Angelís and a preface, notes, and commentary by Carlos Lemée. Buenos Aires: Editorial Americana, 1942.

Sánchez, Florencio. *Teatro.* With a prologue by Walter Rela. Montevideo: Colección Clásicos Uruguayos, vols. 121–22. Ministerio de Cultura, 1967.

Sarmiento, Domingo Faustino. *Argirópolis.* Buenos Aires: La Cultura Argentina, 1916.

——. *Condición del extranjero en América.* Buenos Aires: La Facultad de Juan Roldán, 1928.

——. *Conflicto y armonias de la razas en América.* With a prologue by José Ingenieros. Buenos Aires: La Cultura Argentina, 1915.

——. *Educación común.* Buenos Aires: Ediciones Solar, 1987.

——. *Educación popular.* With an introduction by Ricardo Rojas. Biblioteca Argentina, vol. 4. Buenos Aires: Librería La Facultad, 1915.

——. *Facundo: Civilización y barbarie.* Madrid: Alianza Editorial, 1988.

——. *Viajes.* 3 vols. Buenos Aires: Librería Hachette, 1955–1958.

Smiles, Samuel. *The Autobiography of Samuel Smiles.* Edited by Thomas Mackay. New York: E. P. Dutton, 1905.

The Southern Star / La Estrella del Sur, facsimile ed. With a prologue by Ariosto D. González. Montevideo: A. Barreiro y Ramos, 1942.

El Torito de los Muchachos, facsimile ed. With a preliminary study by Olga Fernández Latour de Botas. Buenos Aires: Instituto Bibliográfico Antonio Zinny, 1978.

Torrejón, Cipriano, with the collaboration of Lucía Aïn de Torrejón. *Lectura de economía doméstica.* 7th ed. Buenos Aires: Angel Estrada, n.d. Archived at BNM.

Trostiné, Rodolfo, ed. *Cancionero de Manuelita Rosas.* Colección Buen Aire. Buenos Aires: Emecé Editores, 1942.

Varela, Jacobo A. *Informe correspondiente al año 1887.* Montevideo: Imprenta El Siglo Ilustrado, 1887. Archived at MPJPV.

——. *Memoria correspondiente a los años 1879 y 1880.* Vol. 1. Montevideo: Imprenta de La Idea, 1881. Archived at MPJPV.

Varela, José Pedro. *Memoria correspondiente al período transcurrido desde el 24 de agosto de 1877 hasta el 31 de diciembre de 1878.* Vol. 1. Montevideo: Imprenta a vapor de La Tribuna, 1879. Archived at MPJPV.

———. *Obras pedagógicas: La educación del pueblo.* With a prologue by Arturo Ardao. Colección Clásicos Uruguayos, vols. 49–50. Montevideo: Ministerio de Instrucción Pública y Previsión Social, 1964.

———. *Obras pedagógicas: La legislación escolar.* Colección Clásicos Uruguayos, vols. 51–52. Montevideo: Ministerio de Instrucción Pública y Previsión Social, 1964.

Vásquez Acevedo, Alfredo. *Serie graduada de libros de lectura, libro tercero.* 2nd ed. Montevideo: Galli, 1887. Archived at MPJPV.

Vázquez Cores, Francisco. *Cuadernos Vázquez Cores: Curso práctico y teórico de escritura; Letra americana.* Montevideo: Librería-Imprenta Vázquez Cores y Montes, n.d. Archived at MPJPV.

———. *Cuadernos Vázquez Cores: Curso práctico y teórico de escritura; Letra gótico-alemana.* Montevideo: Librería-Imprenta Vázquez Cores y Montes, n.d. Archived at MPJPV.

———. *Cuadernos Vázquez Cores: Curso práctico y teórico de escritura; Letra gótico-inglesa.* Montevideo: Librería-Imprenta Vázquez Cores y Montes, n.d. Archived at MPJPV.

———. *Cuadernos Vázquez Cores: Curso práctico y teórico de escritura; Letra inglesa.* Montevideo: Librería-Imprenta Vázquez Cores y Montes, n.d. Archived at MPJPV.

———. *Cuadernos Vázquez Cores: Curso práctico y teórico de escritura; Letra redonda.* Montevideo: Librería-Imprenta Vázquez Cores y Montes, n.d. Archived at MPJPV.

Wagner Sosa, Petronila. *Patria, hogar y fraternidad.* Buenos Aires: Angel Estrada, 1910. Archived at BNM.

Wilde, José Antonio. *Buenos Aires desde setenta años atrás (1810–1880).* Buenos Aires: Editorial Universitaria de Buenos Aires, 1960.

Williman, Claudio. *Banco de la República Oriental del Uruguay: 1896–24 de agosto–1917.* Montevideo: A. Barreiro y Ramos, 1918.

Zinny, Antonio. *Efemeridografía argirometropolitana hasta la caída del gobierno de Rosas.* Buenos Aires: Imprenta del Plata, 1869.

———. *Historia de la prensa periódica de la República Oriental del Uruguay, 1807–1852.* Buenos Aires: Imprenta y Librería de Mayo, 1883.

Zorrilla de San Martín, Juan. *Tabaré.* With a prologue by Alberto Zum Felde. Colección de Clásicos Uruguayos, vol. 18. Montevideo: Ministerio de Instrucción Pública y Previsión Social, 1956.

Secondary Sources

Abella, Gonzalo. *Mitos, leyendas y tradiciones de la Banda Oriental.* Montevideo: BetumSan Ediciones, 2001.

Achigar, Néstor, Hugo Varela Brown, and María Beatriz Eguren. *Hermano Damasceno: Un aporte a la cultura uruguaya.* Montevideo: Colegio Sagrada Familia, 2003.

Achugar, Hugo. "Blanes y el cuerpo de la patria: Apuntes acerca de las imágenes fundacionales." In Achugar, *Planetas sin boca: Escritos efímeros sobre arte, cultura y literatura,* 181–200. Montevideo: Trilce, 2004.

———, ed. *Derechos de memoria: Nación e independencia en América Latina.* Montevideo: Universidad de la República, Facultad de Humanidades y Ciencias de la Educación, 2003.

———. "Foundational Images of the Nation in Latin America." In Acree and González Espitia, 11–31.

———, ed. *La fundación por la palabra: Letra y nación en América Latina en el siglo XIX.*

Montevideo: Universidad de la República, Facultad de Humanidades y Ciencias de la Educación, Departamento de Publicaciones, 1998.

———. "Parnasos fundacionales, letra, nación y estado en el siglo XIX." In Achugar, *La fundación por la palabra*, 39–77.

———. *Poesía y sociedad (Uruguay, 1880–1911)*. Montevideo: Arca, 1985.

———, and Gerardo Caetano, eds. *Identidad uruguaya: ¿Mito, crisis o afirmación?* 2nd ed. Montevideo: Ediciones Trilce, 1992.

———, and Mabel Moraña, eds. *Uruguay: Imaginarios culturales; Desde las huellas indígenas a la modernidad*. Montevideo: Ediciones Trilce, 2000.

Acree Jr., William G. "Jacinto Ventura de Molina: A Black *Letrado* in a White World of Letters, 1766–1841." *Latin American Research Review* 43, no. 2 (2009): 37–58.

———. "Luis Pérez, A Man of His Word in 1830s Buenos Aires and the Case for Popular Literature." *Bulletin of Spanish Studies* 88, no. 3 (2011): 367–86.

———. "La otra batalla: *The Southern Star*, la *Gazeta de Montevideo* y la revolución de las formas de comunicación en el Río de la Plata." In *En torno a las "invasiones inglesas": Relaciones políticas y culturales con Gran Bretaña a lo largo de dos siglos*, ed. Ana Frega and Beatriz Vegh, 13–22. Montevideo: Facultad de Humanidades y Ciencias de la Educación, 2007.

———, and Alex Borucki, eds. *Jacinto Ventura de Molina y los caminos de la escritura negra en el Río de la Plata*. 2nd ed. Madrid: Iberoamericana; Frankfurt am Main: Vervuert, 2010.

———, and Juan Carlos González Espitia, eds. *Building Nineteenth-Century Latin America: Re-Rooted Cultures, Identities, and Nations*. Nashville: Vanderbilt University Press, 2009.

Alonso, Paula, ed. *Construcciones impresas: Panfletos, diarios y revistas en la formación de los estados nacionales en América Latina, 1820–1920*. Buenos Aires: Fondo de Cultura Económica, 2003.

Altamirano, Carlos, and Beatriz Sarlo. "The Autodidact and the Learning Machine." In Halperín Donghi et al., 156–68.

———. *Ensayos argentinos de Sarmiento a la vanguardia*. Buenos Aires: Centro Editor de América Latina, 1983.

Amante, Adriana. "Género epistolar y política durante el rosismo." In Schvartzman, *La lucha de los lenguajes*, 487–525.

Andermann, Jens. *The Optic of the State: Visuality and Power in Argentina and Brazil*. Pittsburgh: University of Pittsburgh Press, 2007.

Anderson, Benedict. *Imagined Communities: Reflections on the Origin and Spread of Nationalism*, rev. ed. New York: Verso, 1991.

Andrews, George Reid. *The Afro-Argentines of Buenos Aires, 1800–1900*. Madison: University of Wisconsin Press, 1980.

———. *Afro-Latin America, 1800–2000*. New York: Oxford University Press, 2004.

———. *Blackness in the White Nation: A History of Afro-Uruguay*. Chapel Hill: University of North Carolina Press, 2010.

Annino, Antonio, and François-Xavier Guerra, eds. *Inventando la nación: Iberoamérica siglo XIX*. México, DF: Fondo de Cultura Económica, 2003.

Ansolabehere, Pablo. "Ascasubi y el mal argentino." In Schvartzman, *La lucha de los lenguajes*, 39–58.

Araújo, Orestes. *Historia de la escuela uruguaya*. With a prologue by Abel J. Pérez. Montevideo: Imprenta El Siglo Ilustrado, 1911.

Arredondo, Horacio. "Los apuntes estadísticos del Dr. Andrés Lamas." *Revista del Instituto Histórico y Geográfico del Uruguay* 4, no. 1 (1928): 1–44.

Arrieta, Rafael Alberto. *La ciudad y los libros: Excursión bibliográfica al pasado porteño*. Buenos Aires: Librería del Colegio, 1955.

Arteaga, Juan José, and Ernesto Puiggrós. "Inmigración y estadística en el Uruguay 1830–1940." In Hermán Asdrúbal Silva, 261–372.

Assunção, Fernando O. *Pilchas criollas: Usos y costumbres del gaucho*, rev. ed. Montevideo: Ediciones Master Fer, 1979.

Auza, Néstor Tomás. *La literatura periodística porteña del siglo XIX: De Caseros a la organización nacional*. Buenos Aires: Editorial Confluencia, 1999.

———. *Periodismo y feminismo en la Argentina, 1830–1930*. Buenos Aires: Emecé, 1988.

———. *Sarmiento: Precursor del mercado latinoamericano del libro*. Buenos Aires: Marymar Ediciones, 1988.

Ayestarán, Lauro. *La primitiva poesía gauchesca en el Uruguay*. Vol. 1, *1812–1838*. Montevideo: Imprenta El Siglo Ilustrado, 1950.

Banco Central del Uruguay. *Papel moneda emitido en Uruguay, 1830–1896*. Montevideo, Banco Central del Uruguay, 2004.

Baracchini, Hugo. *Historia de las comunicaciones en el Uruguay*. Montevideo: Facultad de Arquitectura, 1978.

Barcia, Pedro Luis. "Estudio preliminar." In *La lira argentina, o Colección de las piezas poéticas dadas a luz en Buenos Aires durante la guerra de su independencia*, ed. Pedro Luis Barcia. Buenos Aires: Academia Argentina de Letras, 1982.

Barité, Mario. *Guía de revistas culturales uruguayas, 1885–1985*. Montevideo: Ediciones El Galeón, 1989.

Barrán, José Pedro. *Apogeo y crisis del Uruguay pastoril y caudillesco: 1838–1875*. Historia Uruguaya, vol. 4. Montevideo: Ediciones de la Banda Oriental, 1974.

———. *Historia de la sensibilidad en el Uruguay*. Vol. 1, *La cultura "bárbara," 1800–1860*. Montevideo: Ediciones de la Banda Oriental, Facultad de Humanidades y Ciencias de la Educación, 1992.

———. *Historia de la sensibilidad en el Uruguay*. Vol. 2, *El disciplinamiento, 1860–1920*. Montevideo: Ediciones de la Banda Oriental, Facultad de Humanidades y Ciencias de la Educación, 1992.

Batticuore, Graciela, Klaus Gallo, and Jorge Myers, eds. *Resonancias románticas: Ensayos sobre historia de la cultura argentina (1820–1890)*. Buenos Aires: EUDEBA, 2005.

Battistessa, Angel J. Preliminary study to *Fausto: Su prefiguración periodística*, by Estanislao del Campo. Buenos Aires: Academia Argentina de Letras, 1989.

Beltrán, Oscar R. *Historia del periodismo argentino: Pensamiento y obra de los forjadores de la Patria*. Buenos Aires: Editorial Sopena Argentina, 1943.

Bertoni, Lilia Ana. *Patriotas, cosmopolitas y nacionalistas: La construcción de la nacionalidad argentina a fines del siglo XIX*. Buenos Aires: Fondo de Cultura Económica, 2001.

Biagini, Hugo E. *Educación y progreso: Primer Congreso Pedagógico Interamericano* Buenos Aires: Docencia, Centro de Estudios Filosóficos, 1983.

Blanchard, Peter. "The Language of Liberation: Slave Voices in the Wars of Independence." *Hispanic American Historical Review* 82, no. 3 (2002): 499–523.

Blossom, Thomas. *Nariño, Hero of Colombian Independence*. Tucson: University of Arizona Press, 1967.

Borucki, Alex. "La Republicana." Unpublished paper.

Bosch, Mariano G. *Historia de los orígenes del teatro nacional argentino y la época de Pablo Podestá*. Buenos Aires: Talleres Gráficos Argentinos L. J. Rosso, 1929.

Botana, Natalio. *La libertad política y su historia*. Buenos Aires: Editorial Sudamericana, 1991.

————. "Sarmiento and Political Order: Liberty, Power, and Virtue." In Halperín Donghi et al., 101–13.

Bottarini, Roberto. "Leer, escribir, votar: La conflictiva definición del curriculum ciudadano." In Cucuzza and Pineau, *Para una historia*, 75–105.

Boullosa, Virginia, Rosa del Carmen Bruno, and Mélide Cantarelli. "La cultura rioplatense entre 1845 y 1848." In Weinberg, *Florencio Varela*, 263–88.

Bourdieu, Pierre. *The Field of Cultural Production: Essays on Art and Literature.* Edited by Randal Johnson. New York: Columbia University Press, 1993.

Bragoni, Beatriz. "Esclavos, libertos y soldados: La cultura política plebeya en Cuyo durante la revolución." In *¿Y el pueblo dónde está? Contribuciones para una historia popular de la revolución de la independencia en el Río de la Plata*, ed. Raúl O. Fradkin, 107–50. Buenos Aires: Prometeo Libros, 2008.

Brando, Oscar, ed. *Literatura uruguaya y sociedad: Historia y crítica.* Vol. 1, *El 900.* Montevideo: Cal y Canto, 1999.

Braslavsky, Berta. "Para una historia de la pedagogía de la lectura en la Argentina: ¿Cómo se enseñó a leer desde 1810 hasta 1930?" In Cucuzza and Pineau, *Para una historia*, 33–49.

Braslavsky, Cecilia. *Los usos de la historia en la educación argentina: Con especial referencia a los libros de texto para escuelas primarias (1853–1916).* Buenos Aires: FLACSO, 1992.

Buonocore, Domingo. *Libreros, editores e impresores de Buenos Aires: Esbozo para una historia del libro argentino.* Buenos Aires: Bowker Editores, 1974.

Burns, E. Bradford. *The Poverty of Progress: Latin America in the Nineteenth Century.* Berkeley: University of California Press, 1980.

Burucúa, José Emilio, and Fabián Alejandro Campagne. "Mitos y simbologías nacionales en los países del cono sur." In Annino and Guerra, *Inventando la nación*, 433–74.

Burucúa, José Emilio, Andrea Jáuregui, Laura Malosetti, and María Lía Munilla. "Influencia de los tipos iconográficos de la revolución francesa en los países del Plata." In *Imagen y recepción de la revolución francesa en la Argentina*, by the Comité Argentino para el Bicentenario de la Revolución Francesa, 129–40. Buenos Aires: Grupo Editor Latinoamericano, 1990.

Bushnell, David. "Postal Images of Argentine Próceres: A Look at Selective Myth-Making." *Studies in Latin American Popular Culture* 1 (1982): 91–105.

Caetano, Gerardo, comp. *Los uruguayos del Centenario: Nación, ciudadanía, religión y educación (1910–1930).* Montevideo: Ediciones Santillana, 2000.

Cánepa, Luis. *Historia de los símbolos nacionales.* Buenos Aires: Editorial Albatros, 1953.

Canter, Juan. *La imprenta en el Río de la Plata, síntesis histórica.* Buenos Aires: Imprenta de la Universidad, 1938.

————. Introduction to *Gazeta de Montevideo*, facsimile ed., vol. 1, Biblioteca de Impresos Raros Americanos. Montevideo: Facultad de Humanidades y Ciencias, Instituto de Investigaciones Históricas, Universidad de la República, 1948.

Cara-Walker, Ana. "Cocoliche: The Art of Assimilation and Dissimulation among Italians and Argentines." *Latin American Research Review* 22, no. 3 (1987): 37–67.

Carilla, Emilio. *Autores, libros y lectores en la literatura argentina.* Tucumán, Argentina: Universidad Nacional de Tucumán, Facultad de Filosofía y Letras, 1979.

Caruso, Marcelo, Inés Dussel, and Pablo Pineau. *La escuela como máquina de educar: Tres escritos sobre un proyecto de la modernidad.* With a prologue by Cecilia Braslavsky. Buenos Aires: Paidós, 2001.

Castagnino, Raúl Héctor. *El circo criollo: Datos y documentos para su historia, 1757–1924.* 2nd ed. Buenos Aires: Editorial Plus Ultra, 1969.

———. *Circo, teatro gauchesco y tango*. Buenos Aires: Instituto Nacional de Estudios de Teatro, 1981.

———. *Crónicas del pasado teatral argentino, siglo XIX*. Buenos Aires: Editorial Huemul, 1977.

Castro-Klarén, Sara, and John Charles Chasteen, eds. *Beyond Imagined Communities: Reading and Writing the Nation in Nineteenth-Century Latin America*. Baltimore: Johns Hopkins University Press; Washington, DC: Woodrow Wilson Center Press, 2004.

Catálogo especializado de los sellos postales del Uruguay. Montevideo: Ciardi Hermanos, 2006.

Celesia, Ernesto H. *Rosas: Aportes para su historia*. Buenos Aires: Ediciones Peuser, 1954.

———. *Rosas: Aportes para su historia*. 2 vols. Buenos Aires: Editorial y Librería Goncourt, 1969.

Centeno, Miguel Angel, and Fernando López-Alves, eds. *The Other Mirror: Grand Theory through the Lens of Latin America*. Princeton, NJ: Princeton University Press, 2001.

Chambers, Sarah C. "Letters and Salons: Women Reading and Writing the Nation." In Castro-Klarén and Chasteen, 54–83.

Chartier, Roger. *Forms and Meanings: Texts, Performances, and Audiences from Codex to Computer*. Philadelphia: University of Pennsylvania Press, 1995.

Chasteen, John Charles. *Americanos: Latin America's Struggles for Independence*. New York: Oxford University Press, 2008.

———. "Fighting Words: The Discourse of Insurgency in Latin American History." *Latin American Research Review* 28, no. 3 (1993): 83–111.

———. *Heroes on Horseback: A Life and Times of the Last Gaucho Caudillos*. Albuquerque: University of New Mexico Press, 1995.

———. Introduction to *Beyond Imagined Communities*. In Castro-Klarén and Chasteen, ix–xxv.

———. *National Rhythms, African Roots: The Deep History of Latin American Popular Dance*. Albuquerque: University of New Mexico Press, 2004.

———. "Patriotic Footwork: Social Dance, Popular Culture, and the Watershed of Independence in Buenos Aires." *Journal of Latin American Cultural Studies* 5, no. 1 (1996): 11–24.

———. "Violence for Show: Knife Dueling on a Nineteenth-Century Cattle Frontier." In *The Problem of Order in Changing Societies: Essays on Crime and Policing in Argentina and Uruguay*, ed. Lyman L. Johnson, 47–64. Albuquerque: University of New Mexico Press, 1990.

Chávez, Fermin. *La cultura en la época de Rosas: Aportes a la descolonización mental de la argentina*. Buenos Aires: Editorial Theoria, 1973.

Chiaramonte, José Carlos. "Formas de identidad en el Río de la Plata luego de 1810." *Boletín del Instituto de Historia Argentina y Americana "Dr. E. Ravignani,"* 3rd ser., 1 (1989): 71–92.

Chiaramonte, José Carlos, Carlos Marichal, and Aimer Granados, eds. *Crear la nación: Los nombres de los países de América Latina*. Buenos Aires: Editorial Sudamericana, 2008.

Child, Jack. *Miniature Messages: The Semiotics and Politics of Latin American Postage Stamps*. Durham, NC: Duke University Press, 2008.

———. "The Politics and Semiotics of the Smallest Icons of Popular Culture: Latin American Postage Stamps." *Latin American Research Review* 40, no. 1 (2005): 108–37.

Coll, Magdalena. *El habla de los esclavos africanos y sus descendientes en Montevideo en los siglos XVIII y XIX: Representación y realidad*. Montevideo: Academia Nacional de Letras; Ediciones de la Banda Oriental, 2010.

Comisión Nacional de Homenaje a Artigas. *Artigas en la historia y en el arte: Catálogo de la exposición realizada en el Teatro Solís*. Montevideo, 1952.

Consejo Nacional de Educación. *El analfabetismo en la Argentina: Estudio comparativo desde 1869–1943*. Buenos Aires: Consejo Nacional de Educación, 1944.

Conway, Chris. "Letras combatientes: Género espistolar y modernidad en la *Gaceta de Caracas*, 1808–1822." In Poblete, "Cambio cultural," 77–91.

Cucuzza, Héctor Rubén, and Pablo Pineau. Introduction. In Cucuzza and Pineau, *Para una historia*, 9–32.

———, eds. *Para una historia de la enseñanza de la lectura y la escritura en Argentina: Del catecismo colonial a "La Razón de Mi Vida."* Buenos Aires: Miño y Dávila, 2002.

Dabove, Juan Pablo. *Nightmares of the Lettered City: Banditry and Literature in Latin America, 1816–1929*. Pittsburgh: University of Pittsburgh Press, 2007.

D'Alessandro, Sonia. "Los escritos de los héroes: ¿Monumento fundacional?" In Achugar, *La fundación por la palabra*, 135–75.

Darnton, Robert. "What is the History of Books?" In Davidson, *Reading in America*, 27–52.

Davidson, Cathy N., ed. *Reading in America: Literature and Social History*. Baltimore: Johns Hopkins University Press, 1989.

———. *Revolution and the Word: The Rise of the Novel in America*. New York: Oxford University Press, 1986.

———. "Toward a History of Books and Readers." In Davidson, *Reading in America*, 1–26.

de Gandía, Enrique. Preliminary study to *Los Amigos de la Patria y de la Juventud*, facsimile ed. Periódicos de la Epoca de la Revolución de Mayo, vol. 5. Buenos Aires: Academia Nacional de la Historia, 1961.

———. Preliminary study to *El Grito del Sud*, facsimile ed. Periódicos de la Epoca de la Revolución de Mayo, vol. 2. Buenos Aires: Academia Nacional de la Historia, 1961.

de la Fuente, Ariel. *Children of Facundo: Caudillo and Gaucho Insurgency during the Argentine State-Formation Process (La Rioja, 1853–1870)*. Durham, NC: Duke University Press, 2000.

———. " 'Gauchos,' 'montoneros' y 'montoneras.' " In Goldman and Salvatore, 267–92.

Delaney, Jeane. "Imagining *El Ser Argentino*: Cultural Nationalism and Romantic Concepts of Nationhood in Early Twentieth Century Argentina." *Journal of Latin American Studies* 34 (August 2002): 625–58.

———. "Making Sense of Modernity: Changing Attitudes toward the Immigrant and the Gaucho in Turn-Of-The-Century Argentina." *Comparative Studies in Society and History* 38, no. 3 (1996): 434–59.

de Luca, Alejandro. "Consejos escolares de distrito: Subordinación o participación popular." In Puiggrós, *Sociedad civil y estado*, 47–69.

de Miguel, Adriana. "Escenas de lectura escolar: La intervención normalista en la formación de la cultura letrada moderna." In Cucuzza and Pineau, *Para una historia*, 107–48.

de Ugarteche, Félix. *La imprenta argentina: Sus orígenes y desarrollo*. Buenos Aires: Talleres Gráficos R. Canals, 1929.

Devoto, Fernando. *Historia de la inmigración en la Argentina*. Buenos Aires: Editorial Sudamericana, 2003.

Diego, José Luis de, ed. *Editores y políticas editoriales en Argentina, 1880–2000*. Buenos Aires: Fondo de Cultura Económica, 2006.

Duncan Barretta, Silvio R., and John Markoff. "Notes on Civilization and Barbarism: Cattle Frontiers in Latin America." *Comparative Studies in Society and History* 20, no. 4 (1978): 587–620.

Earle, Rebecca. "The Role of Print in the Spanish American Wars of Independence." In Jaksić, 9–33.

Egaña, María Loreto, Iván Núñez Prieto, and Cecilia Salinas Alvarez. *La educación primaria en Chile: 1860–1930; Una aventura de niñas y maestras.* Santiago: Lom Ediciones, 2003.

Elfenbein, Andrew. "Cognitive Science and the History of Reading." *PMLA* 121, no. 2 (2006): 484–502.

Escudé, Carlos. *El fracaso del proyecto argentino: Educación e ideología.* Buenos Aires: Instituto Torcuato di Tella, 1990.

Esteves, Ricardo, and Rosendo M. Fraga, comps. *Mirando al bicentenario: Reflexiones sobre el bicentenario y memorabilia.* Buenos Aires: Grupo Velox, 2001.

Estrada, Dardo. *Historia y bibliografía de la imprenta en Montevideo, 1810–1865.* Montevideo: Librería Cervantes, 1912.

Eujanián, Alejandro. "La cultura: Público, autores y editores." In *Nueva historia argentina.* Vol. 4, *Liberalismo, estado y orden burgués (1852–1880),* ed. Marta Bonaudo, 545–605. Buenos Aires: Editorial Sudamericana, 1999.

Fernández, Juan Rómulo. *Civilización argentina: La obra de "La Prensa" en 50 años.* Buenos Aires: L. J. Rosso, 1919.

———. *Historia del periodismo argentino.* Buenos Aires: Librería Perlado, 1943.

Figueira, José Joaquín. *Comentarios a páginas olvidadas de Marcos Sastre: Su labor periodístico-pedagógica en el Uruguay, 1830–1832.* Montevideo: Imprenta Nacional, 1964.

Fletcher, Lea, ed. *Mujeres y cultura en la Argentina del siglo XIX.* Buenos Aires: Feminaria Editora, 1994.

Fontana, Esteban. "Los primeros textos escolares de historia argentina a nivel primario, 1860–1890: Primera parte." *Investigaciones y Ensayos* 47 (1997): 361–84.

———. "Los primeros textos escolares de historia argentina a nivel primario, 1860–1890: Segunda parte." *Investigaciones y Ensayos* 48 (1998): 267–98.

Foster, David William. *The Argentine Generation of 1880: Ideology and Cultural Texts.* Columbia: University of Missouri Press, 1990.

Fraser, Howard M. *Magazines and Masks: Caras y Caretas as a Reflection of Buenos Aires, 1898–1908.* Tempe: Center for Latin American Studies, Arizona State University, 1987.

Frega, Ana. "Uruguayos y orientales: Itinerario de una síntesis compleja." In Chiaramonte, Marichal, and Granados, 95–112.

———. "La virtud y el poder: La soberanía particular de los pueblos en el proyecto artiguista." In Goldman and Salvatore, 101–33.

Furlong, Guillermo. *Historia y bibliografía de las primeras imprentas rioplatenses, 1700–1850.* Vol. 3, *La imprenta en Buenos Aires, 1808–1810, La imprenta en Montevideo, 1807–1810.* Buenos Aires: Librería del Plata, 1959.

Gandulfo, Alberto. "La expansión del sistema escolar argentino: Informe estadístico." In Puiggrós, *Sociedad civil y estado,* 309–37.

Garavaglia, Juan Carlos. "¿Existieron los gauchos?" *Anuario IEHS* 2 (1987): 42–52.

García, Eustasio Antonio. *Desarrollo de la industria editorial argentina.* With a prologue by Gonzalo Losada. Buenos Aires: Fundación Interamericana de Bibliotecología Franklin, 1965.

Gazzola, Valeria, Lisa Aziz-Zadeh, and Christian Keysers. "Empathy and the Somatotopic Auditory Mirror System in Humans." *Current Biology* 16, no. 18 (2006): 1824–29.

Gellner, Ernest. *Nations and Nationalism.* Ithaca, NY: Cornell University Press, 1983.

Gelman, Jorge. "¿Gauchos o campesinos?" *Anuario IEHS* 2 (1987): 53–59.

Gerassi-Navarro, Nina. *Pirate Novels: Fictions of Nation Building in Spanish America.* Durham, NC: Duke University Press, 1999.

Glauert, Earl T. "Ricardo Rojas and the Emergence of Argentine Cultural Nationalism." *Hispanic American Historical Review* 43, no. 1 (1963): 1–13.

Glenberg, Arthur M. "Naturalizing Cognition: The Integration of Cognitive Science and Biology." *Current Biology* 16, no. 18 (2006): 802–4.

Goldaracena, Ricardo. *El libro de los símbolos: Escudos y banderas del Uruguay*. Montevideo: Arca, 1995.

Goldman, Noemí. *Historia y lenguaje: Los discursos de la Revolución de Mayo*. Buenos Aires: Editores de América Latina, 2000.

———, and Ricardo Salvatore, eds. *Caudillismos Rioplatenses: Nuevas miradas a un viejo problema*. Buenos Aires: Editorial Universitaria de Buenos Aires, 1998.

González, Aníbal. *Journalism and the Development of Spanish American Narrative*. New York: Cambridge University Press, 1993.

González Bernaldo de Quirós, Pilar. *Civility and Politics in the Origins of the Argentine Nation: Sociabilities in Buenos Aires, 1829–1862*. Translated by Daniel Philip Tunnard. Los Angeles: UCLA Latin American Center Publications, 2007.

González Demuro, Wilson. "Un gallego en los orígenes del periodismo independentista: Antonio Díaz y la prensa montevideana, 1814–1823." *Anuario del Centro de Estudios Gallegos* (2006): 87–104.

———. "*El Sol de las Provincias Unidas*: Un comentario sobre el periodismo, la revolución y la difusión de ideas en Montevideo a fines de la época colonial." *Colonial Latin American Historical Review* 13, no. 1 (2004): 53–87.

González-Stephan, Beatriz. "Forms of Historic Imagination: Visual Culture, Historiography, and the Tropes of War in Nineteenth-Century Venezuela." In Acree and González Espitia, 101–32.

———. *Fundaciones: Canon, historia y cultura nacional; La historiografía literaria del liberalismo hispanoamericano del siglo XIX*. 2nd ed. Madrid: Iberoamericana; Frankfurt am Main: Vervuert, 2002.

———. "Showcases of Consumption: Historical Panoramas and Universal Expositions." Translated by John Charles Chasteen. In Castro-Klarén and Chasteen, 225–38.

———, and Jens Andermann, eds. *Galerías del progreso: Museos, exposiciones y cultura visual en América Latina*. Rosario, Argentina: Beatriz Viterbo Editora, 2006.

Gortázar, Alejandro. "Del aullido a la escritura: Voces negras en el imaginario nacional." In Achugar, *Derechos de memoria*, 189–263.

Guerra, François-Xavier. "Forms of Communication, Political Spaces, and Cultural Identities in the Creation of Spanish American Nations." Translated by John Charles Chasteen. In Castro-Klarén and Chasteen, 3–32.

———. *Modernidad e independencias: Ensayos sobre las revoluciones hispánicas*. Madrid: Editorial Mapfre, 1992.

———, and Annick Lempérière, eds. *Los espacios públicos en Iberoamérica: Ambigüedades y problemas; Siglos XVIII–XIX*. México, DF: Centro Francés de Estudios Mexicanos y Centroamericanos and Fondo de Cultura Económica, 1998.

Halperín Donghi, Tulio. "Argentine Counterpoint: Rise of the Nation, Rise of the State." In Castro-Klarén and Chasteen, 33–53.

———. *The Contemporary History of Latin America*. Translated and edited by John Charles Chasteen. Latin America in Translation. Durham, NC: Duke University Press, 1993.

———. *José Hernández y sus mundos*. Buenos Aires: Editorial Sudamericana, Instituto Torcuato di Tella, 1985.

———. *Politics, Economics, and Society in Argentina in the Revolutionary Period*. Translated by Richard Southern. Cambridge: Cambridge University Press, 1975.

———. *Proyecto y construcción de una nación (1846–1880)*. Biblioteca del pensamiento argentino, vol. 2. Buenos Aires: Ariel Historia, 1995.

————. "Sarmiento's Place in Postrevolutionary Argentina" In Halperín Donghi et al., 19–30.

————, Iván Jaksić, Gwen Kirkpatrick, and Francine Masiello, eds. *Sarmiento: Author of a Nation*. Berkeley: University of California Press, 1994.

Hansen, Emilio. *La moneda argentina: Estudio histórico*. Buenos Aires: Ramón Sopena, 1916.

Hobsbawm, E. J. *Nations and Nationalism since 1780: Programme, Myth, Reality*. 2nd ed. Cambridge: Cambridge University Press, 1992.

————, and Terence Ranger, eds. *The Invention of Tradition*. Cambridge: Cambridge University Press, 1983.

Iglesia, Cristina, ed. *Letras y divisas: Ensayos sobre literatura y rosismo*. With a prologue by Cristina Iglesia. Buenos Aires: Editorial Universitaria de Buenos Aires, 1998.

Ingenieros, José. *La locura en la Argentina*, with notes by Aníbal Ponce. Buenos Aires: Ediciones Meridión, 1954.

Islas, Ariadna. *Leyendo a Don Orestes: Aproximación a la teoría de la historia en la obra de Orestes Araújo*. Montevideo: Facultad de Humanidades y Ciencias de la Educación, 1995.

————. *La Liga Patriótica de Enseñanza: Una historia sobre ciudadanía, orden social y educación en el Uruguay (1888–1898)*. Montevideo: Ediciones de la Banda Oriental, 2009.

Jaksić, Iván, ed. *The Political Power of the Word: Press and Oratory in Nineteenth-Century Latin America*. London: Institute of Latin American Studies, 2002.

Johnson, Lyman, and Susan Migden Socolow. "Población y espacio en el Buenos Aires del siglo XVIII." Translated by Sibila Seibert. *Desarrollo Económico* 20, no. 79 (1980): 329–49.

Joseph, Gilbert M., and Daniel Nugent, eds., *Everyday Forms of State Formation: Revolution and the Negotiation of Rule in Modern Mexico*, with a foreword by James C. Scott. Durham, NC: Duke University Press, 1994.

Joyce, Patrick. *The Rule of Freedom: Liberalism and the Modern City*. New York: Verso, 2003.

Kaempfer, Alvaro. "Periodismo, orden y cotidianeidad: *Presentación de la Gaceta de Buenos Aires* de Mariano Moreno (1810) y *Prospecto* de la *Aurora de Chile* (1812) de Camilo Henríquez." In Poblete, "Cambio cultural," 125–38.

Katra, William. *The Argentine Generation of 1837: Echeverría, Alberdi, Sarmiento, Mitre*. Madison, NJ: Fairleigh Dickinson University Press, 1996.

Kirkendall, Andrew J. "Student Culture and Nation-State Formation." In Castro-Klarén and Chasteen, 84–111.

Kloetzel, James E. ed. *Scott 1999 Standard Postage Stamp Catalogue*. 6 vols. 155th ed. Sidney, OH: Scott Publishing, 1998.

Lafleur, Héctor René. *Las revistas literarias argentinas, 1893–1967*. Rev. and enl. ed. Buenos Aires: Centro Editor de América Latina, 1968.

Lamas, Andrés. *El escudo de armas de la ciudad de Montevideo*. Montevideo: Talleres de A. Barreiro y Ramos, 1903.

Leone, Verónica. "Manuales escolares e imaginario social en el Uruguay del Centenario." In Caetano, 139–215.

Levene, Ricardo. *El fundador de la Biblioteca Pública de Buenos Aires*. Buenos Aires: Ministerio de Justicia e Instrucción Pública, 1938.

Lewis, Marvin A. *Afro-Uruguayan Literature: Post-Colonial Perspectives*. Lewisburg, PA: Bucknell University Press, 2003.

Lichtblau, Myron I. *The Argentine Novel in the Nineteenth Century*. New York: Hispanic Institute, 1959.

Linares, María Cristina. "Nacimiento y trayectoria de una nueva generación de libros de lectura escolar: *El nene* (1895–1959)." In Cucuzza and Pineau, *Para una historia*, 177–212.

Loeb, Marcelo. *Ensayo de catálogo especializado de las tarjetas postales ilustradas y los enteros postales editados en la República Oriental del Uruguay*. Buenos Aires: EBD Impresiones, 2003.

Lomnitz, Claudio. "Nationalism as a Practical System: Benedict Anderson's Theory of Nationalism from the Vantage Point of Spanish America." In Centeno, 329–59.

López-Alves, Fernando. "Wars and the Formation of Political Parties in Uruguay, 1810–1851." In *Wars, Parties, and Nationalism: Essays on the Politics and Society of Nineteenth-Century Latin America*, ed. Eduardo Posada-Carbó, 5–26. London: Institute of Latin American Studies, 1995.

Loreto Egaña, María, Iván Núñez Prieto, and Cecilia Salinas Alvarez. *La educación primaria en Chile, 1860–1930: Una aventura de niñas y maestras*. Santiago: LOM Ediciones, 2003.

Lucero, Nicolás. "La guerra gauchipolítica." In Schvartzman, *La lucha de los lenguajes*, 17–38.

Lynch, John. *Argentine Caudillo: Juan Manuel de Rosas*. New and rev. ed. Wilmington, DE: Scholarly Resources, 2001.

———. *Caudillos in Spanish America, 1800–1850*. New York: Oxford University Press, 1992.

———. "From Independence to National Organization." In *Argentina since Independence*, ed. Leslie Bethell, 1–46. New York: Cambridge University Press, 1993.

———. *The Spanish American Revolutions, 1808–1826*. 2nd ed. New York: Norton, 1986.

Macintyre, Iona. *Women and Print Culture in Post-Independence Buenos Aires*. Rochester: Boydell and Brewer, 2010.

Mañé Garzón, Fernando. *El Glorioso Montevideano: Vida y obra del doctor José Manuel Pérez Castellano (1742–1815)*, vol. 2. Montevideo: Ministerio de Educación y Cultura; Archivo General de la Nación, 1999.

Marcó, Susana. *Teoría del género chico criollo*. Buenos Aires: Editorial Universitaria de Buenos Aires, 1974.

Marengo, Roberto. "Estructuración y consolidación del poder normalizador: El Consejo Nacional de Educación." In Puiggrós, *Sociedad civil y estado*, 71–175.

Masiello, Francine. *Between Civilization and Barbarism: Women, Nation, and Literary Culture in Modern Argentina*. Lincoln: University of Nebraska Press, 1992.

———, ed. *La mujer y el espacio público: El periodismo femenino en la Argentina del siglo XIX*. Buenos Aires, Argentina: Feminaria Editora, 1994.

Méndez Vives, Enrique. *El Uruguay de la modernización: 1876–1904*. Historia Uruguaya, vol. 5. Montevideo: Ediciones de la Banda Oriental, 1975.

Mendive, Gerardo, and Oscar Jorge Villa. *La prensa y los constituyentes en el Uruguay de 1830: Fundamentos técnicos, económicos y sociales*. Montevideo: Biblioteca Nacional, 1980.

Merbilháa, Margarita. "1900–1919: La época de organización del espacio editorial." In Diego, 29–58.

Monestier, Jaime. *El combate laico: Bajorrelieve de la Reforma Vareliana*. Montevideo: Ediciones El Galeón, 1992.

Morales, Ernesto. *Niños y maestros*. Buenos Aires: El Ateneo, 1939.

Morgade, Graciela. "La docencia para las mujeres: Una alternativa contradictoria en el camino hacia los saberes 'legítimos.'" In Morgade, *Mujeres*, 67–114.

———, ed. *Mujeres en la educación: Género y docencia en la Argentina, 1870–1930*. With a prologue by Tomaz Tadeu Da Silva. Buenos Aires: Miño y Dávila Editores, 1997.

Myers, Jorge. "'Aquí nadie vive de las bellas letras': Literatura e ideas desde el Salón Literario a la Organización Nacional." In Schvartzman, *La lucha de los lenguajes*, 305–33.

———. *Orden y virtud: El discurso republicano en el régimen rosista*. Buenos Aires: Universidad Nacional de Quilmes, 1995.

Nelson, Ernesto. *El analfabetismo en la república argentina: Interpretación de sus estadísticas*. Santa Fe, Argentina: Instituto Social de la Universidad del Litoral, 1939.

Newland, Carlos. *Buenos Aires no es pampa: La educación elemental porteña, 1820–1860*. Buenos Aires: Grupo Editor Latinoamericano, 1992.

———. "La educación elemental en Hispanoamérica: Desde la independencia hasta la centralización de los sistemas educativos nacionales." *Hispanic American Historical Review* 71, no. 2 (1991): 335–64.

Nouzeilles, Gabriela. *Ficciones somáticas: Naturalismo, nacionalismo y políticas médicas del cuerpo (Argentina 1880–1910).* Rosario, Argentina: Beatriz Viterbo, 2000.

Núñez, Javier. "Signed with an X: Methodology and Data Sources for Analyzing the Evolution of Literacy in Latin America and the Caribbean, 1900–1950." *Latin American Research Review* 40, no. 2 (2005): 117–35.

Nunn, Frederick M. *Yesterday's Soldiers: European Military Professionalism in South America, 1890–1940.* Lincoln: University of Nebraska Press, 1983.

Ong, Walter J. *Orality and Literacy: The Technologizing of the Word.* 3rd ed. London: Routledge, 2004.

Ordaz, Luis. *Breve historia del teatro argentino.* Buenos Aires: Editorial Universitaria de Buenos Aires, 1962–1965.

———. *El drama rural.* Buenos Aires: Librería Hachette, 1959.

———. *Inmigración, escena nacional y figuraciones de la tanguería.* Buenos Aires: Editores de América Latina, 1997.

———. *El teatro en el Río de la Plata: Desde sus orígenes hasta nuestros días.* 2nd ed. Buenos Aires: Ediciones Leviatán, 1957.

Ossanna, Edgardo O. "El problema de la letra en la escritura: La escuela entrerriana a comienzos del siglo XX." In Cucuzza and Pineau, *Para una historia,* 213–28.

Palacio Montiel, Celia del. "Redes de información y circulación de impresos en México: La prensa de Guadalajara en las primeras décadas del siglo XIX." In Poblete, "Cambio cultural," 35–48.

Paladino, Clara. "Fiesta y contrapunto: Miradas en las celebraciones de la independencia en América." In Achugar, *Derechos de memoria,* 123–88.

Palomeque, Agapo Luis, ed. *Personalidades que han contribuido a la consolidación de la cultura y las estructuras educacionales.* Vol. 1. With a prologue and notes by Agapo Luis Palomeque. Montevideo: Cámara de Representantes, 1992.

Pastormerlo, Sergio. "1880–1899: El surgimiento de un mercado editorial." In Diego, 1–28.

Pellarolo, Silvia. *Sainete criollo: Democracia, representación; El caso de Nemesio Trejo.* Buenos Aires: Corregidor, 1997.

Pellettieri, Osvaldo, ed. *La inmigración italiana y teatro argentino.* Buenos Aires: Galerna, Instituto Italiano de Cultura de Buenos Aires, 1999.

Pignatelli, Adrián Ignacio. "Caras y Caretas." In *Historia de las revistas argentinas,* 2:271–348. Buenos Aires: Asociación Argentina de Escritores de Revistas, 1997.

Pimienta, Juan, ed. *Centenario de la ley de educación común.* Temas Nacionales. Montevideo: Palacio Legislativo, 1977.

Pineau, Pablo. *La escolarización de la provincia de Buenos Aires, 1875–1930: Una versión posible.* Buenos Aires: Facultad Latinoamericana de Ciencias Sociales, Sede Académica Argentina, 1997.

Poblete, Juan, ed. "Cambio cultural y lectura de periódicos en el siglo XIX en América Latina." Special issue, *Revista Iberoamericana* 72, no. 214 (2006).

———. *Literatura chilena del siglo XIX: Entre públicos lectores y figuras autoriales.* Santiago, Chile: Editorial Cuarto Propio, 2003.

Poch, Susana. "Aura de inicio, trazas de escrituras: Actas de independencia de América (1776–1903)." In Achugar, *Derechos de memoria,* 59–121.

———. "Himnos nacionales de América: Poesía, estado y poder en el siglo XIX." In Achugar, *Fundación por la palabra,* 79–133.

Pradere, Juan A. *Juan Manuel de Rosas, su iconografía.* Buenos Aires: J. Mendesky e hijo, 1914.

Praderio, Antonio. *Indice cronológico de la prensa periódica del Uruguay, 1807–1852.* Manuales Auxiliares Para La Investigación Histórica, vol. 3. Montevideo: Universidad de la República Oriental del Uruguay, Facultad de Humanidades y Ciencias, 1962.

Prado, Fabricio. "In the Shadows of Empires: Trans-Imperial Networks and Colonial Identity in Bourbon Río de la Plata." PhD diss., Emory University, 2009.

Preston, Catherine, and Anton Rosenthal. "*Correo Mítico:* The Construction of a Civic Image in the Postcards of Montevideo, Uruguay, 1900–1930." *Studies in Latin American Popular Culture* 15 (1996): 231–59.

Prieto, Adolfo. *El discurso criollista en la formación de la Argentina moderna.* Buenos Aires: Editorial Sudamericana, 1988.

———. *Sociología del público argentino.* Buenos Aires: Ediciones Leviatán, 1956.

Puiggrós, Adriana. *Qué pasó en la educación argentina: Breve historia desde la conquista hasta el presente.* Buenos Aires: Galerna, 2003.

———, ed. *Sociedad civil y estado en los orígenes del sistema educativo argentino.* Historia de la educación en la Argentina, vol. 2. Buenos Aires: Editorial Galerna, 1991.

———. *Sujetos, disciplina y curriculum.* Historia de la educación en la Argentina, vol. 1. Buenos Aires: Editorial Galerna, 1990.

Quintana, Raúl. Prologue to *Fausto: Impresiones del gaucho Anastasio el Pollo en la representación de esta ópera,* by Estanislao del Campo. Buenos Aires: Imprenta de la Biblioteca Nacional, 1940.

Radway, Janice. *A Feeling for Books: The Book-of-the-Month Club, Literary Taste, and Middle Class Desire.* Chapel Hill: University of North Carolina Press, 1997.

Rama, Angel. *Los gauchipolíticos rioplatenses.* 2 vols. Buenos Aires: Centro Editor de América Latina, 1994.

———. *The Lettered City.* Translated and edited by John Charles Chasteen. Latin America in Translation. Durham, NC: Duke University Press, 1996.

———. *Literatura y clase social.* México: Folios Ediciones, 1983.

———. *Las máscaras democráticas del modernismo.* Montevideo: Fundación Angel Rama, 1985.

———. *Transculturación narrativa en América Latina.* México: Siglo Veintiuno Editores, 1982.

Ramos, Juan Pedro. *Historia de la instrucción primaria en la República Argentina, 1810–1910 (atlas escolar).* Buenos Aires: Jacobo Peuser, 1910.

Ramos, Julio. *Divergent Modernities: Culture and Politics in Nineteenth-Century Latin America.* Translated by John D. Blanco. Durham, NC: Duke University Press, 2001.

Recalde, Héctor. *El primer Congreso Pedagógico: 1882.* Buenos Aires: Centro Editor de América Latina, 1987.

Rela, Walter, ed. *Artículos periodísticos de José Hernández en "La Patria" de Montevideo (1874).* Montevideo: Editorial El Libro Argentino, 1967.

———. *Florencio Sánchez.* Montevideo: Editorial Ulises, 1967.

Rial, Juan, ed. *Estadísticas históricas de Uruguay, 1850–1930.* Montevideo: Centro de Informaciones y Estudios del Uruguay, 1980.

Ribeiro, Ana. *Los tiempos de Artigas.* Vol. 6, *El largo final.* Montevideo: El País, 1999.

Riekenberg, Michael, ed. *Latinoamérica: Enseñanza de la historia, libros de texto y conciencia histórica.* Buenos Aires: Alianza Editorial, FLACSO, 1991.

Rivera, Jorge B. *El escritor y la industria cultural.* Buenos Aires: Atuel, 1998.

Rodríguez, Lidia. "La educación de adultos en la Argentina." In Puiggrós, *Sociedad civil y estado,* 177–223.

Rodríguez Molas, Ricardo E. "Contribución a la bibliografía de Hilario Ascasubi (1807–1875). *Bibliografía argentina de artes y letras* 12 (1961): 53–85.

———. *Historia social del gaucho.* Buenos Aires: Ediciones Marú, 1968.

———, ed. *Luis Pérez y la biografía de Rosas escrita en verso en 1830.* Buenos Aires: Clio, 1957.

Rodríguez Villamil, Silvia. *Las mentalidades dominantes en Montevideo (1850–1900).* Vol. 1, *La mentalidad criolla tradicional.* Montevideo: Ediciones de la Banda Oriental, 1968.

Román, Claudia A. "La prensa periódica: De *La Moda* (1837–1838) a *La Patria Argentina* (1879–1885)." In Schvartzman, *La lucha de los lenguajes,* 439–67.

———. "Tipos de imprenta: Linajes y trayectorias periodísticas." In Schvartzman, *La lucha de los lenguajes,* 469–84.

———. "La vida color rosao: El *Fausto* de Estanislao del Campo." In Schvartzman, *La lucha de los lenguajes,* 59–81.

Romano, Eduardo. *Revolución en la lectura: El discurso periodístico-literario de las primeras revistas ilustradas rioplatenses.* Buenos Aires: Catálogos, 2004.

Rómulo Fernández, Juan. *Historia del periodismo argentino.* Buenos Aires: Librería del Perlado, 1943.

Rossi, Vicente. *Teatro nacional rioplatense: Contribución a su análisis y a su historia.* Buenos Aires: Solar / Hachette, 1969.

Rossiello, Leonardo, ed. *Las otras letras: Literatura uruguaya del siglo XIX.* Montevideo: Editorial Graffiti, 1994.

Rostan, Elina. "Extensión de una nueva práctica cultural: El niño lector." In *Escenas de la vida cotidiana: La antesala del siglo XX (1890–1910),* by Silvia Rodríguez Villamil, 79–108. Montevideo: Ediciones de la Banda Oriental; Montevideo, CLAEH, 2006.

Rubens Bonino, E., Eduardo Martín Valdez, and Joaquín Villaamil. *Los billetes de bancos oficiales del Uruguay: Catálogo de billetes del Uruguay años 1896–1989.* Montevideo, Banco Central del Uruguay, 1989.

Ruffinelli, Jorge. *La revista* Caras y Caretas. Buenos Aires: Galerna, 1968.

Sabor, Josefa Emilia. *Pedro de Angelis y los orígenes de la bibliografía argentina: Ensayo bio-bibliográfico.* Buenos Aires: Ediciones Solar, 1995.

Sagastizábal, Leandro de. *Diseñar una nación: Un estudio sobre la edición en la Argentina del siglo XIX.* Buenos Aires: Grupo Editorial Norma, 2002.

———. *La edición de libros en la Argentina: Una empresa de cultura.* Buenos Aires: Editorial Universitaria de Buenos Aires, 1995.

Salas, Horacio. *El centenario: La Argentina en su hora más gloriosa.* Buenos Aires: Planeta, 1996.

Sarlo, Beatriz. *El imperio de los sentimientos: Narraciones de circulación periódica en la Argentina (1917–1927).* Buenos Aires: Catálogos Editora, 1985; reprint, Buenos Aires: Grupo Editorial Norma, 2000.

———. *La máquina cultural: Maestras, traductores y vanguardistas.* 2nd ed. Buenos Aires: Ariel, 1998.

Schvartzman, Julio. "A quién cornea El *Torito*: Notas sobre el gauchipolítico Luis Pérez." In Iglesia, 13–23.

———, ed. *La lucha de los lenguajes.* Vol. 2, *Historia crítica de la literatura Argentina.* Buenos Aires: Emecé, 2003.

———. *Microcrítica: Lecturas argentinas (cuestiones de detalle).* Buenos Aires: Editorial Biblos, 1996.

Scobie, James R. *Argentina: A City and a Nation.* New York: Oxford University Press, 1964.

———. *Buenos Aires: Plaza to Suburb, 1870–1910.* New York: Oxford University Press, 1974.

Scott, James C. *Weapons of the Weak: Everyday Forms of Peasant Resistance*. New Haven, CT: Yale University Press, 1985.

————, and Benedict J. Tria Kerkvliet, eds. *Everyday Forms of Peasant Resistance in South-East Asia*. London: Frank Cass, 1986.

Seco, José Armando. "Los primeros tiempos de la Biblioteca Pública." *Anuario de Historia Argentina, año 1941* (1942): 602–5.

Seigel, Micol. "Cocoliche's Romp: Fun with Nationalism at Argentina's Carnival." *TDR* 44, no. 2 (2000): 56–83.

Shafer, Neil, and Colin R. Bruce II, eds. *Standard Catalog of World Paper Money*. Vol. 2, *General Issues*. 7th ed. Iola, WI: Krause Publications, 1994.

————, and George S. Cuhaj, eds. *Standard Catalog of World Paper Money*. Vol. 1, *Specialized Issues*. 9th ed. Iola, WI: Krause Publications, 2002.

Shumway, Nicolas. *The Invention of Argentina*. Berkeley: University of California Press, 1991.

Silva, Hermán Asdrúbal, ed. *Inmigración y estadísticas en el Cono Sur de América*. Serie Inmigración, vol. 6. Montevideo: Organización de los Estados Americanos, Instituto Panamericano de Geografía e Historia, 1990.

Silva, Renan. *Prensa y revolución a finales del siglo xviii: Contribución a un análisis de la formación de la ideología de independencia nacional*. Bogotá: Banco de la República, 1988.

Silvera Antúnez, Marcos. *El correo en el Uruguay*. Montevideo: Ediciones El Galeón, 2000.

————. *Historia del transporte en el Uruguay*. Montevideo: Ediciones El Galeón, 2000.

Slatta, Richard W. *Gauchos and the Vanishing Frontier*. Lincoln: University of Nebraska Press, 1983.

————. "Rural Criminality and Social Conflict in Nineteenth-Century Buenos Aires Province." *Hispanic American Historical Review* 60, no. 3 (1980): 450–72.

Smith, Anthony D. *The Ethnic Origins of Nations*. Oxford: Blackwell, 1986.

Solá, Miguel. *La imprenta en Salta: Cien años de prensa (1824–1924) y bibliografía antigua de la imprenta salteña*. Buenos Aires: Talleres Gráficos Porter Hermanos, 1924.

Soler Cañas, Luis, ed. *Negros, gauchos y compadres en el cancionero de la federación*. Buenos Aires: Instituto de Investigaciones Históricas Juan Manuel de Rosas, 1958.

Solomianski, Alejandro. *Identidades secretas: La negritud argentina*. Rosario, Argentina: Beatriz Viterbo Editora, 2003.

Sommer, Doris. *Foundational Fictions: The National Romances of Latin America*. Berkeley: University of California Press, 1991.

Spregelburd, Roberta Paula. "¿Qué se puede leer en la escuela? El control estatal del texto escolar (1880–1916)." In Cucuzza and Pineau, *Para una historia*, 149–76.

Stabb, Martin S. *In Quest of Identity: Patterns in the Spanish American Essay of Ideas, 1890–1960*. Chapel Hill: University of North Carolina Press, 1967.

Svampa, Maristella. "La dialéctica entre lo nuevo y lo viejo: Sobre los usos y nociones del caudillismo en la Argentina durante el siglo XIX." In Goldman and Salvatore, 51–82.

Szuchman, Mark D. "Childhood Education and Politics in Nineteenth-Century Argentina: The Case of Buenos Aires." *Hispanic American Historical Review* 70, no. 1 (1990): 109–38.

————. "Disorder and Social Control in Buenos Aires, 1810–1860." *Journal of Interdisciplinary History* 15, no. 1 (1984): 83–110.

————, ed. *The Middle Period in Latin America: Values and Attitudes in the Seventeenth–Nineteenth Centuries*. Boulder, CO: Lynne Rienner Publishers, 1989.

Tedesco, Juan Carlos. *Educación y sociedad en la Argentina (1880–1945)*. Buenos Aires: Ediciones Solar, 1986.

Torre Revello, José. *Orígenes de la imprenta en España y su desarrollo en América española.* Buenos Aires: Editorial Araújo, 1940.

Torres, María Inés de. *¿La nación tiene cara de mujer? Mujeres y nación en el imaginario letrado del siglo XIX.* Montevideo: Arca, 1995.

Trostiné, Rodolfo. *Bacle.* Buenos Aires: Asociación Libreros Anticuarios de la Argentina, 1953.

Unzueta, Fernando. "Scenes of Reading: Imagining Nations / Romancing History in Spanish America." In Castro-Klarén and Chasteen, 115–60.

Uriarte, Javier. "Las fechas y la invención del sistema simbólico nacional en América Latina." In Achugar, *Derechos de memoria,* 341–422.

Vanderwood, Paul J. "The Picture Postcard as Historical Evidence: Veracruz, 1914." *Americas* 45, no. 2 (1988): 201–25.

Vanger, Milton I. *José Batlle y Ordóñez of Uruguay: The Creator of His Times, 1902–1907.* Cambridge, MA: Harvard University Press, 1963.

———. *The Model Country: José Batlle y Ordóñez of Uruguay, 1907–1915.* Hanover, NH: Published for Brandeis University Press by University Press of New England, 1980.

Vasen, W., and H. L. Riese. *Catálogo de enteros postales argentinos.* [Buenos Aires?], 1991.

Vaughan, Mary Kay. "Primary Education and Literacy in Nineteenth-Century Mexico: Research Trends, 1968–1988." *Latin American Research Review* 25, no. 1 (1990): 31–66.

Vázquez Lucio, Oscar E. *Historia del humor gráfico y escrito en la Argentina.* Vol. 1. Buenos Aires: Editorial Universitaria de Buenos Aires, 1985.

Verdesio, Emilio. *Génesis de la educación uruguaya.* Montevideo: Imprenta Nacional, 1962.

Weinberg, Félix, ed. *Florencio Varela y El Comercio del Plata.* With an introduction by Félix Weinberg. Bahía Blanca, Argentina: Instituto de Humanidades, Universidad Nacional del Sur, 1970.

———. *Juan Gualberto Godoy: Literatura y política; Poesía popular y poesía gauchesca.* Buenos Aires: Solar, 1970.

———. "El periodismo en la época de Rosas." *Revista de Historia* 2 (1957): 81–100.

———, ed. *El Salón Literario.* With a preliminary study by Félix Weinberg. Buenos Aires: Librería Hachette, 1958.

Werz, Nikolaus. "Reflexiones sobre la imagen de Bolívar y la enseñanza de la historia en Venezuela." In Riekenberg, 103–21.

West, Regina Angela. "Tailoring the Nation: The Narrative of Patriotic Dress in Nineteenth Century Argentina." PhD diss., University of California at Berkeley, 1997

Williams, Raymond. *The Long Revolution.* Peterborough, Ontario: Broadview Press, 2001.

———. *The Sociology of Culture.* Chicago: University of Chicago Press, 1995.

Wilson, Irma. *Mexico: A Century of Educational Thought.* Westport, CT: Greenwood Press, 1974.

Zeballos, Estanislao S. *El escudo y los colores nacionales.* Buenos Aires: Imprenta, Litografía y Encuadernación de J. Peuser, 1900.

Zum Felde, Alberto. *Proceso histórico del Uruguay: Esquema de una sociología nacional.* 2nd ed. Montevideo: Arca, 1972.

Index

Page numbers in bold refer to illustrations.

Acevedo Díaz, Eduardo, 123
Adelante (Figueira), 114, 115
adult education, 92–93, 97, 111, 116
advertisements, 3, 28–29, 53, 186, **187**
Afro-descendants. *See* blacks
Alberdi, Juan Bautista, 70
almanacs, 19, 188
Alsina, Valentín, 71
Amarilla, La (The Yellow School), 165–66
American Bank Note Company, 172, 174, 176
Amigo del Obrero, El, 188
Amigos de la Patria y de la Juventud, Los, 26
Angelis, Pedro de, 58, 68
anonymous authors, 9, 29, 38, 51, 53, 62–64, 69
anthologies, 18, 32–34
Aparicio, Timoteo, 78, 79
Araújo, Orestes, 86, 102, 110, 111, 129, 206n3
Archivo Americano, 68
Arostegui, Abdón, 124
Arriero Argentino, El, 71–72
Artigas, José
    character of citizens and, 31, 95, 127
    as hero, 123, 126, 127–28, 132, **143**, 144,
        199n17 (*see also* Artigas, José, repre-
        sentations of)
    as threat, 22
Artigas, José, representations of
    at celebrations, 29, **147**
    on currency, 178, 179, **180**
    educational media and, 108, **134**, **139**
    on stamps, 168, 172, 173, **174**
    See also Artigas, José: as hero
Ascasubi, Hilario
    influence of, 77, 78, 181
    popularity of, 57, 71, 82, 204n78
    writings of, 51, 57, 71–75, 79

Ateneo, El (The Athenaeum), 87
Avellaneda, Nicolás, 177, 214n25

Bacle, César Hipólito, 47, 58–59
Banda Oriental, definition of, 20, 199n17
banks, 176–80, 213n23
Barreiro y Ramos, Antonio, 100, 108
Batalla de Las Piedras, La (Héquet), 140
Batlle, Lorenzo, 78
Battle of Las Piedras, 140, 173
Battle y Ordóñez, José, 95
Becher, Emilio, 188
Belgrano, Manuel, 126, 127–28, 137, 138, 175
Bernardo (slave), 21–22
Berra, Francisco, 110
Berro, Bernardo, 206n3
Beruti, Juan Manuel, 28, 35–36
Biasotti, Carmen, 88, 142–44, 161–62, 209n83
Biblioteca La Nación series, 188
Biblioteca Popular de Buenos Aires series, 188
Biblioteca Pública de Buenos Aires, 27–28, 42
Biblioteca Pública de Montevideo, 29
bills of sale, 16, 48, 62
blacks
    political messages and, 9, 52–53, 56,
        64–65, 203n41
    in public sphere, 17, 30, 31
    rebellion led by, 21–22
    in textbooks, 126
Blancos
    children as, 121
    conservatism of, 44, 202n2
    documentation issued by, 50, 62
    lemas of, 59, **60**, 62, 68
    opposition to, 45, 70–71, 74, 82
    popular literature and, 9, 46, 51, 64, 68

Blancos (cont.)
 Varela family members as, 206n3
 in wars, 44, 78–80, 122
 See also Oribe, Manuel
Blanes, Juan Manuel, 40, 134, 135, 141, 173, 179
booksellers, 1–2, 69–70, 107–8, 186
borderland. See Uruguay-Brazil border
branding, of cattle, 46, 47–48, 48, 49, 64
broadsheets, 20, 29–30, 67
buen amigo, Un (Figueira), 114, 115

Caceres, Casto, 61
cafés, 20, 25, 91, 191
Cambaceres, Eugenio, 123
Caras y Caretas, 3, 124, 184, 185, 187, 188–89
"Card Game, The" (Ascasubi), 73–74
cards. See collectible cards
Carlos III, 16
Carlota, La (press), 23, 42
Carlota Joaquina, 22–23
Castañeda, Francisco de Paula, 55
Catalá de Princivalle, Emma, 5, 149–53
Catedral stamp series, 172–73, 173
cattle culture, definition of, 198n13
caudillismo, El (Herrera y Obes), 46
Censor, El, 28
centenary of May revolution
 commemorative items for, 137, 173, 185, 186, 187, 189
 definitions of literature and, 124
 periodization and, 205n2
churches
 dress code for, 61–62
 group reading at, 4, 20–21, 25, 191
 public ceremonies and, 30, 41, 69
 See also clergy; religion
cielitos (dance-based poems), 54, 56, 64, 74, 202n17
cigarette boxes, 166, 180–82, 181, 188, 190
circuses, 12, 81, 124, 182, 188
civic education, 11, 96, 120, 149–50. See also lessons in patriotism
cleanliness. See hygiene
clergy, 21, 28, 39, 61, 87, 100, 131, 208n51. See also Castañeda, Francisco de Paula; Larrañaga, Dámaso Antonio
CNE (Consejo Nacional de Educación), 97, 98, 99, 102, 105

coats of arms, 35–38, 36, 37, 42
 on buildings, 35, 144, 166
 on currency, 36–37, 167, 177, 178, 180
 on official documents, 35, 38, 60
 postal imagery with, 167, 168, 171, 172, 173, 174
 in schools, 106, 136, 144
coins. See currency
Colección general de las marcas (Bacle), 47–48, 48, 49
collectible cards, 5, 165, 166, 180, 182–83, 183, 190
Colorados
 attacks on, 62, 64
 blacks recruited by, 65
 children as, 121
 in present day, 202n2
 Varela family members as, 206n3
 at war, 44, 78, 122
 writing of, 69, 71, 82–83
 See also Rivera, Fructuoso
Comercio del Plata, El, 71
Compte y Riqué, Enriqueta, 105, 118, 208n66
Consejos a mi hija (Palma), 154, 155, 212n55
constitutions
 anniversary of, 175
 celebrations of, 38–42, 40, 65, 201n98
 copies of, 32, 33, 41, 128, 201n98
criollo dramas, 124, 184, 188, 190
Cuadernos Nacionales (notebook series), 108, 138, 139, 140
currency
 coats of arms on, 36–37, 167, 177, 178, 180
 heroes on, 88, 177, 178, 179, 180
 as mass media, 166, 176–80, 190, 193
 on postal items, 167
curricula, 92–93, 94–98, 104, 105, 125, 159
Curso de historia patria (H.D.), 131–32, 133, 134, 135

Darío, Rubén, 123
décimas (poetic form), 53, 62
declarations of independence, as documents, 38–39, 41, 42, 173, 201n88
del Campo, Estanislao, 77–78
del Castaño, Aurora Stella, 153
de María, Alcides, 172
de María, Isidoro, 19, 39, 41, 75, 99, 162
Descripción de las fiestas cívicas, 38

DGIP (Dirección General de Instrucción Pública)
  as distributor of texts, 110–11
  duties of, 97
  notebooks produced by, 108, **109**
  religion in schools barred by, 131
  textbooks and, 87, 97, 98, 99, 100, 105, 114–15, 116
  Varela and, 87
dialogues
  of anonymous authors, 53
  of Ascasubi, 71, 74–75
  of Hidalgo, 31, 34, 50, 54
  of Lussich, 78
  in textbooks, 132, 134, 137–38
Diario de la Tarde, El, 68, 70
Díaz, José Virginio, 121–22
Díaz, Ramón, 34
divisas (ribbons), 57, 61–62, **63**, 121, 203n39
Domador, El, 57
dress
  at celebrations, 35–36, 39–40, **147**
  party affiliation and, 57, 60, 61–62, 63, 121, 203n39, 210n4 (*see also* headbands)

Echagüe, Pascual, 74, 75
Echeverría, Esteban, 70
Economia doméstica al alcance de las niñas (anonymous), 153–54
Educación cívica (Miranda), 128–29
educación del pueblo, La (Varela), 94
Eizaguirre, José Manuel, 1, 129–31
Ejercicios progresivos (Catalá de Princivalle), **112**
elites
  as educational administrators, 90, 131
  European texts and, 26, 70, 207n27, 214n37
  as liberal opposition, 9, 45, 198n13
  national histories and, 33, 126
  newspapers by, 25–27, 71
  popular classes and, 7–8, 17, 27
  popular literature and, 45, 71, 77–78, 80, 123–24, 188
  in power, 17, 33, 46, 76, 80, 213n1
  schools for, 205n1, 207n36
  on social crisis, 83, 90, 91, 94, 96, 190
  Varela and, 87–88, 95, 206n3
  See also Colorados; Unitarians

Ensayo de historia patria (H.D.), 131
Episodios históricos (Araújo), 111, 129
estancieros (estate owners)
  and branding of cattle, 47–48
  criticism of, 70
  height of cattle culture and, 8, 43, 46
  opposition to, 46, 69, 71
  papeletas and, 49, 50, 51
  politics of, 8, 43, 44, 51, 81
  popular literature and, 45, 51
  See also Rosas, Juan Manuel de; Urquiza, Justo José de
Estrada, Angel, 99–100, 109
everyday reading, definition of, 4–7
exams, 111, 113, 114, 142, 144, 209n83

Facundo (Sarmiento), 46, 70
fajas (postage bands), 174
Fausto (del Campo), 77, 78
Federalists
  catchwords and *lemas* of, 46, 59–62, **63**, 67, 68
  cattle culture and, 44, 46, 51–52
  celebrations of, 68–69
  opposition to, 45, 69, 70, 74
  popularity of, 9, 69, 70–71, 202n17
  popular literature and, 9, 45, 51–58, 63–64
  propaganda of, 65–67, 82
  red, as color of, 57, 60, 61–62, 66, 121
  See also Rosas, Juan Manuel de
Feelings of a Patriot (Hidalgo), 30
female students
  teaching as future career of, 102–4, 162
  textbooks for, 11, 116, 122, 125, 148–58, 162, 163–64
  See also Biasotti, Carmen; Pereda, Raudelinda
female students, images of
  in classes, **107**, **150**, **159–61**
  on covers, **110**, **113**
  at events, **146**, **147**
  as readers, **103**, **113**, **115**, **155**, **161**
  as writers, **107**, **110**, **118**, **119**
Fernando VII, 23, 198n11
Ferreyra, Andrés, 99
fiestas mayas (May celebrations), 7, 29, 34, 35, 42, 145, 201n77
Figueira, José H., 114–16

Figueroa, Francisco Acuña de, 41
Figueroa, Julio, 124
figuritas. See collectible cards
flags
   in celebrations, 29, 38, 39–41, 69
   on cigarette boxes, 181
   daily raising of, 145
   on postal items, 168
   slogans on, **133**, 203n41
   in student work, 141, 143, 144, 155
   symbolic repertoires and, 32
   in textbooks, 131, **133**, **136**, 137, 138, 156
   at Varela's burial, 86–87
Fogón, El, 172, 188
folletos (pamphlets), 77, 81, 124, 142, 190
France, La, 86
Fretes, Joaquín, 21–22, 192–93

Gaceta de Buenos Aires, 8, 20–22, 25, 28, 37,
   192–93
Gaceta Mercantil, La, 63, 68
Gálvez, Manuel, 123
Gaucha, La, 52, **53**, 56
gauchesque writing, 12, 44, 51–58, 71–75,
   76–82, 123–24, 190
   trends in, 55, 76–79, 81
Gaucho, El, 50, **52**, 55, 57
Gaucho en Campaña, El, 72, 73
Gaucho Jacinto Cielo, El, **72**, **73**
gauchos (cowboys from the Plata)
   in cigarette marketing, 180–81, 182, **183**,
     183–84, 186
   on currency, 178
   in dialogues, 31, 74
   on educational materials, **133**, 141
   group reading and, 3, 51–52
   myth of, 76, 77, 184
   negative views of, 17, 89–91
   in papers and loose leaves, 50–57, **52**, **53**,
     71–75, **72**, **73**, **75**
   persecution of, 50–51, 76, 77, 80–81, 90
   on stamps, 172–73, **173**
   See also gauchesque writing
Gazeta de Montevideo, 22–24, 200n35
gender identities, 4–5, 11, 122–23, 124–25,
   148–49, 152–64, 190, 213n71. *See also*
   female students; lessons in motherhood;
   women
González, Joaquín, 99

Grito del Sud, El, 24–25
Gualberto Godoy, Juan, 51
Guido y Spano, Carlos, 154
Gutiérrez, Eduardo, 81, 123, 182, 205n101
Gutiérrez, Juan María, 70

H.D. [Hermano Damsceno], 131–32, 211n23
headbands, 4, 46, 74–75
Héquet, Diógenes, 140
Hernández, José, 5, 46, 78, 80–81, 90
Hidalgo, Bartolomé
   influence of, 50, 54, 72, 74
   stature of, 5
   works of, 30, 31, 34, 55, 78
hogar modelo, El (Palma), 111, 154–55
Hogar y patria (Latallada), 147, 212n68
home economics, definition of, 149
Hospital de la Caridad, 201n98
Hudson, W. H., 121
hygiene, 11, 96, 97, 142, 148–52, **150**, 156

immigrants
   cigarette marketing and, 184
   education and, 92, 95, 101, 122, 124, 130,
     205n1
   waves of, 3, 83, 90, 197n6
   See also Angelis, Pedro de; Mailhos,
     Julio
Imprenta del Estado, 16
Imprenta Litográfica del Estado, 47, 58
Independiente, El, 25–26
Indians and indigenous people
   actions against, 50, 58, 76, 90
   declaration of independence and, 39
   visual references to, 35, 181–82
   written depictions of, 32, 126
inspectors, 97, 100, 101, 104, 114, 144,
   208nn62–63
intellectuals. *See* elites

Juan Cuello (Gutiérrez), 182, 188
Juan Moreira (Gutiérrez), 81, 123, 182, **183**, 188
Junta of Buenos Aires, 20–21, 22, 28, 139,
   200n25

Lady Liberty, 174, 175, 178, **179**, **181**, 185. *See
   also* women: as republican symbols
Lamas, Alejandro, 157–58
Lamas, Elvira, 157, 158

Larrañaga, Dámaso Antonio, 30–31, 38, 126, 206n3
Latallada, Felisa, 147, 212n69
Latorre, Lorenzo, 86, 87, 95
Lavalle, Juan, 64
Lavalleja, Juan Antonio, **109**, 126, 132, 144
laws of public education, 94–96, 97, 98, 104, 105, 117, 205n2, 207n38
Lecciones de economia doméstica (Catalá de Princivalle), 149–53
Lectura de economia doméstica (Torrejón), 153
Lecturas ejemplares (Araújo), 110, 129
Lecturas sobre moral, higiene y economia doméstica (Lamas and Lamas), 157–58
legislación escolar, La (Varela), 94–95
Leguizamón, Onésimo, 91
lemas. See slogans
lessons in motherhood
    effect of, 116, 122–23, 124–25, 159–64
    textbooks for, 111, 148–58, 163
    See also gender identities
lessons in patriotism
    effect of, 116, 122–23, 124–25, 141–44, 145, 147, 164
    lessons in motherhood as, 148–50, 156–57, 162–63
    notebooks for, 138–41
    reinforcement of, 144–45
    textbooks for, 125–38, 147, 148, 163
letter-envelopes, 168, 175
liberals. *See* elites
libraries
    collections of, 28, 97, 207n27
    creation of, 27–31, 34, 93, 97–98, 100, 186
    as meeting places, 7, 17, 31, 42, 189–90
    of schools, 95, 97, 99, 101, 111, 114
    See also Larrañaga, Dámaso Antonio
libro del escolar, El (Pizzurno), 111
libros de lectura (textbook genre), 96, 99, 148
Libros de lectura (Vásquez Acevedo), 110
Liga Patriótica de la Enseñanza (Patriotic League of Education), 88
lira argentina, La (anthology), 33
lists of approved textbooks
    by DGIP, 98
    enforcement of, 104, 208n62
    publication of, 100, 108, 208n61

    textbook sales and, 99
    use of, 104
    works excluded from, 131
    works included on, 110, 128, 129–30, 152
literacy rates, 2, 10, 85, 117–18, 120, 190, 197n4, 210n96
literature, definitions of, 5, 6, 123, 124, 165–66
loose leaves
    cigarette ad on, 214n33
    gauchesque writing on, 44, 51, 52, **53**, 56, 62, 68, 71–72, 81, 190, 191
    as mass media, 18, 67, 166
    patriotic verse on, 33, 34, 41
    Rosas regime and, 62
    student work on, 106
López y Planes, Vicente, 25, 34, 70
Luca, Esteban de, 34
Lugares, Pancho, 50–51, **52**, 55–56
Lussich, Antonio, 78–79

Mailhos, Julio, 183–84
Mann, Horace, 93
Manzano, Juan Francisco, 199n9
"Marcha patriótica" (López y Planes), 32, 34–35, 134, 201n77
Martín Fierro (Hernández), 12, 46, 80–81, 90, 182, 183, 205n102
matadero, El (Echeverría), 70
matchboxes, 166, 180
Maternología (Lamas), 157–58
May Revolution of 1810
    definition of, 198n11
    libraries and, 28, 29
    presses and, 16, 20
    See also centenary of May Revolution; *fiestas mayas*
Mejía, José Ramos, 92
memoirs, 28, 61, 91, 100
Método de Caligrafía (Olivera), **110**
military schools, 92–93
Miranda, Francisco, 8
Miranda, Julián, 110, 128–29
Mitre, Bartolomé, 15, 77, 168, 177, 183
Molina, Jacinto Ventura de, 8, 31, 199n9
Monitor de la Educación Común, El (CNE), 100–101
Monner Sans, Ricardo, 134
Monteagudo, Bernardo, 21, 22, 192
Moratorio, Orosmán, 124

Moreno, Manuel, 26
Moreno, Mariano, 19, 20, 25, 27–28, 126, 128
mosaico argentino, El (Igón), **136**
motherhood, lessons in. *See* lessons in
motherhood
Museo Pedagógico José Pedro Varela, 88, 118

Nariño, Antonio, 8
national anthems
at celebrations, 32, 34–35, 145
in schools, 132, 134, 145, **160**
symbolic repertoires and, 17, 38
Navarro Viola, Miguel, 188
Negrita, La, 52–53, 56
Negrito, El, 52–53, 56, 57
nene, El (Ferreyra), 5, 99–100
newspapers
cigarette marketing and, 180–81, 214n33
educators and, 91, 93–94
elites and, 25, 26
everyday nature of, 6
gauchesque writing and, 50–53, **52**,
54–58, **72**, 77, 190
mailing of, 54, 174
reading aloud of, 4, 20–22, 68, 192
revolutionary era and, 4, 8, 16, 19, 20, 24,
26–27, 189, 191
Rosas regime and, 57, 58, 67–69
scholarship on, 3, 13, 199n10, 204n60
second printing revolution and, 124, 163,
186, 204n85
night schools, 92, 205n1
niña argentina, La (Fraguiero), 156–57
Niños Expósitos press, 15–17, 19–20, 22,
24–25, 26, 34, 42
niño y la patria, El (Alexis), 137–38
normal schools, 89, 93, 102–4, **103**, 150, 205n1,
208n58
notebooks
covers of, 107–8, **108**, **110**, 118, **119**, 138–41,
139, **140**
development and distribution of, 105,
106–9, 138–41, 209n70
identity formation and, 4–5, 10, 85
as indicators of lessons learned, 11, 88,
118–20, 141–44, **143**, 159–62, 193
printers of, 100, 107–9

Oribe, Manuel
government of, 50
lemas of, 59, 61, 62
opposition to, 65, 71, 73, 74
out of favor, 168
support for, 9, 45, 60, 64, 82
See also Blancos
Oriental en Campaña, El, 64
Orientales, as term, 199n17

Palma, Amelia, 111, 154–55, 212n57
Palomeque, José, 91
pamphlets, 77, 81, 124, 142, 190
papeletas (ID cards), 49–51, 62
paper money. *See* currency
Paraguayan War, 77, 122, 205n87
parents
at schools, 113–14, 144, 148, 209n83
teachers' contact with, 113–14, 122, 151
as textbook audience, 101, 111, 116–17, 125,
128, 130, 145
See also reading at home
Parnaso Oriental (anthology), 33
pasaportes (passports), 49–50, **60**, 62
pasquinades, 3, 22, 67, 68, 69
patria, La (Eizaguirre), 1, 129–31
"patria, La" (Monner Sans), 134, 137
patria en la escuela, La (Bernárdez), 129
Patria, hogar y fraternidad (Wagner Sosa), 127
Patriotic and Literary Society of Buenos
Aires, 24, 25
patriotism, lessons in. *See* lessons in
patriotism
Paulino Lucero (Ascasubi), 72–73
Pereda, Raudelinda, 118–20, 144, 159, 193
Pérez, Abel, 114, 208n62
Pérez, Luis
Ascasubi as rival of, 71–72
popularity of, 5, 51–52, 57, 78, 193
Rosas regime and, 57, 58, 82, 203n26
writings of, 50–53, 54–57
Perfiles biográficos (Araújo), 110, 129
Peuser, Jacobo, 99
Phrygian caps, 35–36, 38, 183
Pizzurno, Pablo, 111
plays, 81, 124, 132, 134, 137. *See also* criollo dramas; dialogues; theaters: performances in
poetry. *See* verse

political parties. *See* Blancos; Colorados; Federalists; Unitarians
Popular, La (tobacco maker), 182–83, 214n33
postage stamps, 88, 127, 166, 168, **171**, 172–74, **173**, 213n10
postal services, 54, 167–68
postcards, 3, **146**, 166–72, **167**, **169–71**, 174, 175–76, 190, 213n10, 213n15
practice schools, 150
primary schools
  age of students at, 205n1
  curricula of, 92, 94–98, 105, 159
  establishment of, 9–11, 85, 89, 94–98, 102, 117, 205n2, 207n38
  expansion of, 100, 117, 190
  materials for, 85, 92, 104–11, **106**
  other types of schools and, 92, 150, 205n1
  as solution to social crisis, 89–91, 96
  See also Sarmiento, Domingo; Varela, José Pedro
primer libro de las niñas, El (Mareca), 155–56
print culture, definition of, 3–4
printers and print shops
  number of, 24, 186, 204n85
  overseas, 172, 174, 176, 178, 179
  of revolutionary moment, 7, 15–17, 18–20, 22–25, 42, 189
  Rosas's actions against, 58–59
  of school materials, 99–100, 105, 107–9
  See also individual presses
private schools, 124, 131, 209n91
prizes, 32, 41, 111, 114, 182, 209n84
prospectos (newspaper introductions), 22–23, 24–25, 26
pulperías (country stores), 3, 4, 20, 51–52, **54**, **55**, 89, 91, 191
Purple Land, The (Hudson), 121

¿Quieres leer? (Figueira), 114–16, **115**

race, 64–65, 79, 90. *See also* blacks; Indians and indigenous people
Rama, Angel, 55, 78, 166, 205n90, 213n1
Rasgos de la vida publica de . . . Rosas (compilation), 65–66
reading and writing, as school subjects
  chalkboards for, **106**
  extracurricular instruction in, 93
as key to other subjects, 96, 105
  methods of teaching, 100–101, 102–3, 105–8
  notebooks for, 105, 106–9, **110**, 118–20
  student practice of, **103**, **107**, 118–20, 142–44, **143**, 161–62, **161**, 165
  textbooks for, 11, 98, 109–10, **112**, **113**, 114–16, **115**, 204n70, 209n74
reading at home
  bureaucratic framework and, 97
  encouragement of, 101, 102–3, 110–11
  as everyday activity, 4, 192
  images of, **112**, **113**, **155**
  lessons on, 111, 154, 212n54
  reports of, 161
  textbooks used in, 4, 6, 11, 101, 116, 131, 148
Regules, Elías, 124
religion
  schools and, 87, 95, 96, 105, 131, 155
  in state ceremony, 41
  See also churches; clergy
Republicana, La (tobacco factory), 183–84, 214n34
Republicano, El, 64
ribbons (*divisas*), 57, 61–62, **63**, 121, 203n39
Rivadavia, Bernardino, 16, 33–34, 59, 138, 168, 174
Rivera, Fructuoso
  images of, 108, **109**, **177**, 178
  partisan texts and, 64, 65, 67, 71, 73–74
  on passenger list, 62
  in school materials, 108, **109**, 126
Rodó, José Enrique, 123, **147**
Rodríguez, Cayetano, 34
Rojas, Ricardo, 123
Rojo y Blanco, 188
rosa de marzo, La (Aguilar), 66–67, 204n59
Rosas, Juan Manuel de
  as caudillo, 43, 48, 81, 82
  negative views of, 43, 76, 126–28, 168, 182
  opposition to, 71, 73–74
  political trajectory of, 45–46
  praise and support of, 9, 53, 55–63, 65–69, 75
  presses and, 57–59, 68, 203n27
  See also Federalists
Rosas, Manuela, 65

Sánchez, Florencio, 123
San Martín, José de, 35, 126, 127, 138, 174, 186
Sarmiento, Domingo
    as educator, 2–3, 10, 91–93, 100
    Estrada and, 99, 100
    as exile, 59, 70, 91
    government of, 80
    images of, 168, 177–78
    stature of, 89, 120, 126, 168
    writings of, 2, 46, 70, 91
Sastre, Marcos, 69, 204n70
seals. *See* coats of arms
secondary schools, 9–10, 97, 205n1, 207n36
second printing revolution, 123–24, 163–64,
    190
"Sembrador de abecedario" (Lima), 86, 206n4
Siglo, El, 86–87
slaves, 17, 21–22, 28–29, 65, 200nn25–26
slogans
    on printed materials, 59–62, **60**, 67, 68,
      133
    on textile items, 4, 46, 57, 63, 74–75,
      203n41
Smiles, Samuel, 186, 214n37
Society of Friends of Public Education
    (Sociedad de Amigos de la Educación
    Popular), 87, 93, 94, 100, 207n27
Solá, Victorino, 16
Southern Star, 18, 19
Southern Star press, 19–20, 42
Suarez, Joaquín, 168

Tambor de la Línea, El, 65
teachers
    administrators and, 3, 97, 104
    as authors, 99, 107, 110
    in countryside, 104, 121–22
    directives disregarded by, 95, 104
    parents' interactions with, 113, 122, 151
    partisanship and, 61, 121–22
    textbook sections for, 111, 116, 130, 132, 158
    textbook selection by, 99, 104, 107
    training of, 89, 93, 102–4, 205n1
    women as, 102, 162, 208n57
Teatro infantil (Monner Sans), 134, 137
Teatro Solis, 87, 173
textbook selection
    committees for, 97, 98–99
    criteria for, 102

    genre-defining effect of, 99, 207n45
    identity formation and, 10–11, 85
    legislation of, 97, 98
    national similarity of, 116
    and sales, 99, 100, 109–10, 114–16
    teachers and, 99, 104, 107
    See also lists of approved textbooks
theaters
    performances in, 12, 30, 32, 41–42, 81, 188
    as premier location for events, 87, 114
Thirty-Three Uruguayans, 38, 126, 132, 133,
    135, 144
Torrejón, Cipriano, 153
Trabajo (Figueira), 114, 115
tres gauchos orientales, Los (Lussich), 78–80
Trienta y Tres Orientales (Thirty-Three
    Uruguayans), 38, 126, 132, 133, **135**, 144

Unitarians, 44, 62, 67–71, 77–78, 82–83
Urquiza, Justo José de, 61, 71, 72, 168, 177
Uruguay-Brazil border, 81, 102, 104, 113

vademécum del hogar, El (del Castaño), 153
Varela, Felipe, 17
Varela, Florencio, 71, 193, 204n76, 204n78,
    206n3
Varela, José Pedro
    family of, 206n3
    libraries and, 100
    portraits of, **147**, **150**, 166
    Sarmiento and, 2–3, 93
    stature of, 86–89, 120
    vision of, 10, 89, 90–91, 93–95, 127
Vásquez Acevedo, A., 110
Vázquez Cores, Francisco, 108
Vázquez Cores notebook series, 107–8, 138
Vera, Jacinto, 208n51
verse
    celebrations and, 31, 41
    displays of, 29–30, 69, 81
    gauchesque, 55–56, 71–74, 80–81, 82, 77
    legislation against, 58
    party identity and, 46, 51, 63, 71–74,
      81–82, 192
    patriotic, 16, 18, 29–30, 32–34, 129, 189
    printing revolution and, 4, 7, 16, 20, 42
    recitation of, 56, 103, 205n102
    Rosas and family honored in, 53, 57, 69
    in textbooks, 110, 125, 129, 137

Vértiz y Salcedo, Juan José de, 15–16
Vida (Figueira), 114
vida practica, La (Palma), 154–55

Wagner Sosa, Petronila, 127, 163
Wilde, José Antonio, 32, 49, 61, 201n77
women
    exhortations to, 21, 61–62 (*see also* lessons
      in motherhood)
    libraries and, 31
    literary role of, 78

as partisans, 52–53, 56, 61–62, 65
as republican symbols, 178–79, 181 (*see
    also* Lady Liberty)
social status of, 17, 162
as teachers, 102, 162, 208n57
See also female students; gender identities
writing, as component of education. *See* reading and writing, as school subjects

Zeballos, Estanislao, 35
Zinny, Antonio, 17

CHRISTOPHER ALBI

re almost a textbook model of the way to respond to a potential
he" (89).
s book is exemplary of the best in interdisciplinary scholarship
mportant contribution to the field of natural-disaster history.

Ted Steinberg
Case Western Reserve University

y Reading: Print Culture and Collective Identity in the Río de la Plata,
10. By William Garrett Acree, Jr. (Nashville, Vanderbilt Univer-
ss, 2011) 304 pp. $55.00

ina and Uruguay, on either side of the Rio de la Plata estuary,
highest literacy rates and most vibrant literary cultures in Latin
Acree argues that this exceptional intimacy with the printed
an even before the advent of mass literacy at the end of the
century. From the installation of the first printing press in
res in 1780, everyday forms of writing and reading shaped the
re in the region like nowhere else in Latin America. Acree
ly but nimbly over a variety of quotidian reading material,
apers and patriotic verse to textbooks and postage stamps.
a deep analysis of print media with vivid sketches of the
ers, and readers who participated in this unique print cul-
ly, however, in a monograph of fewer than 200 pages of
two countries over a long and tumultuous period, histori-
ation is thin, and several important questions remain un-

ines three key moments in the relationship between
lic sphere in the Rio de la Plata region. First, he looks
f print that accompanied the rebellion against Spanish
ting in 1810. Newspapers and patriotic pamphlets
l revolution, introducing new symbols for the fledg-
gentina and Uruguay. Second, Acree focuses on the
elebrating gaucho life that emerged as cattle raising
he regional economy during the 1830s. This prose
aloud at social gatherings, validated the authoritar-
llos Juan Manuel de Rosas in Buenos Aires and
ntevideo and demonized their liberal enemies. It
tone during the 1860s, as modern agriculture be-
anging gauchos obsolete.
ith popular modes of print means that he does
celebrated piece of gauchesque literature—
cundo (Buenos Aires, 1845). A stinging indict-
l culture, written by a liberal exile for an urban
uld not have been read aloud in the taverns of

REVIEWS | 505

Finally, Acree examines the role of public primary education in creating a mass reading public by the turn of the twentieth century. His
analysis of how children's textbooks instilled patriotic and republican
values, including gender identities, is particularly effective in showing
the relationship between print and group identities.

Historians will note a few shortcomings in Acree's work. He may
exaggerate the exceptionalism of rioplatense print culture prior to mass
literacy. Mexico, for instance, had printing presses since the sixteenth
century and a sophisticated reading public when Buenos Aires and
Montevideo were still raw contraband ports. Acree also does not fully
explain why Argentina and Uruguay succeeded in promoting mass literacy through public education when the rest of Latin America came up
short. Moreover, he concludes on a weak note, discussing stamps, currency, and cigarette cards; a treatment of the popular print media of
Buenos Aires and Montevideo in 1910, such as the illustrated magazine
Caras y Caretas, would have been a better complement to his examination of the revolutionary press of 1810. It could have shown how print
facilitated the process by which European immigrants pouring into Buenos Aires became good citizens (and consumers).

These caveats aside, this elegant volume makes a significant contribution to our understanding of how print culture shaped collective
identities during the era of nation-building in Latin America. Its brevity,
sparkling prose, and well-selected illustrations recommend it for all
scholars interested in print, literacy, and education in Argentina and
Uruguay.

Christopher Albi
State University of New York, New Paltz

Damascus after the Muslim Conquest: Text and Image in Early Islam. By
Nancy Khalek (New York, Oxford University Press, 2011) 224 pp.
$74.00.

Today, the Umayyads make a more appealing subject to Western historians than to historians from the Islamic world because this first Islamic
dynasty, though proudly Arab and vigorously involved in the spreading
of Islam, has been increasingly acknowledged for its continuation of the
practices and structures of Late Antiquity. Having chosen Bilad al-Sham
(the Roman Oriens or the Holy Land), a thoroughly Christianized
country, as their seat, the Umayyads both appropriated and were influenced by the composite religious, cultural, and material and artistic features in this former Byzantine land. Many scholars have argued this
point so compellingly that the currently accepted end date for Late Antiquity is the early Abbasid period.

In Damascus after the Muslim Conquest, Khalek wants to problematize
the continuity discourse by insisting that the Umayyads' identity itself
was molded within the confines of Byzantine culture in Syria. The

E
178
sity

Argent
have th
Americ
word be
nineteent
Buenos A
public sph
roams wid
from newsp
He balances
printers, writ
ture. Inevitab
text, covering
cal contextuali
addressed.

Acree exam
print and the pu
at the explosion
colonial rule sta
stoked the politic
ling republics of A
popular literature
came to dominate t
and verse, often read
ian rule of the *caud*
Manuel Oribe in Mo
assumed a more elega
gan to make the free-

Acree's concern w
not discuss the most
Domingo Sarmiento, Fa
ment of caudillos and rur
elite audience, *Facundo* w
the Río de la Plata.

of 1768 are almost a textbook model of the way to respond to a potential catastrophe" (89).

This book is exemplary of the best in interdisciplinary scholarship and an important contribution to the field of natural-disaster history.

Ted Steinberg
Case Western Reserve University

Everyday Reading: Print Culture and Collective Identity in the Río de la Plata, 1780–1910. By William Garrett Acree, Jr. (Nashville, Vanderbilt University Press, 2011) 304 pp. $55.00

Argentina and Uruguay, on either side of the Rio de la Plata estuary, have the highest literacy rates and most vibrant literary cultures in Latin America. Acree argues that this exceptional intimacy with the printed word began even before the advent of mass literacy at the end of the nineteenth century. From the installation of the first printing press in Buenos Aires in 1780, everyday forms of writing and reading shaped the public sphere in the region like nowhere else in Latin America. Acree roams widely but nimbly over a variety of quotidian reading material, from newspapers and patriotic verse to textbooks and postage stamps. He balances a deep analysis of print media with vivid sketches of the printers, writers, and readers who participated in this unique print culture. Inevitably, however, in a monograph of fewer than 200 pages of text, covering two countries over a long and tumultuous period, historical contextualization is thin, and several important questions remain unaddressed.

Acree examines three key moments in the relationship between print and the public sphere in the Rio de la Plata region. First, he looks at the explosion of print that accompanied the rebellion against Spanish colonial rule starting in 1810. Newspapers and patriotic pamphlets stoked the political revolution, introducing new symbols for the fledgling republics of Argentina and Uruguay. Second, Acree focuses on the popular literature celebrating gaucho life that emerged as cattle raising came to dominate the regional economy during the 1830s. This prose and verse, often read aloud at social gatherings, validated the authoritarian rule of the *caudillos* Juan Manuel de Rosas in Buenos Aires and Manuel Oribe in Montevideo and demonized their liberal enemies. It assumed a more elegiac tone during the 1860s, as modern agriculture began to make the free-ranging gauchos obsolete.

Acree's concern with popular modes of print means that he does not discuss the most celebrated piece of gauchesque literature—Domingo Sarmiento, *Facundo* (Buenos Aires, 1845). A stinging indictment of caudillos and rural culture, written by a liberal exile for an urban elite audience, *Facundo* would not have been read aloud in the taverns of the Rio de la Plata.

Finally, Acree examines the role of public primary education in creating a mass reading public by the turn of the twentieth century. His analysis of how children's textbooks instilled patriotic and republican values, including gender identities, is particularly effective in showing the relationship between print and group identities.

Historians will note a few shortcomings in Acree's work. He may exaggerate the exceptionalism of *rioplatense* print culture prior to mass literacy. Mexico, for instance, had printing presses since the sixteenth century and a sophisticated reading public when Buenos Aires and Montevideo were still raw contraband ports. Acree also does not fully explain why Argentina and Uruguay succeeded in promoting mass literacy through public education when the rest of Latin America came up short. Moreover, he concludes on a weak note, discussing stamps, currency, and cigarette cards; a treatment of the popular print media of Buenos Aires and Montevideo in 1910, such as the illustrated magazine *Caras y Caretas,* would have been a better complement to his examination of the revolutionary press of 1810. It could have shown how print facilitated the process by which European immigrants pouring into Buenos Aires became good citizens (and consumers).

These caveats aside, this elegant volume makes a significant contribution to our understanding of how print culture shaped collective identities during the era of nation-building in Latin America. Its brevity, sparkling prose, and well-selected illustrations recommend it for all scholars interested in print, literacy, and education in Argentina and Uruguay.

Christopher Albi
State University of New York, New Paltz

Damascus after the Muslim Conquest: Text and Image in Early Islam. By Nancy Khalek (New York, Oxford University Press, 2011) 224 pp. $74.00.

Today, the Umayyads make a more appealing subject to Western historians than to historians from the Islamic world because this first Islamic dynasty, though proudly Arab and vigorously involved in the spreading of Islam, has been increasingly acknowledged for its continuation of the practices and structures of Late Antiquity. Having chosen Bilad al-Sham (the Roman Oriens or the Holy Land), a thoroughly Christianized country, as their seat, the Umayyads both appropriated and were influenced by the composite religious, cultural, and material and artistic features in this former Byzantine land. Many scholars have argued this point so compellingly that the currently accepted end date for Late Antiquity is the early Abbasid period.

In *Damascus after the Muslim Conquest,* Khalek wants to problematize the continuity discourse by insisting that the Umayyads' identity itself was molded within the confines of Byzantine culture in Syria. The